INTEGRITY AI

The last ten years have seen the application of market values bring about far-reaching changes in the structures and culture of our public sector institutions. *Integrity and Change: Mental Health in the Marketplace* examines how workers in the caring professions might preserve their integrity and ability to reflect and act purposefully in the face of such rapid and extensive change.

With contributions from well-known clinicians, academics and organisational consultants, *Integrity and Change* explores experiences and dilemmas common to a range of settings. The book is both topical and diverse; it includes examination of:

- the management of institutions in transition
- political analyses of the impact of market values on public services
- possible ways of developing and maintaining creativity in a market culture
- leadership dynamics
- the case for the provision of long-term therapy in public settings.

This thoughtful exploration of pressing issues will be of interest and relevance to academics, managers and clinicians. All those working in the caring professions in education, health, statutory and voluntary social services will find *Integrity and Change* provides the impetus for constructive reflection on the experience of coping with current constraints.

Edited by **Eileen Smith**, Head of the Counselling Service, University of Hertfordshire.

Contributors: Michael Brearley, Paul Hoggett, Jean Hutton, Julian Lousada, Valerie Sinason, Ralph Stacey, Moira Walker, Jean White, Peter Wilson.

INTEGRITY AND CHANGE

Mental health in the marketplace

Edited by Eileen Smith

London and New York

First published 1997
by Routledge
11 New Fetter Lane, London EC4P 4EE

Simultaneously published in the USA and Canada
by Routledge
29 West 35th Street, New York, NY 10001

Typeset in Times by Florencetype Ltd, Stoodleigh, Devon

Printed and bound in Great Britain by
Redwood Books, Trowbridge, Wiltshire

British Library Cataloguing in Publication Data
A catalogue record for this book is available from the British Library

Library of Congress Cataloging in Publication Data
Integrity and change: mental health in the marketplace /
edited by Eileen Smith.
p. cm.
Includes bibliographical references and index.
1. Mental health promotion. 2. Mental health services – Marketing.
I. Smith, Eileen, 1948–
RA790.5.I516 1997   96–16170
362.2–dc20   CIP

ISBN 0–415–14139–7 (hbk)
ISBN 0–415–14140–0 (pbk)

CONTENTS

CONTENTS

CONTRIBUTORS

Michael Brearley is a psychoanalyst in private practice in London. He has also worked as a school counsellor, as a psychotherapist in a local authority unit and as a consultant to companies. From 1971 to 1982 he captained Middlesex at cricket, and between 1977 and 1981 played in 39 Tests for England, in 31 of which he was captain. He also writes occasional articles on cricket for *The Observer*.

Paul Hoggett is Professor of Politics and Director of the Centre for Social and Economic Research at the University of the West of England. He has researched upon and consulted to organisations in the public sphere for over 15 years. He is the author of *Partisans in an Uncertain World: The Psychoanalysis of Engagement* (Free Association Books 1992) and numerous articles.

Jean Hutton is a Director of the Grubb Institute of Behavioural Studies, which she joined in 1969 from a background in management and administration. Working within a systemic and psychodynamic frame of reference, she is a consultant to senior managers in the public, private and voluntary sectors.

Julian Lousada is a Senior Clinical Lecturer in Social Work in the Adult Department of the Tavistock Clinic and a Full Member of the British Association of Psychotherapists. He is the co-author of *The Politics of Mental Health* (Macmillan 1985) and has contributed to a number of professional journals. He is currently acting as a consultant to and writing about community mental health centres.

Valerie Sinason is a consultant child psychotherapist at the Tavistock and Anna Freud Clinics and a research psychotherapist at St Georges Hospital Medical School and the Portman Clinic. She is training at the Institute of Psychoanalysis. Her books include *Mental Handicap and the Human Condition* (Free Association Books 1993), *Understanding Your Handicapped Child* (Rossendale 1993), *Treating Survivors of Satanist Abuse*

(Routledge 1994), a poetry collection *Night Shift* (Karnac 1995), *Memory in Dispute* (Karnac 1996). She specialises in disability and abuse.

Eileen Smith has worked in education as a teacher and psychodynamic counsellor for many years. She began her career as a teacher of English. Developing interests led her to an MA in Cultural Studies, a training in counselling and further study of group and organisational processes. She is Head of the Counselling Service at the University of Hertfordshire and is now working on a book on long-term counselling.

Ralph Stacey is Professor of Management and Director of the Complexity and Management Centre at the Business School of the University of Hertfordshire. He is also a consultant to managers at all levels across a wide range of organisations in many countries and the author of a number of books and articles including *Managing Chaos* (Kogan Page 1992) and *The Chaos Frontier* (Butterworth-Heinemann 1991). His most recent work is *Complexity and Creativity in Organisations* (Berrett-Koehler 1996).

Moira Walker is a psychotherapist who is currently head of the Counselling Service at Leicester University. She is involved in training counsellors and supervisors and writes and edits books on counselling and psychotherapy. She is the author of *Surviving Secrets* (Open University Press 1992) and *Women in Therapy and Counselling* (Open University Press 1990). She has also co-edited the series *Counselling in Context* and *In Search of a Therapist* (both Open University Press).

Jean White is a psychoanalytic psychotherapist. She has worked in the Student Health Service of the London School of Economics, as a member of the Training Committee of the Guild of Psychotherapists and as a member of an Inner London Health Authority. She has also been an organisational consultant and supervisor to various university and community-based counselling services.

Peter Wilson is Director of Young Minds. Peter Wilson began his career as an unattached youth worker and trained as a psychiatric social worker before moving to work in the United States, in New York, in a residential treatment centre for disturbed adolescents. He returned to this country and trained as a child psychoanalyst at the Anna Freud Centre. Since then he has worked in a variety of community and residential settings in London. The positions he has held include Principal Child Psychotherapist, Camberwell Health Authority; Senior Clinical Tutor at the Institute of Psychiatry; Director of the Brandon Centre, Kentish Town; Consultant Psychotherapist at the Peper Harrow Therapeutic Community. For the last three years he has been Director of Young Minds, the National Association of Child and Family Mental Health.

ACKNOWLEDGEMENTS

The chapter, *Captains and Cricket Teams: Therapists and Groups*, by Michael Brearley originally appeared in the journal *Group Analysis* (vol. 27, 1994). For permission to reproduce it here thanks are due to Sage.

I would like to thank all the contributors for their good humour and willingness to undertake yet another task on top of their other responsibilities, all friends and colleagues who were generous with their time in reading chapters and discussing the ideas behind this project and the University of Hertfordshire for providing an institutional base for the conferences and for giving me the time to complete the editing of this collection.

1

INTRODUCTION

Eileen Smith

The years since 1979 have seen far-reaching changes in the policy and funding of our public sector institutions. There have been major shifts in organisational structures and culture. The chapters in this book address the effects of these changes on those who use or work in education, health or social work services in the public and voluntary sectors and consider actual and potential responses to the impact of market values on these areas of provision.

The contributors include clinicians, academics and organisational consultants; some have expertise in more than one of these roles. In their different ways the writers explore experiences and dilemmas common to a range of settings. They ask a number of pressing questions and raise some crucial issues for debate:

- Does the market culture allow for any sustained contact with and knowledge of human complexity and pain – of one's own or of others?
- How are individual and group processes, organisational structures and political/cultural forces interrelated?
- Is it possible for people in the caring professions to work creatively and with integrity in the present climate?
- Which strategies and ways of thinking might help combat demoralisation and a sense of being overwhelmed?
- Are there possibilities for positive change and development in the current situation?

The idea for this book arose from a series of conferences organised by a counselling service in a new university; the original versions of many, but not all, of the chapters were conference papers. The particular university context is more fully described in Chapter 5. The rapidity and extent of change there in the last few years provided the impetus for the thinking that led to this publication. Since 1988 the university has trebled its student numbers, undergone two major changes in status, expanded its portfolio of courses and access for students and radically altered its ways of providing teaching and learning. Such speedy and extensive changes,

effected without adequate increases in resources, have weakened containing structures and forced a reconsideration of working practices and
values on all members of the institution. The university counsellors were
affected both as employees and as recipients of distress as they encountered students who were more seriously disturbed. The conferences were
established as one of a number of projects to help make sense of this
experience through contact and shared thinking with colleagues inside and
outside the university.

The first conference was entitled *Depression and Disadvantage* and
attempted to explore the relationship between individual difficulty
and the recession. Josephine Klein was the keynote speaker then; her
paper can be found in her own recent collection (1995: 31–44). The interest
in the impact of the prevailing culture on forms of individual distress
is taken up in this volume by Jean White in Chapter 11 where she
draws on Lasch and Bollas to describe students suffering from 'normotic
illness'. (For further clinical examples see Brooks 1995.) The second
conference, *Integrity and Change*, where Peter Wilson and Valerie
Sinason painted vivid clinical pictures in their arguments against reduction in services, began to consider the impact of change on professionals
and to ask how they might preserve quality, reflectiveness and a sense of
satisfaction in their work despite economic and institutional pressures. The
following year's conference was entitled *Make It or Break It: Creativity
and Destructiveness in Organisations*. Rosemary Gordon spoke of the
psychological processes involved and Paul Hoggett discussed managers in
destructive organisational settings – the first version of the paper included
here. The fourth conference, *Hope: A Risk Worth Taking?*, with speakers
Moira Walker and Julian Lousada, considered how to avoid either false
self-deceiving optimism or cynical pessimism. The latest conference of the
series – *Regeneration: the Importance of Play* – pursued this key idea by
turning again to the themes of creativity and renewal and exploring
how positive changes – organisational and cultural – might be initiated
and integrated. Ralph Stacey and Jean White introduced the debate on
that occasion.

Conference speakers had a range of professional and theoretical interests, conceptualisations of change and political analyses. Nonetheless, the
emotional response and thoughtful exchanges evoked by the themes and
papers confirmed that the issues identified were of general concern. This
committed interest led to the idea of this collection and the commissioning
of extra papers for it.

THE CONTEXT

Given the rethinking and restructuring of the institutions of the welfare
state since 1979 and the radical changes put in place since 1987, it is

not surprising that so many people in the caring professions should be preoccupied by the effects of these changes on the quality of their work, their own morale and the continued existence of their jobs. Undoubtedly, some questioning of existing assumptions and practices was necessary and productive; all well-functioning organisations are open to outside influences, have mechanisms for self-review and are able to respond creatively to shifting circumstances. Recent changes however have challenged some fundamental beliefs; education, health, the statutory and voluntary social services have all been profoundly affected by the introduction of the mechanisms and values of the market.

As Hutton (1995) has pointed out, some of the impetus for change came from the world recession of the 1970s, which resulted in high rates of inflation and unemployment in Britain. The extent of economic difficulty under Keynesian management lent credence to the attempt of the ascendant New Right in the Conservative party to implement the doctrine of monetarism, with its emphasis on sound money, and supply-side economics, with its extolling of enterprise.

Although the Conservative government was later to abandon the extremes of monetarism, it never ceded its preference for the application of market criteria and solutions in the public sector. Large-scale public expenditure on the welfare state was seen as undesirable on the grounds of expense, inefficiency and lack of competitiveness. Moreover, it was believed that leaving the market free would create more wealth which would eventually trickle down to benefit all members of society. It is beyond the scope of this introduction to analyse the phenomenon of Thatcherism, which is the subject of a wide literature and a variety of interpretations. (For a more detailed commentary see Chapter 11 and for a summary of the debate see Gamble 1994: 174–206.) What is incontestable is the Thatcherite project to challenge the post-war consensus about the desirability of state provision of services and to make profound changes in their delivery.

The arguments for reforming the welfare state were not simply economic. The virtues of self-reliance and individual responsibility were opposed to those of dependency on the so-called 'nanny state'; the importance of choice was insisted on by addressing parents and patients as consumers rather than passive recipients of the attentions of professionals whose credibility was questioned. The devolution of responsibility to a more local level – hospital trust, fund-holding practice or local school – was portrayed as an attack on bureaucracy and a way of ensuring much greater accountability for the use of public funds. The principles of competitiveness and costing in purely economic terms were inserted into every sphere of public life.

Government spending on education fell by 10 per cent in real terms between 1979 and 1986 (McVicar 1992: 133) although it has since risen

3

slightly. Teachers' pay was curbed by the abolition of the Burnham Committee. Parental choice, national standards, preparation for employment, accountability and competitiveness became watchwords of educational policy. Perhaps the most crucial changes in education were those instigated by the Education Reform Act of 1988. This instituted the national curriculum and testing for all pupils at four different ages, thereby allowing for the production and publication of league tables of schools' academic success. This Act made it possible for schools to opt out of local authority control (grants were made available to those which did so), abolished the Inner London Education Authority and introduced local management of schools. It made polytechnics independent corporate bodies, put in place some competitive tendering for students and gave the newly constituted institutions governing boards slanted towards commerce and industry, whose interests were also represented on the new Funding Councils. Increases in the number of places available in higher education have not been matched by increased funding for either students – who must rely increasingly on loans, or institutions – which must compete for public money in repeated research assessment exercises, seek help from the private sector and generate extra income themselves.

Similar principles of establishing accountability, consistent standards, devolution and choice were applied to the National Health Service. In their early years in power the Conservatives encouraged the continuation of private medicine by a number of measures, including the retention of pay beds in NHS hospitals and legislation for tax relief on health insurance. They tried to reform management structures and instituted competitive tendering for ancillary services. However, it was the 1989 White Paper *Working for Patients* (Department of Health 1989) which introduced the most radical changes by recommending the establishment of internal markets which would separate the functions of purchaser and provider. It encouraged the creation of NHS Hospital Trusts which would provide services independently of health authorities which would become purchasers. Larger GP practices would have the option of becoming fund holding and buying selected services for their patients directly. In this way, competition – supposedly in the service of greater efficiency and consumer choice – between Trusts was encouraged. New contracts were introduced for all GPs; these sought to set standards across practices and put more emphasis than previously on service payments. Through fund holding and locality commissioning, responsibility for some health rationing was shifted to GPs who were asked to decide spending priorities.

The split between purchasers and providers was established in personal social services too. The National Health Service and Community Care Act of 1990 enjoined local authorities to move towards becoming largely purchasers of care; they were required to become 'care-managers', inviting tenders for the provision of care rather than necessarily offering it themselves. The idea was to develop a 'mixed economy of care' with considerable reliance on private and voluntary sources. Hence the voluntary sector was also affected by the introduction of market mechanisms. As social service departments and health authorities invited tenders for services, voluntary agencies competed with them and with one another for funding, with possible deleterious effects on the pay and conditions of their employees. (Mayo 1994: 29) Their campaigning voice and advocacy role were somewhat muted by the need not to alienate the purchasers. Meanwhile, there was a continual questioning of the role of social workers who were attacked for failing to prevent child abuse tragedies but also for breaking up families by being over-zealous in sexual abuse cases and being soft on crime by indulging young offenders.

Mental health services in the different sectors of public provision have been profoundly affected by these changes. The drive to close long-stay psychiatric wards and replace the care offered there with care in the community was potentially humane but the implementation was affected by lack of sufficient funds; there has been considerable public concern about occasional violent episodes involving mentally ill patients released without adequate support. The need for mental health services to be local militated against the possible benefits of the purchaser/provider split. Social workers asked to assess mental health needs have been faced with dilemmas about assessing in terms of need or in terms of available facilities.

There have been attempts, some successful, to close institutions or units offering a psychotherapeutic approach to psychological distress. To name just a few examples: Peper Harrow, a therapeutic community and school for disturbed adolescents, was closed in the early 1990s as social service purchasers became less willing to fund long-term placements; the Cassel Hospital, which offers psychoanalytic individual and family therapy to young people and families, was threatened with closure in 1990 – again on the grounds of expense – and reprieved only after a sustained political campaign (for an account of the effect of this on staff and patients see Hartnup 1994); the College Health Service which provided medical and psychotherapeutic services to students at a number of north London colleges was closed in 1989. Jones and Bilton (1994: 41) argue that 'Mental health services for children are particularly at risk from problems of fragmentation, depending as they do on close collaboration between health, education and personal social services.' They refer to the withdrawal of staff from some child guidance and child and family consultation centres. Many units which have survived in name have been under intense pressure to make radical changes in the kind of service they offer while clinicians in the public sector have worked on justifying their

5

psychotherapy services in market terms. (See, for example, Healy 1994 and Denman 1994.) The NHS has invested increasingly in brief and cognitive analytic therapies while the space for preventative and individual work in social work practice has been reduced.

All change involves loss and requires time for working through and readjustment. Change is also essential for growth and the creation of new life, as Chapter 6 by Jean Hutton and Chapter 12 by Ralph Stacey insist. The changes outlined above were, however, rather extraordinary. So much reorganisation in such a short time (much of it threatening jobs, established roles and working practices) and so many new requirements – imposed from above rather than developed organically – have inevitably led to insecurity, overwork and stress. Julian Lousada in Chapter 4 explores the processes necessary for integrating ideas originating elsewhere. The professional autonomy of teachers, social workers and, to a lesser extent, doctors has been challenged and they have been made more accountable to managers and, theoretically at least, to users. The pressures have been exacerbated for many workers by the conflict between the values of the new culture and their professional and personal beliefs. Doubtless, some re-examination and exposition of these was healthy but many felt their principles were compromised by the new order, that they did not have the resources to provide quality services or the space to be thoughtful about their work. It would seem that the values associated with psychoanalytic psychotherapy, or indeed with humane care in health, education or social work – such as allowing time for development, understanding people's need for dependence and tolerating ambivalence and ambiguity – fit uncomfortably within the discourse of cost effectiveness, efficiency and throughput. Holmes argues that 'the market constantly replaces inner structures with outer appearances' (1992: 9) and sets up 'a servicing mentality in which needs are bureaucratised, fragmented and met piecemeal, with little attempt at containment or metabolism of the enduring reality of persistent pain and loss that are central features of psychiatric work.' (10).

The process of implementing change has not been straightforward. There are different and sometimes contradictory strands in conservative philosophy and in the opposition to it. Public protest, especially about the NHS, has prevented some reforms being pushed as far as New Right rhetoric might have suggested was desirable. However, the last 15 years have profoundly altered not just the structures of provision but the terms of the discourse about public services and welfare. Mayo argues that 'the parameters of the debate have been shifted. Fundamental assumptions have been challenged, including fundamental challenges about the role of the state, the private sector and the voluntary and community sectors.' (Mayo 1994: 5). A new common sense is emerging. Stuart Hall argues:

To a significant extent, Thatcherism is about the remaking of common sense: its aim is to become 'the common sense of the age'. Common sense shapes our ordinary, practical, everyday calculations and appears as natural as the air we breathe. It is simply 'taken for granted' in practice and thought, and forms the starting-point (never examined or questioned) from which every conversation begins, the premises on which every television programme is predicated. The hope of every ideology is to naturalise itself out of History into Nature, and thus to become invisible, to operate unconsciously.

(Hall 1988: 8)

THE CHAPTERS

Many of the chapters in this book draw attention to the operations of the new common sense, the entrenchment of the values of the marketplace. The head teacher in Valerie Sinason's chapter who refused to facilitate the continuing provision of therapy for one of his pupils or the management committee in Moira Walker's which welcomed work with survivors of sexual abuse as 'a nice little earner' are obvious examples of considering only the immediately measurable economic costs of any intervention and of ignoring possible human consequences. Jean White describes clients who found it impossible to develop in any depth because of a perceived need to turn themselves into marketable commodities. She also unpacks the language of health service planning to demonstrate sets of assumptions about priorities. Many chapters describe the prevalence of competitiveness and survivalism in different public sector settings.

The chapters collected here explore a variety of strategies for making space for thought and maintaining morale in these difficult circumstances. The approach is not uniform. The writers have a variety of views on the opportunities presented by change which they approach with differing degrees of optimism or pessimism. What they share is a commitment to continuing engagement with the issues. It is hoped that an encounter with their views may help lessen the isolation and misplaced sense of personal responsibility which can make it difficult to think and work creatively.

Peter Wilson's chapter is about integrity and identity in therapy and makes a case for the provision of long-term therapy in public settings. Using a powerful and moving example of the patient and imaginative work he undertook with a largely silent adolescent girl who was enabled to find her voice through the therapy, he argues forcefully for the need to allow sufficient time for therapy if real change is to take place but questions whether, given the demands of the market, a space for such work – which he sees as necessary for at least some patients – can be preserved. Wilson doubts whether 'the current management ethos can ever get to grips with the process of helping people with emotional or psychological difficulties'. The work, he suggests, does not make sense to 'accountants and managers' who may settle 'for determining outcome according to cost factors rather than in terms of human factors'.

Valerie Sinason's chapter takes up this theme. She describes how restricted resources and changing values in the public sector are preventing professionals doing their work properly, inducing unhelpful rivalries and threatening the integrity of practitioners. She argues that we need to acknowledge our own helplessness and powerlessness in the face of the disintegration of public services rather than omnipotently and at great personal cost trying to put everything right. She gives an extended and moving clinical example – of an abused and potentially abusing boy – who was denied all the help he needed and explains how she acknowledged this with him. She concludes: 'To admit to our patients when we cannot offer the right service and may never be able to helps all of us to maintain integrity. To be properly in touch with helplessness provides us, ironically, with strength.'

The following chapter moves on to consider the processes which may occur in the course of making space for the development of new good practice. Julian Lousada writes as both a therapist and an organisational consultant. He is interested in how ideas come to be formed and translated into action. He explores the fact and metaphor of adoption to examine one way in which this can happen. His clinical understanding of the experience of adoption is used to illuminate a consultation to an agency which was struggling with an imported anti-racist policy. The chapter examines how change may be an escape from pain and individuals or organisations may clutch prematurely at new ideas or projects when hopes or expectations of the future have been grievously disappointed. The writer considers the loss and sense of failure which must be worked through and the complexities which must be tolerated before new ideas can be integrated and offer the possibility of real progress. He rejects the simplicity of a fundamentalist morality and, like the other contributors, insists on the importance of maintaining space for thought.

The case study of a university counselling service (Eileen Smith) explores some of the opportunities and tensions arising from being a therapeutic unit within a large and rapidly changing educational institution. The background to setting up such services is explained and the current nature of the demands outlined. The impact of changes in the wider organisation and culture on clinical, educational and preventative work is discussed. Some of the difficulties, dilemmas and responses of the staff team and different ways of understanding these are considered.

Jean Hutton uses the concept of organisation-in-the-mind. She draws on her experience of consulting with managers in human service institutions to discuss the importance of reflective and imaginative thinking for effective leadership. She gives a number of fascinating examples to illustrate different aspects of the management role in a time of change, suggesting how managers might interpret and contain the emotional life of their organisation, help hold onto core values, use different parts of themselves as situations change and re-interpret their context to allow for growth. She argues that all human service organisations are in the business of having to respond to a societal dimension as well as to individual need; the unspoken requirement to manage some larger conflict may interfere with provision but an understanding of the wider dimension is necessary if managers are to work effectively.

Michael Brearley also addresses management issues although he draws on a very different background: he combines his experiences as an England cricket captain with those as a psychoanalyst to consider the dynamics of teams. Basic assumption theory is used to examine the working of cricket teams and their relationship to their captain. The paper's relevance here is its discussion of the prevalence of basic assumption functioning, of what makes a good team and of the positive exercise of leadership. Brearley's thinking about the role of the captain and how he might use, rather than – like the therapist – interpret an understanding of group behaviour and psychological processes, offers us insights into possible good management practice.

Moira Walker's chapter echoes some themes developed in previous chapters – the need for long-term therapy for some people and the extra cost to clinicians of undertaking already demanding therapeutic work in the current climate when they may feel themselves unhelpfully 'sandwiched between the needs of the client and the demands of the institution'. Using examples from case material about working with abused survivors within an institutional setting, she argues that counsellors in institutions may feel that they themselves are abused by their organisations and explores how a counsellor or therapist can hold on to hope and maintain resilience despite organisational pressures. Walker argues that, like survivors of abuse, counsellors need to acknowledge both external and internal realities, to work with the negative aspects of their experience without being completely overwhelmed by them, to use their anger constructively, to establish where they are truly powerless and where they may have some influence and to learn sometimes to put difficulties to one side without denying them. She advocates holding on to faith in the value of the work, using supervision and finding a helpful balance between 'objective distancing and more active involvement'.

Paul Hoggett's chapter offers an uncompromising analysis of the current state of our public services, where market values have triumphed and the ethic of public service has been replaced by that of 'public enterprise'. He describes increasingly destructive regimes where workers are dominated by fear and feel 'trapped within a regime which is abandoning the principles which drew many of them to work there' and challenges contemporary management theory's unthinking embrace of change. His case study of working with a group of senior managers describes how one woman becomes a casualty; it concludes sombrely that 'If there was fighting to be done, so it seemed, they would choose each other as victims.' Drawing on the writings of Levi, Havel and Lasch, Hoggett charts a range of possible responses to the threatening new order. He describes the roles of victim, collaborator, survivor, resister and partisan but argues that the boundaries of these roles and choices are blurred and ambiguous. For all the pessimism of its analysis, this essay is a powerful endorsement of the importance of reflective action, passion and commitment.

Jean White agrees with Hoggett about the inevitability of moral dilemmas and being compromised for those currently working in the public sector. She discusses how market principles have been applied to the NHS, considers the normalising language of the new regime and looks at some of the effects of recent changes. Although critical of the application of these ideas in this context, she does believe there was need for change. She considers what possibilities there might be for subversion and appropriation of the 'reforms' in the service of creative policy-making. In particular she sees scope for positive developments in the areas of consumer consultation, participation and feedback, the growing sophistication of computerisation and the shift of resources to primary care. She argues for an increase of psychological understanding in the health service – of both the needs of patients and of the mechanism of projection which is frequently used as a defence against the distress and anxiety the NHS would ideally own and contain.

Jean White's second chapter develops the concept of internal space and its relationship to cultural space. She critiques some dominant aspects of New Right ideology, with particular attention to its operation in education, the arts and political action and argues that within these fields 'space for thinking critically or independently, space for imaginative re-elaboration has been dramatically reduced'. She describes a culture which relies increasingly on basic-assumption mentality, giving rise to a growth in narcissistic personality disorders and 'normotic illness'. She goes on to consider how, despite the damage caused by the normalising effects of the hegemony of the market, creativity might be developed in educational, political and cultural contexts.

Ralph Stacey's closing chapter brings a fresh perspective to the issues explored in this collection by focusing on underlying ways of conceptualising societies, organisations and individuals. He critiques both neo-classical and Austrian economic theories and the social theories connected to them and draws attention to UK governments' contradictory and confusing applications of both. Like Jean White he is interested in possible interventions to promote more creative ways of living – particularly in organisations. He draws on complexity theory with its origins in the natural sciences to demonstrate interconnectedness, agency and intrinsic value and to argue that creativity is possible only at the edge of chaos. He posits a place on the boundary – which he compares to Klein's depressive position or Winnicott's transitional space – between total disintegration and stable equilibrium, between collaboration and competition, where new life can develop out of creative play. For this to happen, organisations and their members must, he suggests, be able to tolerate unpredictability and anxiety, put aside the illusion of control and concentrate on providing space for collective and playful reflection.

This collection is going to press close to an election at a time of considerable debate about the priorities and principles which should govern our public services. Reviews of higher education recruitment and funding and of mental health provision have been instituted. It is unclear what difference a new government would or could make, which recent policies might be reversed or creatively developed and which have come to embody the new common sense and are embedded in practice. It is not the purpose of this publication to indulge in nostalgia for some mythical golden age or to suggest that there are easy solutions to questions of policy and practice. Rather, we hope that the publication of these contributions may stimulate critical reflection and discussion on the crucial issues and values they address.

REFERENCES

Brooks, O. (1995) 'Loss of Feeling in the University Counsellor: Some Clinical Illustrations of Personal Illness in a University Context', *Psychodynamic Counselling* 1, 4: 600–12.

Denman, F. (1994) 'The Value of Psychotherapy', *British Journal of Psychotherapy* 11, 2: 284–9.

Department of Health (1989) *Working for Patients*, Cm 555, London: HMSO.

Gamble, A. (1994) *The Free Economy and the Strong State*, London: Macmillan.

Gordon, R. (1994) 'Loss, Change and Creativity', paper given at the conference, *Make It or Break It* (unpublished).

Hall, S. (1988) *The Hard Road to Renewal*, London and New York: Verso.

Hartnup, T. (1994) 'The State, the Institution and the Patient: a Three-way Collision at the Crossroads as a Hospital Fights Closure', *Psychoanalytic Psychotherapy*, 8, 1: 3–15.

Healy, K. (1994) 'Why Purchase Psychotherapy Services?', *British Journal of Psychotherapy* 11, 2: 279–83.

Holmes, J. (1992) 'Psychiatry without Walls', *Psychoanalytic Psychotherapy* 6, 1: 1–12.

Hutton, W. (1995) *The State We're In*, London: Cape.

Jones, A. and Bilton, K. (1994) *The Future Shape of Children's Services*, London: National Children's Bureau.

Klein, J. (1995) *Doubts and Certainties in the Practice of Psychotherapy*, London: Karnac.

Mayo, M. (1994) *Communities and Caring*, London: Macmillan.

McVicar, M. (1992) 'Education Policy: Education as a Business?' in Savage, S. and Robins, L. (eds) *Public Policy under Thatcher*, London: Macmillan.

2

A TIME TO THINK

Peter Wilson

INTRODUCTION

I'd like to begin with an image: an image of a face and of a posture. It comes from television, and stands out in my mind because of its simplicity and power. It flashes through in the midst of frantic news coverage of a refugee camp in Bosnia Herzogovina. There are pictures of the injured, the terrified and the dispossessed. It is all catastrophe and madness. Yet, in its midst, sitting silently and unmovingly, is a young woman. She is quite still, just looking, nothing dramatic. Her ordinariness is impressive; so, too, her pride and integrity. It transpires that she is a young woman who has been in the refugee camp for two months. Throughout that time, she has not spoken a word.

As the image passed away, I found myself staying with this young woman – struck by her extraordinary presence and her apparent resolve and stoicism. Whoever she is, I thought, she is standing or sitting for something; she is not going to be moved, shaken out of it, cheered up, changed into what is required of her. Her refusal stands firm. Her silence prevails.

SILENCE AND INTEGRITY

Silence in therapy, as in life, speaks volumes. And the more persistent it is, the more voluminous. Without doubt, it can be a very potent weapon in the many dramas of transference – it can be used to defy, attack, frustrate, confuse, seduce or cajole. It can effectively provoke action and excite communication. It can often, too, carry a lot of anger – and a great deal of resistance to the flow of ideas and the progress of therapy. We cannot forget, as well, that many people in silence are confused and unable to formulate and find words.

These are some of the distinct flavours of silence. But perhaps beyond all these, or indeed as some sort of compilation of them all, there is the silence of the private self. This is the self that is hidden, secret, not to be played about with – never easy to define and all too readily dismissed.

I am referring here to the essential core of the self, which I think lies at the heart of integrity, of the individual's sense of personal coherence. I think this matters to us all. I have been particularly struck by its force in my understanding of severely sexually abused adolescents. For what is most striking for some of the more cruelly sexually abused adolescent girls is their air of detachment and rigidity. Despite their audacity, effrontery and general way of coming on, they are curiously unspontaneous and afraid of risk and uncertainty. Despite their overt liveliness, they seem frozen and inert – and it is quite clear that internally they keep themselves well beyond being touched or messed about with. What they show above all else is their determination to protect themselves, to keep out of reach their inner core – they effectively do not open up or allow for any form of contact. I often refer to one particular young woman who had been sexually abused in her childhood by her father – always incidentally in silence. She summed up her memory of it all quite simply: 'I just lay there dead. He never really touched me at all.' There is in this something heroic – what she retained was the inviolability of her self and spirit, no matter the extent and ravage of the abuser.

Winnicott wrote most clearly of the essence of all of this: 'This preservation of personal isolation is part of the search for identity and the establishment of a personal technique for communicating which does not lead to violation of the central self' (1965: 190). Winnicott's persistent concern was for the development of the core or true self, uncompromised or intruded upon by the external world. In adolescence, this core self is in a state of delicate or partial formation and requires both protection and leaving be. Adam Phillips, who has written an excellent and succinct book on Winnicott, summarises this paradox of psychotherapy with adolescents. He writes: 'the paradox that he [Winnicott] had begun to formulate was that the infant – like the adolescent – was an isolate who needed the object above all to protect the privacy of his isolation' (1988: 145). For Winnicott, the essence of trauma is the threat to this isolated core, the threat of being found, altered, communicated with. The ultimate catastrophe is the annihilation of this core self by intrusion. The sexual abuse of young women is traumatic not only in terms of its bodily invasiveness but in terms of its potential intrusiveness into their sense of self. But this, they did not ultimately allow.

What is important above all else here is the sanctity and the dignity of the life of the self – whatever it is that is idiosyncratic or special to our existence and individuality. Silence is a particularly determined and resolute expression of this; contained within it is the core, the essence of integrity.

Integrity essentially is about a quality or condition of being complete, entire and unimpaired. It refers to a kind of honesty, of being true to oneself, and derives from a process of bringing and holding together many fragments of one's experience. The achievement of integrity is not of course a one-off. Integrity is a condition that is constantly being had and lost in the continual process of growing up – of integration and disintegration, progression and regression. Children, adults and the old are always seeking integrity, much as they seek homeostasis. It is in many ways a narcissistic pursuit, a search for a cohesive self.

The relationship between integrity and change is a constant tussle – because change is fundamentally about altering and making things different. The quest for integrity on the other hand is at any given moment an attempt to hold things together. Integrity attempts to strike and keep something new and true from what has existed; change brings about the loss of what went before and in so doing threatens the new integrity. It is like a kaleidoscope: the bits are constantly forming into new patterns to capture a new sense of integrity but are then so easily shaken into something else.

PSYCHOTHERAPY AND RESISTANCE

Change is thus a constant irritant to integrity, or at least its latest moments. Similarly, psychotherapy must be a nuisance to its clients. There is a never-ending tension in the business of helping people, for the stimulus to the whole enterprise is the demand for change – whether the source of that demand is internal or external. Get better, be happier, be more productive, be more compliant, be more obedient, be more creative, be more loving, be more relating. All commendable, possibly – but the final requirement is to be more something other than what you presently are. This is the ultimate threat, to be withstood at all times. 'No, I won't'; 'Don't help me'; 'Leave me as I am'. Psychotherapy is the story of resistance and what you do about it.

The first to agree would of course be Freud himself. Throughout his clinical life he explored many facets of resistance. Beyond 'repression resistance', he wrote at length of the resistance of the transferences, of secondary gain from illness, of super-ego disapproval. He even went further into what he called id resistance – something inherent and glue-like within our natures, holding back from change, seeking a status quo ante – that does not move forward. Freud's life was in fact beleaguered by patients who refused to free-associate, who became infatuated with him or overly furious with him, who retreated from the prospect of recovery and who entrenched themselves in states of stuckness and what he called 'psychic inertia'. They all in effect refused to cooperate with the enterprise of change. Freud struggled on – indeed as we all do – and in so doing managed to move from his initial impatience and insistence that the patient cooperate (for example, through his early procedure of 'pressure on the forehead') to 'seeking to overcome' the resistances to finally understanding the nature of the repetition compulsion and the need for time and working through.

Working through is a central concept in the understanding of integrity. Basically, it refers to a process in which different facets of the personality – thoughts, memories, ideas, wishes, desires – are bit by bit brought into consciousness and into some new kind of pattern and awareness. Working through is about repeating and registering anew. It is about mastery. It is about taking time to assimilate the past and the present. It is, in fact, a form of mental work which everyone has to undertake in any process of change. The title of Freud's seminal paper (1914) on this was simply *Remembering, Repeating and Working Through.*

Working through, of course, takes time – time to go through all those diverse and complex processes that give direction and meaning to our lives and make for our uniquely human experience. Working through is in fact about the time to think. Thinking is about a lot of things – reflecting, considering, anticipating, rehearsing, expecting, contemplating, meditating, remembering, creating ideas, having fantasies and so forth. And, of course, much of it goes on in silence in private.

CASE ILLUSTRATION

I would like to give a brief example here to illustrate some of the major themes considered so far – namely, the significance of silence as an expression of integrity, as a manifestation of resistance to external demands and as a process of working through. The case that comes to mind is that of a young adolescent girl aged 15 whom I saw several years ago. I saw her in a regular individual weekly therapy for three years and subsequently kept in correspondence with her. In many ways, she is reminiscent of the young woman in Bosnia. She had not of course undergone the same catastrophes of life. However, her life had its own particular disruptions and traumas about which she felt very strongly. And, like the young woman in Bosnia, she chose to hold on to her own particular experience in resolute silence.

I shall call this girl Susannah. Susannah was referred to the clinic because of very difficult and at times violent and threatening behaviour at school. At home she was described as moody, often not speaking to her parents for days on end. As is often the case in referrals of this sort, her behaviour before all of this erupted had been apparently good, compliant and hard-working. She presented a mystery – an alarming one at that.

I shall describe her background only briefly. She lived with her natural parents and two sisters in this country. Her parents had left her as an infant with her grandparents in her country of origin in order to come to England to work. On two or three occasions as a little girl she had been

16

brought to England for holidays and then returned home. At the age of nine, however, she had been brought again with her grandparents to this country for what was understood to be another holiday. This time, though, she had fallen seriously ill and had been kept in hospital for two months. She could not speak English and was in great pain. Whilst in hospital, her grandmother returned home without telling Susannah. When Susannah came out of hospital she found herself living with her natural parents who were in effect strangers to her. She had no choice but to stay. She felt betrayed by her grandparents and resentful of her parents. Nevertheless, she complied as she must. The atmosphere in the family remained tense.

The most striking feature of the therapy with this girl was its silence. Particularly in the beginning, Susannah hardly spoke a word. She sat inert, taut, tense – quite still and statuesque. She looked away from me and had very little eye contact. Her moods changed, but I could only sense them, with very little clue as to what they were about. Basically, I was required to attend closely, and invent out of the silence and the space some sort of understanding. At times she seemed inscrutable and devoid of feeling. But it became increasingly clear that she was in fact in great distress. In some sessions she sat silently tearful and weeping. She was invariably slow to leave sessions.

In all of this, I simply felt at a loss. All of my customary approaches were of no avail and all attempts to offer words seemed futile. The more I tried, the more I seemed to miss or intrude. There seemed little more I could do than to sit and wait. Silence was the fact of the matter – it was Susannah's mode of being. Certainly, at one level, it expressed her refusal to communicate or comply. However, equally, I think it conveyed her attempt to share. She never missed sessions, and I was never at ease. To challenge such silence simply as defiance would have been a violation and a misunderstanding of what was going on. Susannah was in silence and she was using silence – for good reason, though what about was not clear. Ultimately, she and the silence had to be respected.

For much of the time I was left to guess what was in her mind, and this was a tricky business. I found myself fearful of getting it wrong yet always hopeful that I would make some connection. In the beginning I tried to think about the things that were occurring at school and how Susannah was dealing with all of them. She did not of course reply verbally but I got nevertheless a distinct sense of her hurt and rage. I tried to focus on the issue of separation and openly recalled the events of Susannah's life as I knew them and of her feelings of fear, dismay and anger. I wondered how far the silence she created in the therapy was some kind of reliving of those awful experiences. I did in fact get some nodding confirmation from her when I spoke of her 'protest at a world that suddenly changed too much'. It was in moments such as this that Susannah wept, but she never let go her grip on her silence. At such times I became increasingly aware of Susannah's terror of letting go, of opening her mouth, for fear of what might come out, of what destructiveness might unfold. I also thought she was afraid of what I might do in response – that I might leave, disappear, get rid of her, condemn her as mad.

All of this was very intense and I found myself filled with a kind of diffuse anguish, which I am sure is what she was feeling too. For a long while, the therapy seemed stuck in what I can only describe as a turgid mass of muteness. All I could do was either to sit with it or talk into it. Mercifully, however, events took a turn, for Susannah for some reason started to write letters to me between sessions. In these letters, she wrote of her experiences and feelings and effectively gave me something more concrete to work with. We developed in fact a very particular and peculiar dialogue – a silent session, her letter to me, my verbal commentary on her letter in the next session, her silence, another letter and so forth. Into the silence, I spoke: and from it, she wrote.

Her letters were long and full and expressed many of the preoccupations that I had imagined with her before. She described people she was very angry with – her teachers and parents in particular – and her fury at their deceit, indifference and betrayal. She spoke of her wish for revenge and her determination never, ever to give in to them. There was much in this that was quite tortuous and desperate and I talked into our silences of the hurt and the anger that she wanted me to know about and to link these feelings as before with earlier events in her life.

For a while this seemed to be a satisfactory if curious arrangement – we were, in fact, getting somewhere. However, as time went on, I increasingly found it a very limiting and frustrating experience. I became unexpectedly impatient with the palaver of it all and the sheer unrelentingness of her silence. It was so powerful and obdurate. I was beginning to feel weary of being made to feel stupid and left out. I could of course appreciate her evident wish to share and I could make sense of my own feelings as reflecting feelings of hers. But, despite all that, I began to question the purpose of carrying on week after week in this way – unless she began to show some preparedness to talk to me. Eventually, I spoke to her about this – in effect saying 'enough is enough'. For a while I got the usual silence and the letters stopped. After a few weeks, however, she wrote again to me saying that what I had said made 'common sense'.

The letters that she subsequently wrote were very powerful and, although she was not able to talk very much, she began to make efforts to say something. Her letters were of course a gift and now gave me so much more to go on. This was a critical period in the therapy, because so much was now written and acknowledged of her intense anger and disappointment. She could not forgive her parents and teachers for not listening to her and for expecting too much of her. She was acutely aware of her fear of her violence and her need to keep her mouth shut – to hold tight through gritted teeth. The meaning of her silence became increasingly clear. Spoken words were simply too dangerous. They were impossible for her. They could not convey the congestion of feeling that was within her. As she later put it, 'There is a rage and pain that can only be expressed and held in silence – a silence that speaks louder than the words that could come out.'

It seemed too that in silence she held on not only to a control of her fury but to a protection of something important of herself. Her silence was a state of being with me in which she could hold a boundary and keep what in fact she called her 'core', which she thought I could never get to. Again, as she put it later:

> writing to you is a way out but only to the backyard. To do it the other way – through talking – would be opening the front door and out into the open ... saying it out verbally is like losing a part of yourself and I cannot and won't do that. The closeness of the relationship would be too much. Silence is my own world and neither you or anybody can take it away with their persistence of wanting to know about it.

With this understanding I finally stopped 'fighting' the silence. I allowed the silence and I allowed her to be – not expecting her to be other than what she was. I entered a curious state of suspension – sitting with her, looking out of the window, thinking and caring about her, thinking too about myself, and finding words that hopefully might resonate with what she was feeling – always at a distance and not too much. Paradoxically, it was a relationship that was very different from that with her mother and yet evocative maybe of an earlier infantile experience when, as she put it, 'the silences were not hell'. In a subsequent letter, after therapy had finished, looking back on all of this she recalls, 'It was just something that had to be done at that time. It was just looking out of the window and letting your thoughts drift outside and come together.'

DISCUSSION: IMPLICATIONS FOR PSYCHOTHERAPY AND SERVICE PROVISION

I have chosen to discuss this case for three main reasons. Firstly, this young teenager exemplifies the strength of the striving for integrity amongst those most pressured and vulnerable (not least, adolescents). Throughout the time that I knew her, there was a clear resolve on her part not to compromise with the requirements of others. No teacher, parent, therapist or manager was going to take away from her that which mattered the most to her, her integrity and sense of justice. Secondly, she expressed most powerfully the meaning and importance of silence, both with respect to its control over internal violence and to its preservation of her private self. Thirdly, she went through an experience in psychotherapy that was in many ways unusual and not immediately impressive, yet which proved most productive. The outcome was positive. Short-term gains were not, of course, apparent. There was no way that she could immediately comply with the demands around her. However, in her second and third years of therapy, she began to settle at home and at school and study as well. She succeeded academically, went on to higher education and held down a responsible job. In addition, she increasingly enjoyed life, taking an active interest in the arts and sports. Her relationship with her parents improved and she was able to talk more freely.

By all accounts, this was an effective piece of psychotherapy. Yet it took three years and for most of the time it proceeded in strange silence. I should also add that it took place in a public clinic several years ago, before the present-day rush of marketeers and managers. It took place in a climate that allowed for time to be taken and for outcome to be uncertain. It proceeded without rigid requirements for detailed accountability and cost effectiveness. It allowed for Susannah not to be shut up.

The question has to be asked now, however, as to how well such an experience might survive in the current situation of service provision. In the midst of the prevailing concerns about public spending pressures, market-led resource allocation, contract specifications and so forth, who is to have the time or take the responsibility for an angry and recalcitrant girl such as Susannah, who frightens her teachers, confounds her parents and frustrates all those who try to help. Does any of this matter? Is it of sufficient priority? Who decides? What purchaser knows?

There is a distinct danger that in the turmoil of our times, and through the monetarist and individualistic solutions that exist, such a child as Susannah will get overlooked and simply rushed out of the way. I doubt whether the current management ethos can ever get to grips with the process of helping people with emotional and psychological difficulties. Accountants and managers, with totally different trainings, values and aspirations, cannot make sense of much of this work. The danger is that in their frustration they will impose systems of management and accountability that make sense to themselves but that will be intolerable for practitioners. They will settle, too, for determining outcome according to cost factors rather than in terms of human factors. How can they define quality of service in this field?

It is my fear that under the prevailing market economy – where there is no restraining force or strategic overview from central or regional government – a management ethos will prevail that will be essentially impatient with the integrity of the individual and will impinge destructively on the process of psychotherapy and counselling. The over-riding demand will be for cost reduction and this essentially will be for time reduction. The call for short-term, time-limited, contract-defined packages of psychotherapy is already under way. The pressure will be for the therapist to hurry up and, in turn, for the client to hurry up. The premium will be for quick, effective technique. Clearly, in this climate the behavioural, cognitive and family therapies will be much in demand. These approaches are of course appropriate in certain cases. However, there are many young people and families with complex and entrenched difficulties who cannot and should not respond to such work. Susannah was one such case. She needed time to think. It was vital that she was not rushed to give account of herself. She needed time to think – to slowly and properly integrate her experiences and feelings. What was needed above all else was respect for her integrity.

Ann Alvarez, in her moving account of her treatment of a sexually abused child, describes very clearly this essential respect and the time for it:

> I would suggest that a thought becomes thinkable often by a very gradual process, a process which cannot be rushed. The implication for the question of how the abused child may be helped to come to terms with his abuse may be that the 'remembering' may involve a million tiny integrations taking place, each one under conditions where other aspects of the abuse, other integrations can afford to be forgotten. . . . Freud said of the work of mourning that each single memory had to be dealt with and mourned and relinquished. In the same way maybe each single aspect of the abuse, the bits and pieces of the experience, particularly if it was chronic may need to be digested one step at a time.
>
> (Alvarez 1992: 153)

REFERENCES

Alvarez, A. (1992) *Live Company*, London and New York: Tavistock/Routledge.
Freud, S. (1914) *Remembering, Repeating and Working Through*, Standard Edition 12, London: Hogarth
Phillips, A. (1988) *Winnicott*, London: Fontana Press.
Winnicott, D.W. (1965) 'Communicating and Not Communicating Leading to a Study of Opposites' in *Maturational Processes and the Facilitating Environment, Studies in the Theory of Emotional Development*, London: Hogarth Press.

3

WHAT PRICE TRUST?

The struggle against personal corruption in straitened circumstances

Valerie Sinason

In the relatively short period of time since Eileen Smith organised her innovative conference on Integrity and Change at the University of Hertfordshire, changes in public service have gathered momentum. Whilst all changes evoke the possibility of hope and loss, the political and psychological intentions that drive external change are powerfully transmitted. Learning-disabled adults who are moved into group homes in the community for genuine rehabilitative reasons adapt very differently than those who are moved for financial reasons.

The conference that formed the crucible for this book was highlighting a significant change for the host body. The institution was a former polytechnic that had just become a university. It seemed to me particularly hopeful that an academic institution experiencing such a change should host the first national conference on this topic. It occurred to me that the best personal way for members of a new university to keep their integrity was to avoid suddenly denigrating all polys and colleges and assuming a grandiose status in which a past 'humble' history was to be hidden. All of us face internal pressure at times of change which can lead us to mock what we have lost, regardless of whether it was good, bad or indifferent.

For example, first-year university students may have to resist the urge to mock younger colleagues studying for their GCSEs. 'Oh, that is so simple compared to what we do now,' said one first-year student to a fifth-form high school friend. At each change in life there is the task of struggling to avoid denigrating what came before. Whilst training to be a teacher I remember hearing of the 8-year-old who, on meeting a Professor of Ancient History, said rather contemptuously, 'But we finished all about the Romans last year!' It was infinitely rarer to come across 6-year-old Gary who could say to his 4-year-old brother, 'I think you will really like it when you start big school and I will meet you at playtime so you don't feel shy.'

When change occurs due to progress there is still a feeling of loss and a struggle against denigrating what we have left behind. So what happens when things change for the worse? I want therefore to concentrate on the struggle against corruption when the change is not a positive one.

In hearing case presentations from nurses, social workers, psychologists and psychiatrists over the last two years a certain pattern has been very noticeable. Professionals, from a range of settings, have been describing external factors that stop them doing their work properly. For example, an educational psychologist had assessed a learning-disabled boy from an abusive home. She recommended that for the boy's needs a therapeutic boarding placement was optimum. She was told most categorically that as her borough did not have such a therapeutic boarding school and as the budget could not extend to paying for such an out-of-borough placement, she would have to reword her statement of the child's needs or lose her job. As a newly qualified educational psychologist she did not feel able to be a whistle-blower, so she rewrote the statement of special needs. It is due to all the re-writings of statements for similar reasons that led to major therapeutic institutions like Peper Harrow being closed down.

A social worker working with chronically abused children was interviewed by a newly appointed business efficiency manager. He was carrying out a time and motion study. He drew a graph for her and said:

> We can see that you currently see clients for around 30 sessions and it seems to me that you work first to get a disclosure, then to deal with Court and then to help the child after. Now all you have to do is speed up your technique so you can get to the disclosure in three meetings, pick up the pieces in another three and if you were able to help each child go through at that accelerated rate, our through-put would increase dramatically and we would have many more referrals.

Now she actually did move to another borough but the remaining social workers there, for fear of their own possible job losses, mortgages, everything else, weren't necessarily in a position to feel free to blow the whistle and, as Peter Wilson pointed out at the University of Hertfordshire Conference, time to think is itself chronically attacked.

A nurse made an emergency home visit to a severely learning-disabled adult, who had a coexisting mental illness, at the request of her ageing parents with whom she lived. In spite of medication, this woman broke down periodically and needed hospitalisation. Previously, this was quickly arranged through the psychiatrist or social services who combined to pay for it together, knowing that they were very lucky that the parents were carrying the bill for this woman's primary care all the rest of the time. On this occasion when the nurse visited and found the woman in a mad, manic state, throwing furniture and crockery and the old parents terrified and helpless, she phoned the psychiatrist to request an emergency in-patient admission but was told there were no longer any beds available and nothing was possible unless social services could pay. She phoned the social services, who said they had no money for another three months. She was the one at the most junior level who was left trying to deal with those parents.

Those three examples are representative of hundreds that we are all hearing about and workers presenting such vignettes at seminars are expecting to hear a psychodynamic formulation of how they should deal with their clients and are expressing their own despair and guilt at not putting the service right. What had they done wrong? Who had they failed to contact? Should they go to the level above? Should they change their line management? As well as guilt, there was splitting and blaming. The nurse was sure that the psychiatrist and social worker who failed to admit her patient were 'mad' and it was because of them that the system was not working. The social worker in the child abuse case was sure that the business efficiency manager was 'mad'. The educational psychologist was sure her borough was 'mad and corrupt'. What it became crucial to realise was that all these individuals and, indeed, most of us are operating within a system that takes away professional judgements and autonomy. We do not have a fantasy of being helpless – we are. Only when it is actually acknowledged that the public service, outside of a few growth areas, is disintegrating and at a fast rate and that we cannot omnipotently put it right – only then can we get strength from our inner resources.

This means acknowledging the helplessness, commenting on it and merging the personal and political in a non-retaliatory integrated way. Having blamed the level above me on many occasions in exactly the way I am describing, consultations to organisations have actually led me to be concerned at the near-suicidal feelings of the people on the highest service planning levels at the impossibility of the job they have been given. And I have been feeling more and more that it is a defence against helplessness and fear of change that makes us imagine that the level above us is the withholding mother, not giving us the milk.

Mother, after all, is the first capitalist, withholding milk supplies and, after a short period of time, retaining private ownership! Being deprived of resources brings out infantile losses in us. It can be hard for us to realise that there is a metasystem which has made whole line management structures helpless. At director level, an awareness of not being able to provide the service that is wanted can be so intolerable that it gets passed and passed down the levels. Think of the army wisdom contained in the statement that the colonel tells off the sergeant who tells off the private who kicks a stone. The trouble, of course, is that in society the child is the stone that is kicked at the end of the chain of command downwards.

If professionals are able to say, 'I am sorry. You need X and because of the financial problems you are only getting Y' there would be a greater sense of integrity. However, as professionals, we are experiencing in our work the same dynamics as abused children. The first response is to internalise the despair of the abuser and be responsible for the cushioning and maintaining of a service that we are not equipped to cope with. As a defence against powerlessness we blame ourselves or just one parent, one borough, or one line manager. Finally, without treatment, we sink into low self-esteem, run away from 'home' into another borough, burn out, break down, or overwork to cover up the fact that something is not working.

These situations I have described exact an emotional price and are inextricably linked to economic prices, and so my title "What Price Trust?" is intended to make a pun between the new Trusts and the ludicrous attempt actually to try and cost something that has no place in a marketplace whatsoever. Let me mention my favourite author on this subject, Daniel Defoe. This has remained my emotional text. In 1711 he wrote:

> I tell you all gentlemen, in your poverty, the best of you will rob your neighbour; nay go farther . . . you will not only rob your neighbour, but if in distress, you will EAT your neighbour, ay, and say grace to your meat too – distress removes from the soul all relation, affection, sense of justice, and all the obligations, either moral or religious, that secure one man against another. Not that I say or suggest the distress makes violence lawful; but I say it is a trial beyond the ordinary powers of humane nature to withstand. Necessity is the parent of crime.
>
> (Defoe 1711)

Daniel Defoe understood over 280 years ago what periods of recession teach us now. Unemployment, poverty, poor housing, health and environment lead to rises in child physical abuse, marital violence and marital and social breakdown. John Major's infamous comment that we should 'understand less and condemn more' sits uneasily with our hard-won but ignored knowledge of how unemployment depletes the cushioning that keeps people away from their inner disturbance. Insurance companies, like our best politicians, however, are well aware of the impact of negative circumstances – bereavement, divorce, redundancy, AIDS. They are our way of counting up the cost of external traumas that wreak their internal havoc. Cicero over 2000 years ago could comment that:

> I refer to poverty, failure, low birth, loneliness, bereavement, physical agony, ruined health, paralysis, blindness, national collapse, exile, slavery. All these states of affairs, and others besides, may easily befall even the wisest of men, since they are the products of chance, from which no man, however wise, enjoys immunity.
>
> (Cicero in Grant 1982)

How well are we standing up to the attacks on our integrity? How much are we turning to the language of audit, customer satisfaction, service users, mission statement, flag statement, costing? What used to be a free intellectual networking, colleague to colleague, now has a cash register linked to it.

In two different clinics I worked in, when a colleague from a similar or linked profession wrote in who wanted help with a specialist subject, a standard letter would be sent stating, 'Do come to our workshop and talk about it and we can all think together.' There was no question of that being paid for. Then came the directive that we had to charge for all consultations, and I think it is very important to note the ways our language and inner views have changed. Here are two statements, made by same person, with one year's gap between them. 'I think it is important to provide a space for Health Service colleagues to come and discuss their problems as quickly as possible.' That is the first one. Now it's, 'I think it is important to charge a proper economic price to colleagues from other boroughs. Otherwise we are subsidising their service to the detriment of ours.'

I have been noting such language in order to ward off the fear that I would hear myself uttering such words. When I was asked to charge for attendance at previously free discussion groups I ran, we sent out a political letter stating, 'I am afraid because of the breakdown in the Health Service as we know it we are now expected to ask you to pay £50 to bring a problem for discussion to our workshop. We are extremely sorry about this. Please let us know if you can't get funding and we will arrange something anyway'. We considered that was the only way we could morally manage. The biggest shock we got after instituting this practice was a letter which said: 'Thank you so much for being willing to fit us in. My management has agreed to pay and I am looking forward to coming.' Now that really knocked us out. We were experiencing our new position as a pimping one and there was the first punter saying, 'I am delighted to pay you'. It was a more corrupting, disturbing feeling than anything that had gone beforehand.

I have noticed rivalry between colleagues take a new form. 'Of course our service is more profitable. We are answering a real need – much more so than the X service. We should increase our charges as we are certainly worth twice as much as them.' In the new context, the glossy brochure detailing more and more costing breakdowns on less and less patients, the outside counts more than the inside and whistle-blowers are economically reprehensible as they affect the reputation of the seller.

Instead of 'Who is the fairest of them all?' we have 'Who is the richest of them all? Who is going to bring in the money from outside? Who is going to bring in the extra contractual referrals?' We can already hear amongst ourselves, 'Well, if that place is charging so much a year to place a child and they have only had this training, then maybe we should be charging this price because what would it mean if we said we did not cost as much as them?' This is the ugly way in which some of us join in with accommodating corruption and an abuse of integrity.

CLINICAL ILLUSTRATION

Here is a clinical case where I actually was helpless in the final result. (A full-length description of this child's treatment can be found in Sinason 1993.) This is about an abused boy. The reason for bringing him as an example is, I think, to show the way we struggle with accommodating corruption or speaking out against it. This is very much the process our most abused clients have gone through and are bringing to us. The boy concerned was severely learning-disabled and very emotionally disturbed and I was only able to see him because I was a child psychotherapist in a school for disturbed children. His parents were not the kind who would have ever managed to bring him to a child guidance clinic (had there existed a local child guidance clinic!). He was the kind of boy who made himself known to any stranger with a stupid smiling expression and the question 'Alright? Alright?' Anybody who keeps asking 'Alright?' is telling you that they are not alright and checking whether you are alright enough to bear it. I am using the word 'stupid' deliberately in that we tend to forget it means 'numb with grief'.

The boy, who I will call Ali, in his first year of therapy showed no symbolic play, never played with his toys and would each week evoke in me the question, 'What on earth am I seeing him for?' Slowly, I became aware of a driving idea that I should bring some larger toys into the therapy room and I brought a teenage Barbie doll, an Action Man and a plastic baby boy doll. It was difficult for me to add to the traditional child psychotherapy tools of trade. The toys we use for children – tiny animals and doll families (in addition to drawing equipment) – are almost the same as those the pioneers Melanie Klein and Anna Freud used in the 1930s. When they were first brought in they were highly fashionable toys whereas now, over sixty years later, because of the influence of psychoanalytic thinking on nursery and infant education, they are not high-status toys. Those of us working in the field of abuse are very aware that such tiny dolls cannot be undressed or take particularly rough treat-ment. The pioneers who introduced the toys were not orthodox, but followers can transform a revolutionary idea into arch-conservatism! There can be an element of personal corruption and lessening of personal integrity in the way we fail to retain a freedom to question that our most revered pioneers had! I became aware that by carrying my own internal orthodoxy around in my head I was not providing Ali with what he needed in order to communicate with me. So, after one year of therapy in which very little happened, I gave him two weeks' advance notice that there would be some new toys in the room.

In the first session with the new dolls he picked up the teenage girl doll and said in perfectly fluent English, 'Hello, dolls! Hello, dears! Wanna fuck?'

Now this was a boy who had said, 'Alright? I help. I sleep. Tired.' English was not his first language. No one had ever heard him speak a complete sentence. Speech therapy had not made any impact on him. As a result of my realising that I had not supplied him with adequate means of communication he was able to show me that he had gone through an experience that had abused his language as well as his intelligence. Over the next few months his descriptions of abuse at the hands of a paedophile ring became clearer. It is always a painful experience to hear of the way a child's vulnerability is systematically exploited and abused. However, this was 1983 and there was an added difficulty. Apart from a very small band of professionals who recognised this problem of child abuse, the vast number were not yet aware of its significance.

However insightful and committed we may be to our patients, we are also a product of our own historical time. Just as we only properly understood the extent of physical abuse in the 1970s (ten years after America) we would only begin to acknowledge the problem of sexual abuse in the mid-1980s. Indeed, I consider we are now in a similar position with regard to multiple personality disorder and ritual abuse that we were to physical abuse in the 1960s.

In the case of Ali, not only was he talking of ring abuse at a time when the existence of abuse was still in doubt, he was also severely learning-disabled. At that point, no one had written about working with such a disabled child whose language, upon revealing abuse, showed such dramatic change. This meant good colleagues genuinely doubted my sanity and my memory.

I remember seminars at which I was asked, 'Are you sure you did not imagine the child saying a normal sentence because he so projected into you his longing to speak normally?' I truly wished it might be true that I was hallucinating because then I would neither have to deal with the concerns of colleagues or the painful predicament of the child. Indeed, when asked on a radio show after my book on the treatment of survivors of satanist abuse (1994) came out, 'What do you say to the thousands of people out there who do not believe a word you are saying?' I was able to truthfully answer again, 'I wish I was one of them.'

But each week Ali added more. He spoke of the nature of the videos, the men and the women. But outside of the therapy room he could not write his name, he could not draw, he could not dress himself. His parents had little English and were mildly learning-disabled themselves. There was at this time in the East End of London rather an abuse of political correctness. It was considered that such handicapped non-English parents could not be abusive.

Slowly, the impact of the therapy generalised and he was, after two years, able to have a disclosure interview with the school psychiatrist. The most wonderful sign of change in him was that he was able to talk to her in the same way as he had to me. She was so relieved I was not mad, her relief was almost as great as mine! Indeed, this whole experience showed how painful it is to be the only one who has seen or experienced something. Without corroborative evidence, one is discredited.

However, the point of bringing this case is to recount what happened in the second stage. (A full account of his therapy is in Sinason 1993.) I had kept my internal resources and Ali had kept his and his improvement meant that he was moved from the school for emotionally disturbed children into a school for severely learning-disabled children. As it happened, a local decision was made shortly after to close the EBD school (Emotional and Behaviour Disturbance) because of a political climate in which such specialist schools were seen as scapegoating and labelling children.

I followed Ali to his next school to continue work with him (unpaid) as he was the first learning-disabled child with whom I had worked: he is the reason why I have stayed in the field of abuse and disability. The head teacher of this school was willing to give me a room at the school where I could see him. Ali carried on improving and was then moved to a school with children with a mild learning disability. This is where a serious problem began.

The head teacher there was not prepared to see there was a problem. Ali was able to talk in the classroom, was beginning to be interested in writing and, as for things like hanging round the toilets and looking up little girls' skirts and trying to encourage small boys into the toilet, well, that was normal adolescent behaviour. This was a school where there was categorically no abuse and this head teacher considered the 'new-fangled' ideas of abuse were scaremongering and clearly thought that I was mad and my views could be discounted.

Ali had been in therapy from the age of 7 and now at 13 was suddenly terrified on hitting adolescence that he might repeat what had been done to him. He started talking worriedly about his little cousins and giving me clear evidence of his concerns. He became sure he would abuse a child, and I did not think he would manage to avoid this – despite his treatment – although I knew he would not be a group or sadistic abuser. The head teacher could not be convinced in any way so I started writing those letters of semi-processed anger where you have 'cc to 30 eminent people' at the bottom of the page! I said I would consider the school guilty of professional negligence if the child's therapy did not continue; that he was in danger of succumbing to the experiences he had gone through now he had reached adolescence; that small children were at risk and I considered, given his parents' inability to travel, that it would be criminal for an escort not to be found.

29

However, the Inner London Education Authority (ILEA) was dying and with it the whole escort service. Under the much-vaunted own-budget process the school was given its own sum to organise its services and it instantly dropped the escort service. Under the name 'Community Service', parents as volunteers helped to take children to treatment but for a child like Ali whose parents were not capable of such things there was no escort.

When I started work at the Tavistock Clinic I tried but failed to get funding for escorts. There was a big enough problem for patients already there, let alone Ali who was yet again an unwelcome dowry I had brought to several places. However, with the support of colleagues at the Tavistock, my letters finally made some impact on the head who said he would provide an escort for one term so long as I stopped then. Cowardice and corruption entered me, in that I agreed: I had done the fighting of which I felt personally capable.

What I want to do now is provide an image of that final term which was in a way both Ali's struggle to deal with my cowardice and corruption and my struggle to speak out about it in a way that would allow him some help. He knew that we had one term of therapy and he was informed of all the negotiations, just as he had been in all the schools he had moved to. His first response was to go 'stupid', putting on a false, handicapped smile. A major finding in my work with learning-disabled children and adults was that in the face of trauma there is a defensive way of surviving by 'smiling' and looking friendly and being 'stupid'. Stupidity has nothing to do with disability, which is an issue of deficit. Stupidity means becoming numbed with grief and through that being unable to have access to intelligence that is possessed.

In one session at this point he told me a dream he had had about Frankenstein (meaning the monster). 'Frankenstein has a hole in his head and so did Jaws have holes from where they shot him. Frankenstein had drill holes in his head. The man drilled holes in his head, terrible, terrible, holes that should not be in a head. Drill, drill, drill in poor Frankenstein's head.'

I commented on these terrible holes that were made in the wrong place, the terrible experiences he had had in his bottom hole and now the holes I and his head teacher were making over his therapy. After this, he was in hospital with a severe throat infection. It became clear he had become speechless over the ending. When he recovered he told me that while in hospital he saw a little girl who was a friend. He said she was handicapped and she had a hurt tongue and could not speak. Also there were tubes all around her face so she had to whisper. 'I said, "Hello, Tracey". I thought she would say "Hello, Ali" but she could not speak and my dad and my mum and me were sad to see a friend like that, all handicapped with tubes.' He wiped a tear from his eye. 'My mum cried too, so sad to have a friend like that unable to have a tongue to speak.' I said that he

30

had been a poor sick Ali who didn't have a tongue to speak and he knew what it felt like. Today he had all his thoughts and feelings and could speak with them and he had compassion for his handicapped self, not hate or despair. But he was worried whether he would be able to keep his tongue when we stopped.

At the next session he said, 'Such a lot has happened, Mrs Sinason, now I'm older and we're in your new room. Last time I was talking about the poor handicapped girl and she is still in hospital.' He picked up a teddy bear and wiped away a tear. I said he was an older, thinking boy and he felt sad for the poor handicapped Ali who had had no tongue but just horrid things done to him like the girl in the hospital. He hugged the bear and looked at me in a truly loving way before his expression became eroticised and he asked me to suck his penis – something he had not said for several years. I could remind him of the way it was that when he was most distressed he had sexy feelings that were not friendly.

In the penultimate session he spoke in a long monologue – the difference between his initial language and this was breathtaking. 'Can I tell you something, Mrs Sinason? I watch all the Frankenstein films and I want to talk to you about them. Frankenstein has this bolt around his neck. If it was a human person they'd die, but he doesn't. But when he wakes up and lives, his neck hurts and then he puts his hands round his neck and then he strangles someone.' Ali demonstrated. I said he had always worried about strangling and being strangled. I asked if he remembered that the reason Frankenstein's monster felt his neck was because he had been put together from the body of a hanged man. 'Yes. Hanged and strangled,' said Ali. 'And poor Frankenstein, he cannot speak at the beginning and he runs to a priest who is blind and nice and the priest helps the handicapped Frankenstein to speak but then the people warn the priest about a monster and the priest gets scared of Frankenstein but the priest shouldn't because Frankenstein is nice to children. Sometimes they scream and run away but they don't have to because he is only cruel to animals.'

I said he wanted me to know that a monster, Ali, couldn't hurt me because monsters were nice to children, that he wanted me to know that monsters could be sad and lonely and he was going to miss me next term. Perhaps, too, I seemed like a stupid blind priest. It was fine when I didn't see what a monster I had, but now I really knew him I was running away, not fighting his head teacher anymore. He knew I had hoped to find an escort for him and he knew we had not been able to. In fantasy he saw me running away from the wounded monster just as he had learned to speak and just as his little cousins might be in danger.

On the last session he came looking pale and awful and said he was going to the toilet to be sick. He told me he felt sick and ill and asked me if I had an aspirin. I said no wonder he felt sick and ill, it was our last session. At the moment, there was no hope of an escort and no hope of another time next term. He put his head in his hands. 'I might as well just leave now and go swimming. The head teacher told me he didn't like me missing swimming to come here. I could be swimming instead of being here with you feeling sick on our meeting.' I said he felt the head was stronger than me and he had disagreed with me when I said that Ali needed more therapy. Now Ali felt that as the head was stronger than me – what was the point? 'He's stronger than you,' said Ali. I reminded Ali of when he was at his last school and he managed to say 'No' to bullies even though they still hurt him and were stronger. I reminded him of how even if he did say 'No' there would always be somebody bigger and stronger. But it did matter to say 'No'. I said even though I was losing over therapy, I had still said 'No' to it stopping. I had said, 'Ali needs therapy' and the head had said, 'No, Ali needs school most.' I had lost that fight but I was still sending letters and trying to find an after-school escort. I was still saying therapy mattered even if I did not win. 'I do need my therapy, but they will never let me come. I feel sick.' I said if we really could not find an after-school escort then the only thing we could think about would be in a few years' time when he was older, if he learned to be able to come by himself. 'Yes,' he said. 'When I am older I could get a bus pass.'

He took a game of Ludo out and threw the dice. He burst out crying. 'How can I play? How can I move without therapy?' I agreed. I said there were further moves he could not make without therapy. But a couple of months ago he could not even play a game and a couple of years ago he could not even speak. He cried and wiped his eyes. 'I will fight. I will say I need my therapy.' I said he could fight to continue therapy and it still might not happen until he was older. His face went thick and his stupid smile returned. I said, 'Poor Ali. This is sad for both of us. We know it is not the right time to stop so it gives you that sick and stupid feeling you used to have.'

Two months later I arranged to visit him at his school. He was smiling stupidly and was very demanding in the classroom. The class teacher, who did not know anything about the background, said she was concerned by his eroticised behaviour and the way he approached little children. I was pleased she had understood and told her the background. It made no difference to the head. Therapy was still ruled out. Ali has not yet come back to me.

I am ending with that rather dispiriting study knowing that he will have abused. He needed several years' more treatment. But even saying 'No' and admitting we are not giving the right length of treatment is still one way of keeping integrity. To admit to our patients when we cannot offer the right service and may never be able to helps all of us to maintain integrity. To be properly in touch with helplessness provides us, ironically, with strength. Only if we are in touch with our own real helplessness do we actually gain the strength to help to be able to build our clients' strengths.

REFERENCES

Cicero, Marcus Tullius 'On the State' and 'Discussions at Tusculum' in Grant, M. (trans.) (1982) *Cicero: On the Good Life*, London: Penguin.

Defoe, D. (1711) A Review, vol. 8, entry for Saturday 15 September. Quoted in Boulton, J. T. (ed.) (1965) *Daniel Defoe*, London: Batsford, pp. 130–1.

Sinason, V. (1993) *Mental Handicap and the Human Condition*, London: Free Association Books.

Sinason, V. (1994) *Treating Survivors of Satanist Abuse*, London: Routledge.

4

THE HIDDEN HISTORY IN AN IDEA

The difficulties of adopting anti-racism

Julian Lousada

This chapter began its life as a presentation to a conference on *Hope: a Risk Worth Taking?* Given the symbolic meaning of the millennium it seemed to me to be an extraordinarily provocative theme. We are in a period of such rapid change, economically, technologically and ideologically, that it is very difficult to identify hope, if by that we mean a sense of optimism about the social as a site of change.

It seems to me that many patients enter psychotherapy with the hope that the therapist will somehow provide something magical. Anger and depression frequently accompany the discovery that the therapist has no magic and, to make matters worse, expects the patient to take responsibility for thinking. The disappointment that is inevitably part of this discovery can indeed undermine the ambition implicit in hope.

For those professions such as social work that are concerned with the boundary between the personal and the social, the result is a considerable difficulty in arriving at a set of ideas around which they can cohere. Constructing the social as a site for hope is difficult in a period where the certainties of essentialist politics and grand narratives are thought of as being so fractured. It is as if ideas, whether they be philosophical, religious or political, are either subject to tremendous suspicion for the audacity of their large-scale projects or, at the other extreme, are attacked as fundamentalist. There is a longing for simplicity and a denial of complexity. At the same time there is a fascination with management, with its mission statements, goals and tasks, and the implicit suggestion that there has been a discovery of a sense of purpose.

The reality is that there remains a vitally important contest of ideas concerning the objectives and practice of welfare. It seems to me that one of the essential ingredients of hope is the capacity to think and to have some understanding and curiosity about where ideas come from and, dare I say it, some ideals against which to test them. There are many routes by which ideas become formed and translated into action, and in this chapter I want to draw attention to one route only.

My proposition is that in a period which is characterised by an attack on ideas, considerable anxiety is produced in those who are expected to have them. The attack on the chattering classes, on the 'ologies' is fundamentally nothing more or less than an attack on thinking as an activity. What is so insidious is that it is not just the content of thinking that is subject to denigration, but the act of enquiry – rooted as it must be in not knowing – and the necessary intercourse between complex ideas. Put another way, rather crudely, the argument seems to suggest that the relations between the economic, the social, and the personal, can be understood as if they were simply commodities of the 'dynamic' marketplace. In effect, such an attack is aimed at the fertility of ideas, that is to say, how ideas are transacted across boundaries. Infertility damages the capacity to reproduce, and it may not be fanciful to think that the capacity to think may also be subject to damage. Raymond Williams makes what I think is an important point when he writes:

> Bad governments damage many things – they can even damage the intelligence of their opponents. A government may be so bad that it seems necessary to remove it; anything else would be an improvement. This is good rhetoric but bad intelligence. Even under closed tyranny, opponents must think very hard about how to overthrow a regime and how to prevent it coming back ... Equally, no new government can do much with the assembly of negative forces generated by a previous bad government: the central activity by which a new government stands or falls is the very difficult process of converting enough of these negations into positive ones for practical construction.
>
> (Williams 1989: 141)

There is, I think, a dangerous omnipotence which avoids the painful truth that the capacity to think can also be damaged under certain personal or social conditions of threat, trauma or anxiety.

I want to suggest in this chapter that one of the many routes to the acquisition of ideas is adoption. I want to use this concept, as a metaphor, to explore the experience of an agency in its attempt to 'adopt' a specific idea – namely an anti-racist practice. Implicit in my argument is that there are different dynamics involved in the process of adoption as compared to giving birth, and that this may be true for the development of ideas as well. This argument is not, I should emphasise, a judgement upon the quality of the idea of anti-racism, nor on the agency I later describe, but rather predicated on the belief that the differing dynamics, of 'birth' and 'adoption' provoke different experiences which need to be understood in the service of the idea.

35

THE DYNAMICS OF ADOPTION

As the frequency of low sperm counts increases, there is evidence of real anxiety about the possibility of infertility; this anxiety may be exacerbated in generations who have practised contraception, may have had abortions, and may be subject to unconscious guilt about dead babies. Likewise, in the context of ideas, their adoption takes place in the company of those ideas that could not be given birth to naturally, or, to put it another way, in the context of ideas that may have been 'forgotten' or 'killed off'. So the adoption of an idea, which is so often imbued with tremendous hope, can also take place in the context of a guilty preoccupation with the fate of the idea that could not be given birth to naturally. I want in what follows to think about some of the difficulties associated with adoption. I will start by describing experience and thoughts that arise from my treatment of a young adopted woman, and in the substance of the chapter I will be concerned to raise some issues that I think confronted an agency, with whom I did some work, in their attempt to adopt an anti-racist practice.

Thinking about these ideas, I was reminded of one of my adopted patients who had over the years found it so extraordinarily difficult and painful to imagine the circumstances of her conception. Was it, she wondered, casual? Was there any love? Was she a mistake? A product of a violent act? Could she detect in her past any evidence of a hope for her future? What was, and remains, so very much in her mind was the question as to the nature of the intercourse that gave her life. Her concern was not just to try and discover the circumstances of her conception: importantly, it involved a quest for meaning. These considerations were very significant in her therapy; time and again she returned to them and found their repetition in the transference, in the 'accidental' and 'arbitrary' nature of her 'selection' of me as her therapist. For myself, I was aware not just of a strong desire to be good enough but of a longing to replace her absent birth-parents in her mind: in effect, to render them obsolete, as if they represented something that could not be thought about. This wish for obsolescence had been in us both, but ghosts, or perhaps the shadow of the biological parental objeci was never far away, and constantly vied for attention with the adoptive parental experience. For those of us who know our biological parents it is hard to comprehend the impact of this primary loss. It is of course not the loss of a known object but a loss predicated on ignorance and the unknown. My wish to be a good and reparative therapist draws attention to the intense loneliness of her project. More than with any other patient I have been forced to interrogate my reasons for the adoption of my chosen work and, indeed, she has been constantly preoccupied with this question.

As I pondered this issue and how to manage it within the treatment, I became aware of what is, it seems to me, an absolutely central reality for

the child adopted by parents unable to have their own biological child –
namely, the absent child in the parents' minds. Not only has the adopted
child to come to terms with two parental experiences – one known and
the other not – so, too, the parent struggles to manage the child s/he has
– and the child they failed to conceive.

I recently did an assessment with a mother of two adopted children,
who said the following:

> I love my two children very much, but I have an inner fantasy that
> I would never admit to other adoptive parents – they'd think I was
> disloyal. I would like to see the face and body of the biological child
> I couldn't have. We have gorgeous people in our family, bright people
> with brilliant minds ... I am sure it would have been a wonderful
> child.

By all accounts these were very successful adoptions; however, what she
drew my attention to was the environment into which her adopted children came, an environment informed in part by failure, disappointment
and a preoccupation with an absent child who was very much in her mind.
The disloyalty that accompanies these thoughts can provoke guilt in the
mother, and a sense of confusion in the adopted child. In both parties
therefore there is a concern with what is lost and unobtainable; there is
also, I suspect, a knowledge that the Other has these thoughts but there
is a real inhibition and anxiety about confronting what is experienced, as
it were, as the squatter in the other's mind.

In spite of having very considerable talent and being blessed with
good looks, my patient who was concerned about the circumstances of
her conception was nonetheless constantly aware of the possibility that
she would be 'discovered', 'found out', and expelled from her treatment.
Unlike the infant *in utero* pushing against the boundary, who experiences
its containment, she seemed to predict its collapse and being exposed
to some awful truth. The sense of pessimism and absence of hope was
pervasive. I felt a tremendous pressure, in effect, to 'jolly her along'. One
particularly painful day she said, 'I bet you are bloody sick of me and
wished you had never taken me on'. Instantly I wanted to refute this, but
actually she was right; the truth was that I was increasingly frustrated and
angry at having to rise at 6 a.m. for a 6:45 session, only to have frequently
to sit on my own. It was not just anger and frustration that I felt but,
above all, a loneliness devoid of hope. It was as if she were vividly demonstrating what could not be brought together. The intensity associated with
her absence contrasted with the nervous way she approached and
conducted the sessions to which she did come, as if they were delicate
and had to be treated carefully. The location of gratitude and revenge in
different places produced a split that was very hard to reconcile, and drew
attention to the very considerable difficulty she encountered in resolving

the Oedipal dilemma. Ronald Britton describes a similar patient when he writes:

> Internally she had one self in loving union with an idealised mother (i.e. birth mother) and another self in alliance with a father (adoptive/therapeutic) seen as epitomising anti-mother love. The link between these two selves was missing, as was the link between the internal parents.
>
> (Britton 1989: 93)

What this drew to my attention was how hope for change cannot survive without some very robust and active companions, companions that can tolerate not only curiosity, uncertainty and ambivalence, but also aggression, pain, loss and the wish for revenge. Reparation and the experience of change depend upon this companionship. For my patient to have confidence in these companions was extremely difficult as they were always experienced as coming from two irreconcilable places. What I am drawing attention to here is something that all infants encounter but, as Jill Hodges argues, there is a particular difficulty for the adopted infant:

> All adolescents have the task of freeing themselves from the emotional ties to the idealised infantile object. This means achieving some integration of fantasy and reality to the parents ... But perhaps the inner conflict cannot, for the adoptive child, be fought on firm ground. It cannot be fought in one arena, because it has occupied two psychological spaces throughout the child's development.
>
> (Cohen 1983: 174)

What I want to draw attention to is how adoption takes place in the context of an intense and frequently painful preoccupation with the past. On the one hand are the unknown birth-parents, and on the other the unknown birth-child. The reception that awaits all babies depends upon where the baby is located in the unconscious world of its parents, and the corresponding complexity of the meaning of the baby to the mother. With this in mind there must be a complicated overlap between the experience of the birth and the adopted child. However, whilst many mothers may give birth in the context of abortions, or miscarriages or stillbirths, etc., nonetheless they have the mitigating experience of conception. For the adopting mother, however, there is the experience of the failure of conception, the attendant investigations, the lengthy and invariably intrusive (though not necessarily unhelpfully so), experience of vetting. The psychoanalyst Joan Raphael-Leff writes so movingly about the relentless quality of this experience:

> While trying to conceive, each month becomes a cycle of elation and deflation, each fertile outsider a potential reminder of their 'failure'.

When a couple find they are unable to produce a baby of their own making the impact of this incapacity pervades their present relationship and invades past and future. Genetic immortality is curtailed. Lovemaking becomes baby-making. Persecutory guilt, mutual recriminations, sorrow and the non-materialisation of their joint procreative project are coupled with an irrational sense of personal inferiority. In the case of assisted conception, invasion of their sexual privacy by technology and experts reawakens heightened feelings of childish incapacity and shame alongside renewed hope, deep gratitude, rage and bittersweet dependency.

(Raphael-Leff 1993: 26)

The psychological management of this experience, together with the couple's own unconscious history, provides the complex terrain into which the adopted child is placed. In the context of the adoption of an idea, I want to suggest that something similar may take place.

THE AGENCY AND ITS PROJECT

The agency I have in mind is a rapidly growing and innovatory provider of adult mental health services in the community. It has a number of units which offer residential provision for ex-psychiatric patients. Explicitly, as is the case in many such agencies, it had committed itself to the adoption of an anti-racist and anti-discriminatory strategy. This policy had been engaged with seriously and with sensitivity. What was a surprise, I think, was the discomfort and anxiety that accompanied the adoption of these policies. I first became aware of this discomfort when, on my first visit, the team presented a case of a very disturbed young black woman, Ms I, who spent much of her time trying to gain access to Glyndeborne and other classical concerts for which she had no money. The team was concerned to explore how it was that she had become so alienated from her 'own' culture, adding with some emphasis that she had been adopted by a white middle-class family. Three thoughts came to me. Firstly, I had been invited as an institutional consultant and not as a supervisor and so I could not help but wonder what it was that the selection of this case was meant to represent about the agency in question. It was as if my attention were being drawn to the staff group's experience of alienation within their own organisational state of mind, as if they were, in some unnatural way, being required to take on something that had not naturally originated from within themselves, and they too were experiencing the process of an adoption. However, there was a sense of unease – of alienation – as if something could not be processed. Their experience struck me as having parallels with that of the young woman they were describing.

Secondly, the metaphor of adoption seemed very powerful to me. In the first instance it drew my attention to an idea or practice that is not 'conceived and given birth to' but rather is achieved via an arrangement that always involves others – what I refer to as a bureaucratic arrangement. Thirdly, what came to mind was a 'disturbance in timing'.

Adoptive parents often report and comment upon the lengthy selection process, and contrast it with the suddenness of the arrival of the child, and how disturbing this lack of notice can be. Likewise for the agency, there seemed to be a disturbance in timing which affected their capacity to consider how best to integrate this new idea/practice. This was not a question of sincerity but of preparedness. I was struck by how this agency thought that it could 'adopt' an idea without confronting the painful reality that the idea was not natural, not spontaneous. The idea had to be arranged; especially catered for.

An essential requirement for the vetting of potential adoptive parents is a consideration of how they have processed their failure to 'create' their own child. At best, this is a considerable narcissistic blow to the relationship, but it can also come to symbolise failure of quite a profound nature. A manic response to this failure is to proceed prematurely with adoption – investing the child with the awesome burden of the eradication of the sense of loss and failure. The 'adoption' of an idea, like that of a child, takes place in the context of something that has been lost, that is, not been able to develop spontaneously. It would be inconceivable for the adopted child not to be compared with the child who might have been. The relationship to the child that has been given birth to must be different, at the outset, to that with the adopted child. To love a child that has grown within must be a different project to learning to love a child that has grown without. The danger is that the urgency to adopt the child obscures the absolute necessity, for the future welfare of all, of staying in contact with what is inevitably a painful past.

It is, I think, not fanciful to suggest that within the agency a similar process was underway. It was as if they were so overwhelmed by the demands of the 'adopted' idea that they were quite unable to think, to plan operational objectives, or to undertake any audit, or evaluatory activity. The manic 'adoption' of the anti-discriminatory nomenclature took place in the context of a belief that the ideas of the past were redundant and obsolete. Hence, the new anti-racist ideas, like an adopted child, were impossibly burdened. They had to be completely right, and were never to provoke any disappointment. It seems to me the project is how to embrace the new idea/child whilst at the same time not forgetting the vicissitudes of the past. Adoption does not entail the sweeping away of the past, nor is it in the context of ideas and practices a revolutionary victory; adoption is in the end a pragmatic response to the painful experience of not conceiving one's own child. A response nonetheless that is invested with considerable hope.

THREE ASPECTS OF THE ADOPTIVE PROCESS

I want, in what follows, to consider three aspects of the adoptive process: 'Trauma', 'The bureaucratic child', and 'A place to think' and ask tentatively whether the metaphor of adoption is helpful in understanding the difficulties that the agency in question was raising. What does seem abundantly clear is that the experience of adopting anti-racist ideas/practices has been hard and is not altogether internalised. The forces of opposition to new ideas are internal as well as external. Understanding the dynamics of adoption may help us to think about our internal resistances and so strengthen us to contend with external forces.

Trauma

There are, it seems to me, two primary traumas associated with racism. The first is the appalling inhumanity and cruelty that is perpetrated in its name. The second is the recognition of the failure of the 'natural' caring/humanitarian instincts and of thinking to be victorious over this evil. We should not underestimate the anxiety that attends the recognition of these traumas. In its extreme form this anxiety can produce an obsequious guilt which undertakes reparation (towards the oppressed object) regardless of the price. What this recognition of a profoundly negative force fundamentally challenges is the comfort of optimism, the back to basics idea that we are all inherently decent, and that evil and hatred belong to others. Being able to tolerate the renunciation of this idea, and the capacity to live in the presence of our own positive and destructive thoughts and instincts is the only basis on which the commitment to change can survive, without recourse to fundamentalism. The longing for painless change, free of anxiety, loss and aggression, is present in us all. However, without the capacity to tolerate frustration there is little motivation to engage in the exploration, uncertainty, and incompleteness that inevitably accompanies change. Paul Hoggett points out that:

> To think critically one must be able to use aggression to break through the limitation of one's own assumptions or to challenge the 'squatting rights' of the coloniser within one's own internal world.
>
> (Hoggett 1992: 29)

One of the most important discoveries for the mother of the newborn is not her capacity to love the child, but the realisation of her capacity for hatred, that is to say, the potential for the failure of love. This realisation can be truly terrifying, necessitating a whole range of defensive manoeuvres the purpose of which is to dilute the knowledge of this capacity. Likewise for the 'caring' professions, what is so hard to come to terms with is not just the 'failure' of their caring, but the anxiety associated with the hateful feelings which are provoked by the client or their condition. There is a delusion that the caring function can be carried out as an act of will and desire, both of which are conceived of as 'natural' functions and as such free of the 'unnatural' forces of hatred. This delusion is not only damaging to the helper and helped alike, but is deeply prejudicial to the project of care inasmuch as frustration in the form of ambivalence, envy, hostility and loss, are evacuated from the process of change. What has to be given up, in the service of change, is the desire to be freed from contradiction and destructive thoughts. Melanie Klein refers to 'the infant's desire for the inexhaustible ever-present breast . . . It is not only food he desires; he also wants to be freed from destructive impulses and persecutory anxieties'. However, as Mrs Klein goes on to point out, frustration is necessary for development. 'For frustration, if not excessive, is also a stimulus for adaptation to the external world and for the development of the sense of reality.' (Klein 1957: 187). The trauma for the adopting parents is not, as I have suggested earlier, just the fact of their inability to conceive but also how this failure can provoke other traumas (i.e. social, sexual, of the relationship, etc.). Likewise, the failure of the institution to 'conceive' a non-racist practice can provoke substantial doubt concerning the integrity of the institution itself, which in turn can inform a sort of manic state in which the tension is reduced by a premature adoption. This, far from protecting the agency, can become the catalyst that destroys it. In the context of anti-racism there is a need for the 'adopting' institution to maintain its capacity to consider its 'failure of creativity'.

Too often in the arena of anti-racism there is a terror of failure. It is as if there has to be a guarantee of success. But success can only be guaranteed when measured against moralistic or fundamentalist certainty. It is precisely the recourse to moralism that has, in my view, done such a disservice to the cause of anti-racism inasmuch as it obscures the complexities of both the political and the psychological factors that produce racism, and the variety of actions that might be deployed to fight it.

The bureaucratic child

One of my adopted patients repeatedly told a story of how her parents had 'chosen' her. She was in a crib in a ward full of other babies and her father had picked her out because of her 'happy smile'. The repetition of this story on each occasion she enquired as to her origins was undoubtedly aimed at mitigating the truth about how incidental he was to the process that placed her with him for adoption. Her curiosity was unbearable for her adoptive parents, principally because they did not have the answers. She was preoccupied with questions concerning the circumstances of her conception, the state of mind of her birth-mother, her adopted parents' experience of failed conception, but also it seemed to me she was drawing attention to a bureaucratic process, that is to say, the experience of parents and baby being 'matched' by others using criteria that she could not be party to but longed to know about.

This might feel like a rather offensive way of describing the adopted child, who is so often so desperately wished for. But to my mind it very usefully draws attention to the extraordinarily difficult process that precedes the child's arrival during the period in which a wide range of others upon whose judgement the adoption depends are involved. Prior to the 'placement' of the infant the parents must be in a relationship of some conformity to the adopting agency. On completion of the legal process the parents are able to reassert their independence from the agency. In effect, they must take authority for how they act and what they consider to be in the best interests of the infant. This separation is clearly important, not just for the confidence of the parents, but also because without it it would be difficult to use and respect the ideas of the agency.

Once more there is an important difference between the adoptive parents' experience and that of the organisation I have in mind. Whereas the adoptive parents can achieve a separation, it seemed to me that it was precisely this separation that the agency could not achieve. It was as if the 'placement' for the 'adoption' of an anti-racist practice came from without, and the judgement as to its success or failure continued to be held without, leaving the organisation no capacity for, or perhaps a fear of, developing the capacity to think for itself as how best to respond to, or develop the interest in, the 'adopted idea'.

Adoption necessarily takes place in the context of what is not known, and hence may generate all manner of toxic meanings, which require a container if they are to be thought about. What I am suggesting here is that this organisation was unable to resolve two principal concerns, and consequently their adoptive project was in some jeopardy.

The first was that they were unable to find a way of thinking about their infertility, that is, why it was they were unable to conceive of an anti-racist policy for themselves. Adoption protected them from a sense of failure. Without the acknowledgement of failure there is no experience of loss, and therefore no mourning capable of resurrecting the object in such a way as to be of value to the adoptive project.

The second was that not being able to make the adoption their own, i.e. free from the 'placing agency', contributed to a persecutory anxiety that they would be judged as having failed in the eyes of the outside world.

What became clear to me as the consultation progressed was the danger of my becoming adopted as a higher moral authority capable of both thinking and knowing what to think about. That is to say, I would be adopted rather than being experienced as a container for their own thinking. It was as if this organisation was urgently seeking solutions in preference to developing a state of mind that could think about the unthinkable . . . racism.

I was very struck when I learned that this organisation accepted new referrals, mainly from psychiatrists, who would not provide them with the medical notes pertaining to the patient's social or psychiatric history. It was as if the patient were split in two – one part remaining in the hospital, the other exported to the community: the psychiatric patient in one place, the citizen in another. This was a mutually collusive project in which the bad patient was in one place and the good citizen became one of their residents, for whom an 'empowered' existence was possible.

The anti-racist project was concerned to elaborate all manner of injunctions and procedures (the manifest aim of which was the production of equity) which, by their very bureaucratic nature, protected them from the split-off, bad patient. As I have already mentioned, the adopting parents' capacity to separate from the placing agency allows for a process in which the 'idea' of the child is given a meaning, that is to say the child becomes a known person, owned as it were by and within the family. By contrast I was struck by a monotonous quality which accompanied any discussion within the organisation of their adoptive project, as if they had truly adopted a bureaucratic baby who was indistinguishable from any other. There is, it seems to me, a deadening uniformity that seems to accompany so much of anti-racist practice. In effect, the subjective experience of Ms I (referred to on p. 39), her disturbance and her need for care were left unattended precisely because to attend to them would by necessity expose the agency staff to primitive feelings associated with being close to the 'foreign object', and having to think.

Let me at this point be a little more speculative. Earlier in this chapter I said how perplexed I was by the difficulties that many organisations had experienced following the adoption of anti-racist policies. I think this way of putting it under-estimates how extraordinarily painful the adoptive process was frequently experienced as being. It was not a process of joining: frequently, the result was one of disintegration and recrimination. Far from there being an enactment of the slogan of 'Black and White Unite and Fight', it was as if something had been imported which severed the links of the very solidarity upon which this view of struggle or action depends. I have suggested earlier that an adoption is predicated on there being a 'child in the mind', but what would happen, if such a thing were imaginable, if no such idea of the child existed? Could in these circumstances such a child, its needs and wishes, ever become established, or known about? The child in the mind of course is as much influenced by the parents' own infantile experience as it is by the thought of the child

44

to be created. Could it be, I wonder, that this organisation's adoptive problem was precisely that the child in their mind had to be disavowed for fear that it might be seen as a racist child?

Adopting something that is 'anti' must I suppose draw attention to something that is being pushed from the mind. What the child is not is perhaps more important than what it is. I suppose in all parents there is the strong wish to reproduce what was so comforting and nourishing from their own childhood experience. Conversely, adults have the fantasy that they will, as parents, make good some deficiency from their own experience as children. However, could a 'good enough' parenting take place in the circumstance of a childhood which is considered so unmitigatingly bad that it has to be eradicated from the mind? In these circumstances, memory, association and so on are experienced as posing an overwhelming threat, no less I think than of the annihilation of the baby. Psychically, I think this state of mind is extremely hard to imagine. What I am nonetheless trying to draw attention to is how for this organisation the content of its mind was, I think, felt to be dangerous for the future welfare of the adopted anti-racist child policy, precisely because of the organisation's unconscious identification with the racist. The result was a policy aimed at keeping child and parent apart, in effect the production (if one could imagine such a thing) of a sort of autonomous child. This could only be achieved by an idealisation of the anti-racist child as a defence against the persecutory anxiety that is provoked by the thought that the child in the parental mind would become active.

I am suggesting that the contents of the mind of this organisation's anti-racist adoptive project were felt to be dangerous, and therefore could not be made available for its project. It is precisely the fear of discovering something within called racism that seeks a solution in adoption. Adoption was a solution inasmuch as it tried to represent the problem as being outside. There is a powerful wish to locate racism in the logic of social policy, as a legacy of imperialism, or as a residue of Thatcherite greed, an ideology. However, it is not the rationality of these policies that on their own sustain racism, but an irrationality that effortlessly reproduces it. Michael Rustin makes the point when he writes:

> It does seem vital to assess correctly what racism is, before deciding upon anti-racist strategies. Theories which characterise racism primarily as an ideology, as a system of false beliefs derived from imperialist history and as representing in a displaced form the interests of conflicting social classes may in part misrepresent the nature of the phenomena, and therefore generate mistaken strategies for dealing with it.
>
> (Rustin 1991: 71)

This is not the place to go in any length into what the 'internal racist' psychically represents. However, I want to end by saying that the racist mind – if there is such a discrete thing, which I personally doubt – depends upon one characteristic above all, and that is the capacity to dehumanise its subject. If the subject does not excite curiosity, ambivalence and thought, in no real way does it exist. Its existence is simply as a vehicle for unwanted projections and, in a more disguised form, envy.

The anti-racist policy of this organisation in its practice produced not a whole object but one that was split between patient and citizen, and was underpinned by an unconscious fear of what would happen if the part-objects were to come together. There is little meaning to the much-flaunted notion of 'working with difference' unless that which is different is capable of being held in the mind as an object that can excite both love and hate. It is, I suspect, the fear of the hateful feelings associated with that which is different that motors so much of anti-racist policy. This has a tendency to produce what can only in the end be a perverse intercourse, and one which depends upon the repudiation of complexity. There is no such thing as a simple anti-racist discourse; without the capacity to embrace complexity there is an alarming similarity between the state of mind of the racist and the anti-racist.

The project of the adoption of anti-racist strategies is clearly of the utmost importance. The metaphor of adoption draws attention to a wish that cannot be realised through a biological conception. The adopted child is no less longed for and cherished; likewise the adopted idea, but it is nonetheless different in some important respects from the conceived child. It is necessary to engage with the difference in character and antecedents of the adopted child or idea if they are to have the possibility of development. Cohen makes a very similar point when he writes:

There is no space here for eccentricities, and little room for doubt. In fact it seems that the more powerless or marginal the individual or group, the greater the pressures to adopt positions of omnipotence from which to broadcast one's views or personal centrality, to cast out the taint of exclusion through the counter-assertion of moral superiority, to exchange negative stereotypes for positive ones. But to uncouple the relation between difference and domination in this way also means to deny the Other within, to forge purified identities in which other classes, other ethnicities and other sexualities have no place. In other words, to repudiate that anxiety of influence through the politics of narcissism.

(Cohen 1993: 2)

A place to think

The accusation of racism can produce a response that, via a reaction-formation, converts the feelings of persecution (implicit in the accusation) into a thoughtless admiration of the victim. This can lead, as I think was the case in this agency, to a practice which in essence is concerned to reduce the anxiety aroused by the accusation, and its embodiment in the black client. Grandiose ambition replaces the reality, conflict, discomfort and modesty of what can be achieved for the client. The wish is that, like some foreign body, racism can be cut out, made obsolete by the adoption of strategies and practices. However, what is avoided here is the fact that racism is the product of a way of thinking or, to be more accurate, a fear of thinking – what Christopher Bollas described as 'intellectual genocide' (Bollas 1993: 207). The capacity to keep in mind the racist is as crucial to the anti-racist practice as keeping the birth mother/parents is to the project of adoption. It seemed to me that the agency longed for a two-person relationship between worker (the rescuer) and client (the victim) and delusionally hoped that this alliance would expel the racist. The help offered then was predicated on not just the denial of the third party, but also a denial of the interconnectedness between the victim and racist.

In conclusion, I have tried to find a way of thinking about how an idea is given life. Adoption is by no means the only route but it is, in my view, an important one. The point I want to stress is that both the adopting parents and the child come together with a conscious and unconscious history. If this history is denied, pushed out of the mind, then something toxic is not dealt with which in turn can be damaging to the project. In these circumstances the adopted child/idea has the awesome responsibility of producing a solution to the anxiety and pain that informed the decision to adopt. It is of course a responsibility that cannot be realised, and leaves the protagonists in a state of mutual and destructive recrimination.

I have suggested that the project of adoption of a child or an idea is different from the experience of giving birth. Both 'projects' involve the bringing up of infants. However, the one is informed by the celebration of creativity and continuity, the other by its failure and the attendant grief, shame and a sense of an encounter with the unknown. Edgar Reitz interviewed about his film *Heimat* says:

> Remembering is a creative act. Our past is a pile of broken pieces. When we remember, we take these little mosaic pieces and build a new life with them. When we write down memories, or make a film about them, we rescue a bit of life from death and out it on a level where it can exist longer. In that there is a kind of love.
>
> (Reitz 1993)

Racism is not, as Michael Rustin above points out, simply or only an ideology, a set of oppressive practices or false beliefs. Racism is a way of managing hatred, of protecting the self against the feeling of fragmentation, which is associated with the outsider. Perhaps for the anti-racist what is most difficult to come to terms with is the familiarity with both hatred and the attendant sense of threat. It seems to me that the anti-racist project can never proceed securely unless it can be approached with the capacity to consider both its social and psychic history. The adoptive project cannot hope to succeed in the circumstances where it is expected to conform to an over-determined programme. The failures and disappointments of the past, together with the necessarily uncertain origins of the adoptive infant, or idea, have to be given their place in the service of an uncertain future.

REFERENCES

Bollas C. (1993) *Being a Character*, London: Routledge.

Britton R. (1989) *The Oedipus Complex Today*, London: Karnac Books.

Cohen P. (1983) 'Summary of Jill Hodges' conference contribution "Oedipus was Adopted"', *Bulletin of the Hampstead Clinic* 6, 2: 171–4.

Cohen P. (1993) *Home Rules*, New Ethnicities Unit, University of East London.

Hoggett P. (1992) *Partisans in an Uncertain World*, London: Free Association Books.

Kline M. (1957) *Envy and Gratitude*, London: Hogarth Press.

Raphael-Leff J. (1993) 'Transition to Parenthood – Infertility', paper given at Family Creation Conference, 1992 and published in Burnell A. (ed.) *Infertility and Adoption Seminar Series* (available from Post-Adoption Centre, London NW5).

Reitz E. (1993) *Observer* (30 May).

Rustin M. (1991) *The Good Society and the Inner World*, London: Verso.

Williams R. (1989) 'Ideas and the Labour Movement', in *Resources of Hope*, London: Verso.

5

COUNSELLING IN HIGHER EDUCATION: WHAT KIND OF CONTRIBUTION IS POSSIBLE?

A case study of a counselling service in a period of change

Eileen Smith

THE CONTEXT

A collage of quotations – from letters, memos, telephone and face to face conversations – may give a flavour of the day to day experience of working in a counselling service in Higher Education now.

'This student's mother is dying – he's been told there's a waiting list. Can you help?' (telephone call from a tutor)

'This student has been discharged from hospital after a serious suicide attempt. He has abused drugs, comes from a family with a history of schizophrenia and doubts his own sanity. I hope that a few sessions of advice and support will help.' (referral letter)

'Could I have two minutes of your time?' (a colleague in a corridor). There followed a 40-minute discussion of one of her students.

'There has been another death – can you be ready to help?' (telephone call at 8.30 a.m.)

'Will you write something for the corporate plan; take part in induction for new students; contribute sessions on tutoring and counselling to a course for new staff; run a course for halls wardens; attend a meeting about local health resources; be represented at a seminar on multi cultural issues?' (a series of memos)

'I wouldn't feel very safe if you were to close.' (a discussion with an academic colleague)

'Why should students have something special – they're already privileged.' 'Surely helping one student can be of benefit to the whole

49

group.' (varied responses from senior academic staff to a presentation about the service.)

'I could counsel the students – I just don't have the time.' (a tutor)

'It must be very depressing work.' (a senior manager)

'Of course you are always going to have to work harder to justify counselling than you would careers or financial advice.' (a manager)

Meanwhile, a range of clients, students and staff come for counselling sessions on three campuses. They arrive with very diverse concerns:

- They may be troubled by their inability to study or to work with others;
- A placement or assignment may have put them in touch with unmanageable memories or emotions, for example, about past sexual abuse;
- They may be concerned about a relationship that has gone wrong, or a difficulty in making relationships;
- They may be trying to cope with a death or an unplanned pregnancy;
- They may be suffering panic attacks or depression.

Some attend for just a few sessions, some need much more prolonged help over the months and years of their courses.

These examples of clients and interactions are not exhaustive but they may convey some sense of the multiplicity of expectations of and responses to one counselling service.

WHY WRITE ABOUT IT?

This chapter is being included for a number of reasons. One purpose is to illuminate the context from which the book arose – the thinking behind the choice of conference themes and commissioned chapters for this book. Another is as a vehicle for thought; the writing coincides with a period of stocktaking and reassessment for the counselling team at the university. My hope was that the writing and discussion of this chapter should stimulate creative reconsideration of the counselling service's history, current situation and task by myself and my colleagues.

However, the main purpose of this chapter is to provide a case study of a particular unit at a particular moment in time. It will give another illustration of the themes of this book by describing and discussing some of the ethical and practical difficulties and dilemmas a group of practitioners in one setting encountered when working in an organisation going through far-reaching and rapid changes. It is the only chapter which deals solely with an educational context, although a number of others describe consulting to and supervising across different kinds of institution, including educational ones. Although each work situation and moment in an organisation's development is unique, many of the issues and processes encountered by the counsellors in one university service may resonate with those of workers with different caring functions in other settings. The aim is not to give answers but to convey the feeling and thinking of one group of mental health professionals as they struggled to preserve their integrity and capacity for reflection in the face of potentially demoralising change.

Some, although not all, of the questions we have been grappling with arise from being part of an organisation which has changed practically beyond all recognition in the last ten years. Changes in government education policy and funding, declining local industry, shifts in the job market, debates about access to and the purpose of education have all influenced the structure and culture of what was originally a local technical college. The number of students in the university has trebled; it has moved from being a polytechnic under local authority control to independent corporate status to becoming a new university, competing with older universities for research funding and standing. The move to university status was accompanied by a major restructuring of staffing which resulted in a large number of early retirements. There have been mergers and rumours of mergers with other educational establishments. The original emphasis on engineering has decreased and the health and human sciences subject area now attracts the largest number of students. Flexibility of course delivery has been a growing priority. There has been a shift – not uncontested – towards a more business-orientated and managerial culture. Financial constraints have been a major preoccupation.

Meanwhile the counselling service has grown only a little in size, has retained the same apparent structure and tried to hold on to a fairly constant set of values and philosophy. However, changes in the wider institution have put considerable pressure on established ways of thinking and functioning. Counsellors have become increasingly stressed and sometimes quarrelsome as the strains, caused partly by changing government and university policy, have brought more and more students to ask for much-needed help.

There are ongoing debates within the service and with managers and referrers about which clients and activities should be prioritised and how the service should relate to others in the university. I have had to ask which aspects of the work are essential and cannot be compromised but also which reactions to change are merely self-righteous and self-protective rather than principled. It has been necessary to consider what the service was doing with the projections it inevitably received, how successfully it was processing and containing them and what counsellors themselves might be projecting into other groups and individuals. I have had to ask too how it is possible to know when feelings are not the result of a failure to process, but a legitimate response to unjust policies or procedures. Such reflections consume a great deal of time and energy. They can divert attention from clients. However, an understanding of the connections between institutional difficulty and the experience of staff and students may enhance the counselling work.

THE BACKGROUND

At the time of writing, almost all British universities provide a counselling service, at least for their student members, although the services vary in size, theoretical orientation and institutional philosophy. A full history of the development of counselling in British education and a discussion of the issues faced by the profession are offered by Bell (1996). Here my interest is in how changing and disputed educational philosophy and practice have impinged upon the philosophy and practices of one particular counselling service.

The last 30 years have seen considerable expansion in the university sector: since the publication of *The Robbins Report* in 1963 there have been successive initiatives to provide for increased student numbers and widen access to higher education. The intention behind these was to reduce the waste of untapped talent which was seen as harmful to both individuals and the economy.

In the 1960s and 1970s there were also very varied signs of interest in emotional states. The 'growth movement' flourished; publications in the field abounded; new courses for counselling and psychotherapy training were set up; the British Association for Counselling was established in 1976. These new developments were not homogeneous nor can they be understood simply. A culture's turning to the personal can be variously interpreted: it may be seen as a disillusioned retreat from the possibility of collective change, or as the result of the achievement of sufficient stability to permit inward exploration. For the individual, the choice to concentrate on the personal may be healthy or evasive or somewhere in between.

However, whatever the mixed motives and many determinants, there was some area of belief shared by educationalists and counsellors in the importance of individual self-development. The Oxbridge concept of the moral tutor was not obsolete and universities accepted some responsibility for the care of their students. It was hoped that counselling services would help promote both personal development and academic achievement – which were seen as linked – and help students make the transition from adolescence to adulthood. A number of services opened and in 1970 the Association for Student Counselling was established. (For a history of this development see Bell 1996.) The Association came to recommend that counsellors in education should have an educational and preventive role as well as a remedial one.

This former college of technology became a polytechnic in 1969; in the same year it set up a counselling service. This was before the days of mission statements but the aim was to provide psychological support for students and back-up for their tutors within a comprehensive system of pastoral care. The current aims of the service are officially defined (by the service itself) as offering high-quality counselling to students and staff, contributing from a counselling perspective to the educational life of the university and contributing to the development of understanding and knowledge in the field of counselling. These are very much in tune with the ASC guidelines. Senior managers have not entered into much debate about these aims but their allocation of resources to the service clearly has a major influence on whether or not they can be achieved.

RECENT CHANGES

Like most other university staff and their counterparts in other institutions, the counsellors have been affected by the profound changes brought about by the implementation of government policy in higher education. Perhaps the most obvious change this service has had to respond to has been the huge growth in student numbers, without a corresponding growth in the number of administrative or counselling staff. In eight years, student numbers have trebled while counselling staffing has been at a virtual standstill. Some of the growth has come about by increasing intake on already established courses but much is the result of mergers with other institutions and hence the acquisition of new areas of work. The changing course profile has meant an increase in numbers of students training for the helping professions who need emotional competence if they are to qualify and practice safely. Teaching methods have been revised quite radically: there is now more emphasis on student-centred learning, group work and group assessment and less contact time with staff; the regular individual tutorial has virtually vanished. Academics have been very stretched; counsellors who do most of their work one to one have also felt stressed by the increased demand caused by these larger numbers.

There seems, moreover, to have been a change in the kind of student being admitted. Polytechnics traditionally recruited students with non-standard entry qualifications and had grown skilled at helping mature students, who often lack confidence initially, make the best of their opportunities. However, the pressure to fill all places combined with the decline in employment opportunities has meant the arrival of some students who are in education not because they missed out first time round but because they cannot find suitable work or think of what else to do. These may come to the university already somewhat disappointed, as may those who have not been accepted by their first choice of university.

Counsellors throughout higher education have commented on an apparent increase in disturbance in the students they encounter. Sixty-nine per cent of higher education institutions surveyed by the ASC Research Sub-committee in 1993–4 reported an increase in psychological disturbance among their clientele. The interrelationship between economic recession, cultural values and individual emotional states is complex and explored elsewhere in this collection. (See, in particular, Jean White's discussion of education in Chapter 11.) What I would argue is that the adaptations made to traditional teaching and pastoral structures which followed rapid expansion have weakened frameworks and attitudes that might have helped contain vulnerable individuals. The number and percentage of suicidal clients and clients with a history of previous contact with psychiatric services have increased as competitive individualism has become more prevalent in the wider society and the time and mental space for giving individual attention less available in the university.

Another major institutional change has been the shift to university status. This has raised staff and student expectations and put increased pressure on staff to do well in the research assessment exercises. But just as the former polytechnic proudly achieved university status there seems to have been a real change in the idea of a university. The vocabulary of accountability, appraisal, performance indicators, audit, line management and acceleration is heard everywhere. There is an acknowledgement of a duty of care to students but the prevailing educational philosophy of the 1960s and 1970s, with its emphasis on self-fulfilment and time to experiment, is in conflict with a much more utilitarian view of the purpose of education. Students are suffering increased financial hardship and insecurity and may have less time and inclination for the disinterested and imaginative exploration necessary for truly productive work and development.

All these changes have had considerable psychological effects on the members of the university. Survival and competition have been key themes. It is almost as if the university has been engaged in a kind of war – dressing itself up for inspection, pushing to extend its frontiers, increasing the sophistication of its armoury. Meanwhile, the ordinary citizens have had to endure hardship and rationing. Moreover, there has been a certain amount of civil war going on in the shape of competition for resources within and between units. For those staff involved in successive restructuring or feeling threatened with redundancy, there have been fears about their own survival as members of the university. Students too share this fear – of not having enough money to live on, of failing their examinations, of not being able to establish themselves in the student role or with their peer group. The preoccupation with survival issues has meant a weakening of the sense of the university as a holding and containing environment in which its members could safely experiment and learn.

WHAT IMPACT HAS THIS ENVIRONMENT HAD ON THE SERVICE?

Not all the difficulties the counsellors have had to face are attributable to these changes. Units which care for people in trouble are rarely likely to be able to get on with their work in a totally straightforward way. Client distress is likely to get into staff teams, who may sometimes be infected as well as affected by the pain they encounter. Providers of care develop their own defensive structures against the anxiety this pain engenders. Moreover, therapeutic units are likely to attract a whole range of irrational feelings from idealisation to envious attack. (For a recent discussion of these dynamics see Obholzer and Roberts 1994.) Psychic pain is not new nor is the use of one individual or group to contain it for the organisation. Much that is enduring or more properly located in an individual or group history may be wrongly attributed to some external agency or change.

Yet the service has of course been profoundly affected by recent changes. It is part of the wider institution, not an independent clinical practice. Therefore it is hardly surprising that it is affected by the same dynamics as the rest of the university. There have been worries about survival, internal competitiveness and rivalry with other units and strong feelings of disappointment. Frequently, counsellors have felt that what they value most highly is under attack, that it is hard to be creative; they are unsure that they want to cooperate with management changes and fear selling out if they do. Clinicians are not immune from irrational behaviour. Just because they can list the common defences does not mean that they never split, deny, idealise or project, or that they do so only consciously.

However, change is not neutral and reactions to it are not necessarily purely psychological. The struggle has been to hold onto both a perspective on the context and a psychological appraisal of oneself and others. In trying to work out what contribution counselling can or should make in this environment, team members have had to try to understand the context better, to question their own professional ideals and assumptions and to cope with very difficult feelings. There have been matters to debate in all the main areas of the work, although most strain has come from the pressures to provide more counselling.

The clinical work

The basic request by senior management, implied rather than explicitly stated, seems to be that the service will somehow accommodate all students in difficulty within the limited resources that are available without making too much fuss about it. There has never been an agreed formula that would match the number of students to the number of counsellors; hence, painful issues about choices and priorities in a time of scarcity have been preoccupying.

The debate about what kind of clinical work it is possible or desirable to undertake in an academic setting is ongoing among psychodynamic counsellors. Noonan (1986) suggests that working with and interpreting unconscious processes are both possible and relevant in this setting. Noonan, May (1988) and more recently Warburton (1995) and Bell (1996) have described the possibilities and limitations of the framework rather differently. However, they would all agree on the centrality of the relationship between counsellor and client and that developing therapeutic relationships takes time.

This service, like other university counselling services, does a great deal of brief work but it also has a tradition of offering some particularly needy students longer-term counselling and has found the time to do so. There have been spells when there was a waiting list but, on the whole, counsellors were able to offer what they judged the client needed and could use.

Over the last few years it has not always been possible to provide effective help to all who asked. In the last three years there has been a 100 per cent increase in the number of clients approaching the service. Moreover, many of these are in considerable need and have come with longstanding and entrenched difficulties rather than to deal with a crisis, life event or developmental period. Although the percentage of mature students seeking counselling is no greater than the norm, they tend to need considerably more long-term help than their younger peers. The percentage of students who are on courses training for the caring professions is high; our statistics show these students are twice as likely to use counselling help. The service has not yet turned people away but it has had to ask them to wait and has considered rationing. Possible alternative sources of help have also been affected by major reorganisations and budget reductions. The increase in student need has coincided with a marked decrease in the availability of psychiatric and psychotherapeutic services in the NHS; local voluntary counselling services are few and normally have lengthy waiting lists and limited funding; hence, the scope for referral has been restricted.

There have been very different responses to our inability to meet all requests adequately. Undoubtedly, counsellors have worked harder and demonstrated their goodwill and professional concern by fitting in extra appointments and finding extra time for the most vulnerable clients. At other times some staff effectively denied the existence of the waiting list or spoke about it as the responsibility of only the Head of Service – who was occasionally seen as persecuting others with reminders of its existence – or of the secretary, the only person everyone felt able to support. There were occasional suggestions to have more drop-in groups and a counsellor permanently on call – to attempt, rather omnipotently perhaps, to eliminate all waiting.

The team did agree a number of responses which have reduced the waiting list. More efficient use of appointments, referral to external agencies when possible, the establishment of a holding group, limited work with staff on the grounds that they are more likely than students to be able to access therapy elsewhere, and continued arguing the case for increased resources have all made some impact. Nonetheless, legitimate requests still exceeded what could be offered and led us to re-examine our sometimes conflicting values and try to establish some priorities. A list of the questions that arose may give a sense of these dilemmas:

- Should we counsel staff at all? Or give them extra sessions on the grounds that they too are stressed by the system and counselling might help them be more useful to the students?
- Is it reasonable to refer everyone we think can pay for private therapy?
- Should we turn away those whom we think might be more appropriately dealt with in the NHS – even though we think they may just sit on a waiting list or be offered only medication?
- How much time can we allow for new and uncertain clients to form an attachment?
- Should we discard those who act out a lot by missing many appointments?
- Is it cynical or sensible to discard from the waiting list those who do not respond to letters?
- Should our criteria be those who can use counselling best? But use what? Supportive or interpretative work? Short- or long-term? Individual or group?
- Should we try to give everyone something? Or is this to give ourselves an impossible or completely frustrating task?
- Would seeing everyone for a limited number of sessions hide the real extent of the problem from management, the rest of the university and ourselves?
- Who should get most or first help?
- Should it be those who are most disruptive to their teaching groups or cause most concern to lecturing or residential staff?
- Or those who are suicidal? Coming up for exams? Talking of leaving?
- Is it reasonable to think about our pleasure and professional development in choosing whom to work with?

This barrage of questions indicates the professional and personal frustrations about not having sufficient resources to provide decently for everyone who seeks help; it is hard for people trained to be aware of the reality and extent of people's pain to dismiss much of it. Moreover, counsellors felt angry that their reports of the problems they encountered and requests for resources were sometimes met with seeming indifference or the suggestion that counselling is something of a luxury. Nonetheless, some further modifications to working practices were thought both possible and ethical.

Given the university's increasing emphasis on students learning and being assessed in groups and the counsellors' sense of the isolation experienced by some students, one initiative was to increase the amount of group work offered – with varied success. In one year, one group was firmly established after initial difficulties, a small eating-disorders group held its membership, a more preventative life-skills group failed to recruit while another group limped along. Sometimes it was hard for students to accept the offer of a group – perhaps because they had so little individual attention elsewhere in the university and were resisting being herded together again. Occasionally, staff were reluctant to refer or accept referrals from colleagues; this may have reflected their need to hold onto their sense of individuality and control over their work. Despite the difficulties, the counsellors wanted to persist with trying to improve this offer. More recently, a project undertaken with another university has helped revive enthusiasm for thinking and experimenting in this area.

A need for training in brief focused work was expressed and a workshop extending over two terms was provided. Yet only one counsellor brought a client who fitted the criteria for the model being presented and the shared experience of learning about and discussing this way of working did not really seem to inform practice in an ongoing way as had been hoped. One difficulty with this initiative was that the training coincided with unpredicted staff changes and the serious illness of one team member, which were preoccupying concerns. Another was the amount of rethinking and adapting of working methods this rigorous approach required. A third was the growing level of disturbance we were encountering, which seemed to call for a great deal of patient holding; many of our clients seemed to lack the ego strength to use this kind of approach.

The waiting list was prioritised on the basis of written reports of assessment interviews. Training in assessment was provided and many clinical meetings were devoted to discussing new clients. It was not easy to establish a group consensus: the manner of writing assessments differed markedly from person to person and discussion in clinical meetings sometimes wandered off course. Some counsellors found it hard to relinquish anyone they had assessed to the waiting list. Officially, there was a limit on the number of clients and proportion of long-term spaces (long-term was not very clearly defined) any counsellor could have, but it proved difficult for everyone to stick to this when confronted with very vulnerable clients.

Why did these apparently agreed and sensible initiatives prove hard to implement? The reasons are complex. There were real practical difficulties:

there was never any let-up in the increase in numbers so the problem expanded all the time; clients did not always appear conveniently ready to be helped by the latest initiative, whether on groups or focused work.

I think too there was considerable resistance to change. Much of this was to do with the effects of the extent and pace of change in the university. Some of the difficulty arose from internal conflicts about what it meant to be an individual within a working group and to be a unit within a larger organisation. What was to happen to personal autonomy given the demands of the service as a whole or the constraints imposed by limited resourcing? What was to happen to people's professional allegiances and judgements? Perhaps some of the difficulty in prioritising students' demands or needs (the choice of word depended on whether compassion or exhaustion predominated) was paradoxically to do with having a highly trained and experienced team, who may have been particularly alert to disturbance and more interested in curing rather than simply holding and caring for clients. For a long period there was some sense that the offer of a group or focused brief work was a second-best alternative rather than a healthy adaptation of skills. Certainly there was frequent reference to professional standards which were seen not to fit in the new business culture of the university.

As a manager I struggled to judge when professional demands were being cited legitimately and when defensively. I asked myself when resistance to change was principled and when defensive. If it was defensive, what was being defended against – the loss of a sense of control of the work, the fear of exposure or inadequacy, having to re-examine cherished values and practices, learn new skills? Probably something of all of these, but what seemed to predominate was a fear of being overwhelmed by need. New clients were often experienced as the bureaucratic children described by Julian Lousada in Chapter 4. One image that surfaced during a training day was of the students in search of adopters and the counsellors as fearful of having too many sick children thrust upon them by an institution which seemed to want to off-load rather than share responsibility for difficulty. The impact of increased numbers of extremely distressed clients made it a struggle to hold onto the beliefs and values that had brought us into this area of work in the first place and to move beyond resentment and rage to reflect on and process our own reactions.

Educational and consultancy work

The clinical work takes up much but not all of the time. For several years the service has undertaken a range of educational activities within the university. These have expanded and developed over time. The purpose here is not to describe them all in detail but to indicate the thinking behind some initiatives. Examination-anxiety workshops are one very practical way of using skills and insights in an area of immediate concern to students. The service has offered several training courses for tutors, courses which attempt to give them a counselling perspective on their students. The most recent course for tutors reflected changing times – an original 60 hours was compressed into 12! We try to work within existing structures and through negotiation with others. Hence, there have been training days for students and staff in particular schools of study and for halls wardens, contributions to the induction programme for new academic staff and the training of Student Union officers and tailor-made groups for early retiring members of staff, personnel managers and new lecturers in radiography. We have worked within the staff development programme to train in stress management and counselling skills and have planned events along with careers advisers and nurses. We offer supervision to both our own trainees and to other local counsellors. The annual lecture and conference are ways of engaging in dialogue with colleagues outside as well as within the university. More recently, we have been developing our research work.

The need for teaching, training and liaison work has been less overwhelming than clinical requests because it is more within our control and because it is easier to refuse a colleague asking for a course than a distressed student asking for help. There are some who would argue that engaging in teaching or committee work may damage the clinical work by blurring the boundaries and muddling the development of transference with actual or potential clients. On the whole, we have felt able to manage these overlaps and have felt less conflicted about this area of our work, although there have been debates within the service and with other colleagues about whether we should continue our diverse offer when demand for counselling is so high. One motive for continuing with this work is to be able to demonstrate the service's usefulness to a larger number of students than those we counsel, as managers are sometimes given to comparing us to other service providers on the basis of who sees most people. This homogenisation and continued demand to justify our worth can be demoralising but we do sometimes respond by head-counting ourselves.

More positively, attempting some educational and developmental work is partly about asserting that we share some tasks with others in the university. For our own sanity and survival we need to be connected to others; we believe that we do not have an exclusive duty of care to the students or monopoly of knowledge about how to provide it. Working with and learning from colleagues are pleasurable activities. Research and writing are easier because we can draw on the expertise and interest of academic staff. We offer courses but we expect to learn as well as teach – from our fellow tutors in joint courses and from the staff and students who enrol. Such activities are usually welcomed although there is sometimes demur at a charge for a course or conference – as if a 'caring' unit is supposed to be different and not subject to the university's internal market.

Preventative work

The service tries to have some effect on the university's policies in those areas where we feel we have legitimate cause for concern and have the knowledge and experience to make a contribution. We have served on some committees and working parties on topics such as access, tutoring and induction. Counsellors are currently working with other members of staff and students on welfare issues for minority ethnic students. An Annual Report is prepared and presented in a range of meetings. When particular issues, such as staff stress or student suicide, come to our attention we suggest ways in which our expertise might be useful.

We do not always feel that our perspective is as heeded as we would like. Sometimes our representations receive no response. An initial reaction to this might be petulance or paranoia but reflection suggests a number of possible explanations. It may be that we do not present our interventions as well as we might: we may sound too accusatory or self-righteous. We may appear not to appreciate the constraints senior management faces. It may be that people are simply too busy to reply to us. The hierarchical structure of the university is such that our attempts to intervene may be seen as puzzling. On the other hand, it may be that what we have to say to senior managers is sometimes too difficult to hear. We remind them of painful experience, of disturbance, of inadequate holding structures, of staff under strain, of the fact that people and systems have breaking-points.

Counselling staff and stress

It must be evident from all this that the service is ambitious in its aims. This, together with pressures from students and staff, makes working here a challenge – on a good day. Being exposed to others' pain is in itself inherently stressful but present conditions exacerbate the toll on staff. Halton (1995) has written vividly about the institutional stresses on counsellors in the current climate. He argues that the fight/flight basic assumption mobilised by a market culture sits ill with the assumption of the potential usefulness of dependency on which counselling operates. He describes how excessive demands, ongoing uncertainty and institutional undervaluing can undermine practitioners' professional attitudes and capacity to work. Brady et al.'s (1995) review of the literature on counsellor stress notes many of the precipitating factors which are common in the service – suicidal clients, severely depressed clients, premature termination, unrealistic institutional demands.

It has sometimes been extremely stressful to work in the service. The stress has shown itself in a number of ways. Counsellors have suffered a fair amount of illness and minor physical ailments, some of which may be attributable to work pressures. Many very difficult feelings have been experienced. There has been a great deal of anxiety about some very worrying clients. Considerable self-doubt has been expressed – sometimes guiltily, for example 'I used to feel more useful to clients, to think I could help people change but now I just feel exhausted by them and that I do no more than hang onto them.' This questioning of one's internal resources has sometimes been experienced as anger. Conversely, there has been a certain amount of denial, of filtering out the most difficult or alarming parts of what is presented so that relief rather than concern is often the predominant feeling when a client cancels or fails to appear. On occasion, it has been hard for people to hold onto the boundaries of their roles or the frame of the work so that either too little or too much has been attempted. Guarding the therapeutic space and holding onto time to think in it and about it have been real challenges. At times, counsellors have withdrawn and distanced themselves from common problems in order to protect themselves and their ability to function personally and therapeutically.

One consequence and cause of stress has been a certain amount of dissension in the team when unprocessed feelings of being undervalued, disappointed, overwhelmed or persecuted have taken over. Sometimes people have felt they are doing more than 'their fair share' of the work or of the most difficult clients. There have been sibling rivalries and leadership challenges. However, we have continued to offer a service, been available for consultation to staff and developed new initiatives. And we have attempted to understand and process our joint difficulties. One of the most useful features of consultation days has been to help us reflect on how our own experience might mirror that of other members of the university. We hope that recognising the parallels may help both us and our clients.

Some themes have been persistent. We are conscious of the students' transference to the university but perhaps less aware of our own. Rapid organisational and ideological change has left us too feeling sometimes uncontained and occasionally paranoid, in a state of hostile dependency on an institution whose values and care for us we may doubt. We, like our clients, sometimes feel like numbers or products, rather than people wanting to develop at our own pace through membership of the organisation. It has not always been easy to deal with our own feelings about difference, success and failure despite or because of their significance in an academic setting. Students – in British universities anyway – have always been in a competitive culture, and comparisons and rivalries with others have always been issues for student counsellors. The state of the economy has exacerbated these concerns; our students now have to compete not just for degrees and good jobs but for any work with graduates from other (more traditional) universities. We have sometimes found it hard to be open about our own competitiveness despite the ongoing rivalries in the different professional bodies to which we belong and our very varied approaches to the work. Sometimes we have felt disappointment or rage that our hopes have not been fulfilled; this may reflect our students' experience. Some of them may also have had grand ideas of what a university might offer and feel let down. These insights do not dissolve our difficulties but they do help us make some sense of them.

CONCLUSION

The title of this section might suggest that the end of a journey has been reached and answers have been found, but satisfactory closure seems impossible and is probably undesirable. I have been describing a living and lively organisation which has been shifting even as I have been trying to capture it in words. Some of this movement, and my own dual role as counsellor and manager, are reflected in the shifting personal pronouns of this chapter – from I to we to it. Like any snapshot, this piece omits as well as reveals and shows only one kind of light and shade. Nonetheless, I would suggest that there are some useful ways of thinking about the issues raised here.

It does seem vital to be able to hold on to a number of different perspectives at once. Counsellors, or other mental health professionals, may need to remember what they know. As individuals, however self-aware, we all come to work with some unresolved personal issues and hence valency for being used by others to carry and express unresolved difficulties. When difficulties or frustrations arise they are usually multi-determined; under stress we all have a tendency to become defensive and resort to blame. We may all have some residual wish that there ought to be an ever-bountiful breast which never runs out of milk, and an accumulated store of resentment when resources dry up. As providers we may find it painful not to have enough to give to all who ask for help or we may feel angry with those whose needs wear us out. We may respond to these feelings by indulging in damaging blaming of ourselves or others rather than a more rational acceptance and assigning of responsibility. The experience of group relations conferences suggests that being part of an organisation can arouse quite primitive anxieties and defences. We know we cannot escape projections; perhaps we could accept and use that reality in relation to the institution as we might with an individual client. We have access to therapy, training, supervision, individual and group consultation to help us process and separate our idiosyncratic individual or group responses from useful counter-transference reactions to the institution.

Whilst not abandoning our understanding of unconscious processes we need to hold onto our political awareness. Understanding the psychological effects of frustrated needs or survival mentality does not justify or change the situations which gave rise to them. The major shifts in public priorities over the last 15 years may now be embedded in the structure of educational and other institutions but these can be challenged. We can campaign both as citizens and as members of our own organisations for more attention to individual need. We can draw attention to the consequences of current policy. Networking with others may strengthen both our case and ourselves. There is a great sense of relief from discovering that we are not alone in feeling overwhelmed, deskilled or demoralised by the circumstances in which we work.

If we are to continue to work in the public sector and offer our clients something, we may need to accept being satisfied with not offering them everything. In student counselling we often begin a piece of work and must settle for not knowing what use is made of it or for accepting that some other practitioner may have the pleasure of finishing what we have begun. We may need to be clear about our limitations – personal and contextual – and accept our own and other people's disappointment about them. But we may need too to assert – to ourselves and our employers – what we can do, what is particular and valuable about our way of understanding and working. We need to be alert to when and why our boundaries are being tested by invitations or temptations to be more practical or to minimise the pain we encounter.

Of course, it is not that simple. Change, whether individual or institutional, creates conflict and confusion, contradiction and uncertainty; every chapter in this collection bears witness to that. Perhaps the distinctive contribution a counselling service can aim for is to try to tolerate and think about these very difficult states without resorting to excessive simplification or despairing paralysis.

NOTE

The original idea, initial thinking and statistics for this chapter came from Lesley Parker. Drafts were discussed with her and with other members of the counselling team. I would like to acknowledge all the help I have received in writing this chapter from ongoing discussions with colleagues inside and outside the University. Nonetheless, the responsibility for the views expressed here is my own.

REFERENCES

Bell, E. (1996) *Counselling in Further and Higher Education*, Milton Keynes: Open University Press.

Brady, J., Healy, F., Norcross, J. and Guy, J. (1995) 'Stress in Counsellors: An Integrative Research Review', in Dryden, W. (ed.) *The Stresses of Counselling in Action*, London: Sage.

Halton, W. (1995) 'Institutional Stress on Providers in Health and Education', *Psychodynamic Counselling* 1, 2: 187–98.

May, R. (ed.) (1988) *Psychoanalytic Psychotherapy in a College Context*, New York: Praeger.

Noonan, E. (1986) 'The Impact of the Institution on Psychotherapy', *Psychoanalytic Psychotherapy* 2, 2: 121–30.

Obholzer, A. and Roberts, V. Z. (eds) (1994) *The Unconscious at Work*, London: Routledge.

Warburton, K. (1995) 'Student Counselling: a Consideration of Ethical and Framework Issues', *Psychodynamic Counselling* 1, 3: 421–35.

6

RE-IMAGINING THE ORGANISATION OF AN INSTITUTION

Management in human service institutions

Jean Hutton

Those who manage institutions today are acutely aware of the rapid changes taking place around them. They are challenged both to react quickly and efficiently to these influences and demands and to anticipate events, even though they feel confused and uncertain.

As consultants in the Grubb Institute, I and my colleagues are working with such managers, seeking to understand how to assist them to think and act under these pressures, while remaining true to their institution's purposes. For those in human service institutions, the tension around the aim of their work and the contradictory demands of the marketplace culture, has been leading many good managers to become caught up in tasks, and to lose sight of the whole picture. This is true in all institutions, but there are particular features in relation to human services, as I shall attempt to show.

In the Grubb Institute we have been working at this by suggesting that managers have more resources at their disposal than they may realise, which can be accessed through developing the reflective activity of imagining and *re-imagining the organisation* of their institution. We call this dynamic experience *'organisation-in-the-mind'*.

As a result of using the tool of *'organisation-in-the-mind'*, managers in human service institutions can stay alert to what is actually happening, and can see whether the way they are structuring and regulating the work supports what we call their 'core technology', that is, the fundamental process of interaction with the client which brings about desired changes.

In this chapter I am drawing on the work of the Grubb Institute over a number of years, and using concepts, fieldwork, reports, books and papers of my colleagues. Their writings inform the following pages without attribution, but I would like to record my debt to them.

ASSUMPTIONS AND DEFINITIONS

The title of this chapter makes a number of assumptions, and calls for some definitions before its theme can be expounded.

One assumption is the *centrality of reflective thinking* as an activity of management. This seems obvious when tasks like planning, forecasting, decision-making, etc. are considered, but here I am saying something more. I would suggest that managers are continually processing data, information, impressions and feelings to learn what they signify, which results in a body of knowledge being assembled in patterns and groupings in their minds. Some file this knowledge away mentally, in drawers to be soon forgotten, while others are selective about what they remember and use it occasionally as appropriate. There are other managers who hold to it and consciously set about making space to reflect on what they are learning. They exercise their minds in trying to interpret the meaning of what is happening currently in the institution and its context, in order to know how to act as managers.

They may go further and, from what they know about the context of their institution, use their imagination in working out plans for the future – they stretch their minds around problems and work their way through obstacles to progress. They do not necessarily remain in control of this conscious activity, as thoughts trigger off anxieties and images conjure up ghosts from the past and their train of thought becomes derailed. While logic may remain the baseline from which they work, they recognise forces and pressures both from within themselves and from without which are affecting them. I would describe this as working with '*organisation-in-the-mind*'.

The use of 'organisation' needs to be differentiated from the terms 'institution', 'company' or 'enterprise'. The latter are legal entities and their character is spelled out and defined in memoranda and articles, constitutions, etc. They are external realities whose survival or growth is dependent upon other realities, for example, resources, products, finance, personnel, results.

'Organisation' is something other. It is constituted by the ways the various elements of the institution are related to each other. This set of relations provides the institution with its identity – a hospital, school or prison. Some of this connectedness is visible but some is not. How the planning of the actual activities relate to one another in specific processes is shown by the configuration and layout of people, resources, equipment and functions which can be defined as the *structure* of the institution. In practice, these processes give rise to emotions, interactions, mistakes and achievements as people demonstrate their varying levels of competence, their attitudes to work and their personal values. The quality of the work and the satisfaction of the workers is inevitably being influenced by, and in turn influences, these capabilities, relations and feelings.

67

The term 'organisation' is the summation of this planned and unplanned connectedness, including its structure. It is seen as a mental construct, which is emphasised by using the phrase 'organisation-in-the-mind', which then becomes a tool for managing.

Experiences of interacting with those working in institutions in many projects has led us to the conclusion that the value of 'organisation-in-the-mind' as a tool is limited to those who actually manage. In a recent international conference, where the opportunity to employ this tool was provided to a mixed membership of executives, managers and management consultants, the consultants (and some were very experienced professionals) could not use the tool with respect to themselves in their role as consultants, though they could understand how the managers did for their institution. It was only when those consultants who had management roles in their professional companies applied it, that its meaning became apparent for them. The other consultants recognised how their client managers were working, consciously or unconsciously, with 'organisation-in-the-mind'.

The reason why this is a tool for managers is that a manager has to be responsible for all the activity of the institution – to regulate the processes which enable the institution to achieve its purpose while being flexible enough to adjust the processes to cope with variations both within and outside the institution.

This requires working from the *boundary* of the institution and only those who are in a position to relate to the entire institution in this way can build up the idea of 'organisation-in-the-mind'. The manager of a subsidiary department can form 'organisation-in-the-mind' for that department, but unless he or she is also a member of the senior management team, they will be unlikely to be able to form 'organisation-in-the-mind' as a tool of the whole. A junior manager can dream about the institution, can speculate about how it can be changed for the better, and can argue about policy, but his own 'organisation-in-the-mind' is likely to prove an inadequate tool to understand the whole.

'Organisation-in-the-mind' is a holistic concept. That is, everything is interconnected. The challenge for managers is whether they can see the significance of working from the boundary, where they can get the overview and see the interconnectedness of the parts, in order to understand the full significance of the institution in its context. Because institutions can be considered as living organisms, which is shown by the shifting patterns of relations and networks of activities and feelings, something is always happening and management's picture today cannot be relied on for tomorrow.

In the course of examining and working with the institution and its parts hidden facts may come to light, new ideas or opportunities may occur, extra resources be added and innovative decisions made; so that all those involved in working on the outer boundary of the institution need to continually re-imagine the organisation of the institution. On occasions like this it may come as a shock to discover that disagreements about future plans and policy can derive from the disclosure that members of management have different pictures of '*organisation-in-the-mind*', which means they cannot proceed without taking the space for reflection and re-imagining among themselves.

EXPERIENCES OF MANAGEMENT IN HUMAN SERVICE INSTITUTIONS

The following case studies illustrate in different ways the significance of the ideas which I have been describing.

Case Study 1: The manager as container and interpreter

The senior management of a local voluntary agency had difficulty in re-cruiting a manager for a hostel working with young people with moderate learning difficulties. They were concerned about how well the two deputies and workers were handling a potentially volatile situation and planned a staff workshop.

A colleague who was leading the workshop invited staff to draw a picture of how they personally were experiencing working at the hostel. One experienced worker drew a picture of himself standing in the staff office within the hostel. On a shelf too high to reach were books which contained the information he needed to do his job and suspended above his head was a ton weight, threatening to fall on him at any moment.

Reflecting on the picture, my colleague suggested it might relate closely with the experience of the hostel residents. Because of their learning difficulties, the skills and knowledge they needed for life seemed to be out of reach, and also they had a constant anxiety that something would happen which would expose them to failure and ridicule (i.e. the 'ton weight' descending). The particular worker and other staff acknowledged the parallel.

An interpretation is that this worker had been sensitive to, and had internalised, the feelings and experience of the young people he was working with. However, he was unable to work with these feelings consis-tently for their benefit. Instead of using them as a resource in understanding how to support residents, the feelings of the residents which he had internalised had undermined his own feelings and confidence about being a worker in the hostel, potentially disabling him because he could not reflect on and use his counter-transference.

Opportunities had been provided for him to examine what was happening through professional supervision with the deputy hostel managers and the agency's senior managers. The sessions were obviously not adequate to enable him to interpret his experience as a function of what was taking place in the hostel as a whole. The hypothesis was that there was no one effectively working on the outer boundary of the hostel who could provide this overview and who could contain the considerable anxieties of the staff and residents. Neither the two deputy managers nor the agency's senior managers were doing so in the absence of a hostel manager. There was nobody to hold the '*organisation-in-the-mind*', which embodied the purpose of the institution.

This agency began as a pioneering venture in the 1920s, based on a belief that those categorised as 'ineducable' could learn and progress. It was that belief which gave those with learning difficulties the necessary hope in the future to face the pain and fear of failing associated with their disability. The worker's anxieties indicated that he had been unable to sustain this core technology and that this weakness could be attributed to the lack of a competent, containing, interpretative management.

Case Study 2: Managing change and keeping the ethos

Three years ago, a colleague and I were carrying out a project to discern the spirituality of a large Christian voluntary institution serving many different community needs. It has a tradition of work with young people for over a hundred years. I was interviewing a group of users at one local association. A young woman, who had been involved with drugs and was homeless and was now living in the adjoining hostel, was asked by me, 'How do you see the organisation?' Her reply was immediate and emphatic, 'They never give up on you'.

In the project I was looking for evidence of the core values of the work which were expressed or implicit in its aim. In the context of her having now joined the association and participating in its activities, her comments said far more than that they were housing her: the association was providing a 'home', where she belonged and could grow. The deeper needs of young people were being catered for.

Over the years the agency's management had provided many different activities in adapting to changing needs in the community, particularly those of young people. Through the honesty and professionalism of these activities the management had been able to communicate enough of their basic belief, so that young persons knew they were valued for who they were, not for what they might become. This young resident had been there for two years. She had been very unstable, had reverted to drugs, and disappeared several times. Her remark revealed that the management had been able to work beyond the presenting needs of a homeless young woman to what they believed was more fundamental, so that she felt treated as a whole person and accepted for herself.

Since its origins well over a century ago, the agency had concentrated on the wholeness of life of young people. While changing social, political and religious environments had qualified their expressions of wholeness, the leaders of the agency in this and other instances we studied were able to adapt their methods to the external cultural changes. Successive generations maintained the practice of wholeness, by keeping it as central to their management policy.

Case Study 3: Management and vocation

Since the early 1980s, the Grubb Institute has designed and run conferences for parish clergy to enable them to work with and analyse their own actual experience of their congregation and parish. Using this experience as a basis, they explore the activities of their parish church and how leadership is being exercised and their church institution is managed.

During the early conferences, clergy presented us with images of a longstanding traditional organisation, often run by people following set patterns, rules, rituals and principles, with the clergy as the professional leaders. They were aware that the community context had been changing dramatically, both societally and ecclesiastically, and recognised that the challenge to them was how to find and take up the role of a manager as they re-imagined the church at a time when authority was being questioned. To start with, most were naive about the whole of management, assuming it could be the answer to their problems, but nevertheless they felt the need for persevering with the approach as economic and staffing issues became more pressing. This emphasis led many clergy to split off their role as spiritual leaders, which became secondary. By the 1990s we found 'management' language and business principles were beginning to be taken for granted. This mirrored the trend in society generally, where secular institutions were responding to new fashions in re-imagining their companies.

Three years ago we took the major step of re-imagining the conferences themselves, under the title 'God's Call', and proposing that vocation to ministry was fundamental to their roles within their parish church, while acknowledging their need to keep on managing their churches as local institutions with their financial, staffing and other responsibilities.

For some clergy, this double approach led to a major re-imagining of their churches. The 'quality management' approach measures success by the number of people engaged in church services and activities. The parish ministry approach involves the minister taking responsibility for all people in the parish boundaries, whether of Christian affiliation or not. What the local church does is therefore done on behalf of the entire parish, whether or not they know it – or even approve it. The focus has shifted from the local congregation being the end to it being the means. To use biblical

71

language, the church is God's servant to bring about the Kingdom of God in the world.

It is therefore possible to hypothesise that as a church conducts its worship its effectiveness on a societal dimension might be judged on whether the local community experiences a sense of well-being, hope and care, a drop in the suicide rate, etc. That is, it is becoming more like the Kingdom of God. Conversely, if there are signs of increased ill-being – such as riots on local housing estates, GPs handing out more and more anti-depressants, etc. – it raises questions about the effectiveness of the parish church, however godly it appears.

Case Study 4: Management and charismatic leadership

Over the space of a few years, a tiny imaginative project to do with housing elderly people so that they would feel part of their local community grew to national proportions. The founder who had the original vision was someone who could work sympathetically with old people and could inspire others with his charismatic leadership. He devised the methodology, and was brilliant at putting it into practice as a worker himself. But as the idea caught on and the charity grew, he became increasingly anxious. The Council of Trustees who had backed him from the beginning knew somehow things were not right. They moved into action and suggested that they should appoint a manager to run the organisation nationally, allowing him to concentrate on the vision and on what he could do well. The council, with his agreement, appointed an excellent manager, who developed the scheme nationally at a great rate. However, the new appointee and the founder soon had great trouble in working together. The founder felt that a key factor of the project – stimulating the community's involvement in caring for their own elderly inhabitants – was misunderstood and devalued. Eventually he resigned and went off to start another similar organisation, while the original one continued to grow.

Here is an example of how difficult it sometimes is for a leader to understand the function of management as the institution's needs grow, even though the council genuinely wanted to maintain the founding vision. The wish to remain at the level of the coalface was the only way for the founder to sustain meaning for himself in the work.

Because the founder was heavily identified with the actual people in the local community he was unable to appreciate some of the management realities in the expansion of the project into a national institution. His withdrawal meant that his founding vision – that they were engaged in a whole community project – could be easily reduced to providing small housing units for the elderly. To use Miller and Gwynne's (1974: 85) expressive words, houses were in danger of being 'warehouses' rather than part of a 'horticultural' task of the community.

Here is a clash of different 'organisations-in-the-mind's which were not able to be reconciled. The success of the idea stimulated enthusiasm for more houses, which spurred on the management but made it impossible for them to appreciate the sensitivity of the charismatic leader to values which were for him essential, but which for them were less vital and left more open.

Case Study 5: Erosion of a service agency

This example concerns the frustration of a Clinical Psychology Service being subject to a variety of external and internal pressures. After three years of uncertainty about where it would be located within the emerging pattern of health trusts and agencies, the Service had recently become a permanent part of a newly formed community health services trust. The Head of Service suddenly found that instead of spending most of his energy in 'holding the Service together' within transient structures, he was having to re-imagine the Service within the still evolving structure of the Trust.

The psychologists working in each of the Service's five specialisms had become engaged with separate multi-disciplinary 'care groups' which were emerging in the Trust in relation to the different purchasers of its services. The Head of Service became concerned that staff were becoming out of touch with the other specialisms and seemed increasingly reluctant to engage with each other. He responded by organising an away-day with one of my colleagues to help staff make sense of working in the new context of the Trust.

What emerged during the away-day was the psychologists' shared sense of pressure from both the increasing numbers of people in the community experiencing *psychological distress* who needed support, and the demands from purchasers around performance data and limiting cost. They felt that they were seeking to work with people as whole persons, in a health service which increasingly treated them as part persons, for example, in terms of their symptoms and their cost implications. It was hard within the pressures to *make space* to engage with integrity with the distress of individuals. The problem was symbolised for the psychologists by a new time-recording procedure, introduced by the Trust at the behest of a major purchaser, which was time-consuming and neither related to the realities of the psychologists' work nor provided a meaningful measure of their effectiveness.

The Head of Service recognised that within the Trust, he had not been able to protect staff from such demands; its managers had accepted a measurement they acknowledged was meaningless, rather than find a more realistic way of meeting the purchaser's underlying concerns. Within the Trust's management group he found himself resisting seeing the community solely in terms of 'business opportunities'. He felt that the Trust was in the position of having to win the confidence of local people before they would want to use its services.

The evidence suggested that the constant political and economic pressures were slowly grinding the role of manager down, and with him the Service itself. The question for the Head of Service was how the clinical psychologists could be sufficiently part of the care groups to influence their development without losing their own sense of vocation. In seeking to re-imagine the organisation of the institution, he had already secured approval for the appointment of a Senior Psychologist within each specialism, to be the key person in both negotiating with the care group and sustaining the psychologists' professional identity. He recognised the need to think further about his own role, both in terms of how far he was becoming the head of a resources group rather than the manager of a unit, and how he took up his role within the Trust's management group where there was a conflict about the *'organisation-in-the-mind'* between himself and the Trust's senior management.

Case Study 6: Management discerning the community context

For four years the Grubb Institute has worked with the Principal and senior staff of a College of Further Education in a borough of East London. The political leadership of the borough had made much of the borough's position as being one of the most deprived in the UK on virtually all measures of poverty. College staff, under the previous Principal, had developed a reputation for being responsive to this deprivation by seeking to alleviate the impact of poverty, unemployment, refugee status and homelessness on students. When our client took over as Principal he recognised that a poor self-image at both individual and borough level was being used in ways which justified the passive acceptance of the situation by both staff and students.

He was convinced that the college staff needed to open their eyes to see the changes that were taking place in East London, not only Canary Wharf but the Docklands Light Railway, the City Airport and other investments taking place along the Thames. They needed to regard these developments not simply as invasions of the traditions and social values of East London, but as the seeds of an economic revival beginning to sprout. The students were coming from the older social communities and structures to which this newness was a threat, which then gave rise to an increased sense of defeat. That sense of defeat was militating against the educational task of the college at all levels.

In re-imagining the context, the Principal interpreted the development in terms of hope of the new rather than in despair of the old. He set out to reinterpret the newness so that people coming to the college could share that hope and therefore engage more fully in their studies. He did not imply that they would necessarily get work in the new businesses, but the new hope represented by Docklands could enable the college to work more effectively as a service institution with the students, in giving them incentive to go out into the world in the same way that they experience the world coming to them. This was reflected not only in how he led and worked with staff, but in the way he reorganised and refurbished the old buildings, particularly around the entrance area to give a sense of value to all who came in to the building, and through setting up a new resource centre.

The Principal made no attempt to deny the negatives of the present but to construe the situation positively as the bedrock from which to build for the future. His re-imagination of the college from a care agency to an educational institution was his strength. Student performance and achievement have now improved so markedly that a recent inspection rated the college very highly.

Case Study 7: Managing the need for security in the community

This example makes a general statement about the Police Service, based on the work of a group of managers in criminal justice agencies which has been meeting at the Grubb Institute over several years, to consider the relation between community stress and the criminal justice process.

The Police Service has a dual task of keeping the peace and upholding the law, which includes catching criminals. Managers in the Police Service are now arguing that the performance measures they are expected to provide do not, and cannot, tell an adequate story of what the Service is accomplishing in the community. Simon Jenkins comments:

> what was being measured was what was most easily measurable. How much security, peace of mind, community relations or victory for good over evil delivered in each area was not measured. To the Home Office ... what was measurable was what mattered.
>
> (Jenkins 1995: 100)

> At no point did Whitehall have at its disposal performance indicators that more than scratched the surface of what the public expected of the police ... As police raced in their cars to improve their '999 call response times', the public did not necessarily feel better protected.
>
> (Jenkins 1995: 107)

Is it possible to measure the value of the constable on the beat, walking down the street, so far as the general public are concerned? The societal dimension of constables' presence in certain areas is that they symbolise authority, which reassures a public anxious about safety and security. Patrolling the streets in this regard is less to do with catching offenders for petty offences, and more to do with enabling society to handle its own problems of criminality, in the sense we all have some lawless tendencies. However, alongside this there are different societal images. For young Afro-Caribbeans in some parts of inner London, the police presence incites rage and adds to their fear and uncertainty of being in a dominant white culture.

Where the integrity of the police is called into question, the safety and security factor is blown away, for instance when a local community considers a wrongful arrest of one of its people has taken place.

> A feature of the 1990s was a public beginning to doubt the virtues of the police monopoly. Neighbourhood Watch proliferated. Businesses turned to the private sector for security – local councils recruited private guards to protect their buildings and housing estates. Non-police vigilantes, night-time citizen patrols and other irregulars emerged, notably among insecure ethnic groups in cities.
>
> (Jenkins 1995: 108)

The task of 'keeping the peace' is a subtle and sophisticated idea which threads through every decision and action of a police officer. This role of being a 'good object' and how to tolerate being a 'bad object' in the changing circumstances needs a special type of leadership, particularly when it is balanced with the other role the police need to take when catching criminals.

In this description we are conceptualising the Police Service as a human service institution. That this is not the whole story is obvious: it is also a criminal justice agency. Our emphasis is that if the *'organisation-in-the-mind'* of the Home Secretary, the Police Authorities and Chief Constable is wholly about criminal justice, then the community's need for security will not be addressed adequately. It calls for re-imagining of the Police Service by some of its managers.

Case Study 8: Management responding to new contexts

The Grubb Institute's early work with local state schools under the old Inner London Education Authority was done in the context of a shared idea between the ILEA and heads about what these schools were for. This agreement, though unstated, enabled my colleagues and I to develop a number of theories about education and the aim and purpose of school and the way it facilitates processes with its pupils. It was only as we moved to schools out of London, and after the dissolution of the ILEA, that it became clear that our theories and hypotheses looked very different in the contexts of other localities.

When the ILEA ceased and the local boroughs took over responsibility for local education under Local Management of Schools, it became evident that we were now dealing with communities with different values and cultures. The strong culture of the ILEA had blocked from view these community variations in its implementation of comprehensive education in schools. Up to that point, the school managers had been responding to the values of the ILEA as expressed through its officers and professionals. Now parents' voices and wishes were being more clearly heard, especially where schools had opted out of local authority control, and it was apparent that schools were now being pressured to respond to the needs of their constituency's culture, placing considerable strain on head teachers used to the old regime.

Existing heads had to re-imagine their schools serving a context whose culture was reflected in the intake of pupils and the policies of the school governors. The education theories of the Grubb Institute as they stood were inadequate to deal with this complexity, which was further complicated by the central government's changing policies on the curriculum. What is now required if school governors are to carry out their responsibilities is for them to hold the *'organisation-in-the-mind'* themselves, and not rely on the head teacher.

This move acknowledges that schools are doing more than meeting the presenting needs of children as individual pupils. What goes on in a school can only be fully understood by reference to culture, and state schools are inevitably processing the culture from which their pupils come. By contrast, independent public schools would take this as basic policy.

Comment on case studies

In the above analyses we have used the overt evidence in understanding the realities of the different situations. The various interpretations in a number of cases, however, rely heavily upon the understanding of the unconscious in institutional life. Case studies which indicate this most clearly are numbers 1, 3, 5 and 7. Managers who are very close to the significant issues in their institution will always find it difficult to get in touch with the unconscious. It is more easily discerned by the observer, which is perhaps where I and my colleagues have been able to clarify the significance of certain aspects of institutional life.

MANAGING ON THE BOUNDARY

In this last section I want to explore these case studies further, using the model of an open system engaging with its context. This involves taking account of the *inputs* to the system, the *transformation processes*, and the *outputs* as shown in Figure 6.1. The *feedback* loop indicates successful outputs generating new inputs.

The diagram is drawn with a double boundary to show that this is where management functions from, regulating the transactions across the boundary of the institution. Management is always on the boundary, whether of the whole system, or of a sub-system within it.

The significance of what happens at the boundary is seen in some of the case studies. Unless management is functioning effectively on the boundary, the pressures from the outside flood in uncontrollably and disrupt the transformation processes within the system. Some of the case studies show how difficult managers find it to sustain their institution against these pressures, which threaten to engulf or divert the core technology and to skew the institution's aim. Thus in the parish church case study (Case Study 3), the assumptions of the adopted management approach had distracted attention from the importance of worship. In the College of Further Education (Case Study 6) the principal inherited a situation in which the community's sense of deprivation had resulted in the core technology of education being submerged by attempts to alleviate that deprivation by 'caring'. In the clinical psychology service (Case Study 6), the values of clinical psychology were under threat from those of the contract culture.

Case Study 1 presents a situation where the ability to sustain the core technology had been undermined by the absence of a manager able to focus on the process. As a result, the residents' fear of failure had swamped staff at the unconscious level and they had not been able to process this to generate hope.

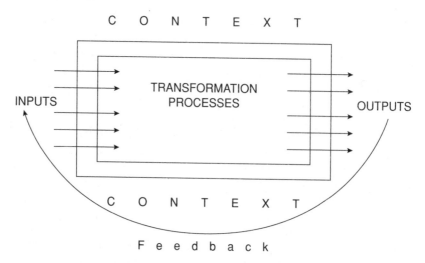

Figure 6.1 An open system engaging with its context

It is vital for the management to be clear about the aim of their institution and the nature of their core technology which enables the aim to be achieved, so that they continually work at creating and sustaining the appropriate environment inside the institution in which the staff can work face-to-face with their clients and deliver the human service to which they are committed. This happens as the manager works with '*organisation-in-the-mind*' as a tool to review and reinterpret the context and how it is impacting on core technology. Thus, the action of the college principal in re-imagining the organisation made it possible to recover the core technology, with considerable effect in terms of educational results. The head of the clinical psychology service was seeking a way of re-imagining the core technology within the new institution.

'*Organisation-in-the-mind*' helps the manager to stay in touch with the nature of the core technology and alerts her or him to the key management issues for ensuring that the core technology is sustained. Figure 6.2 illustrates this for the institutions in the case studies.

Whilst sustaining the core technology within the institution is one aspect of management on the boundary, the other is the 'reading' of the context and alertness to the meaning and demands, conscious and unconscious, on the institution.

The case studies indicate that a human service institution provides the service for some person or persons in need at two levels of interaction:

- The level of the presenting issue, which may be poverty, illness, criminality, lack of knowledge, etc.
- The societal dimension, which has a link with an underlying reason or cause for the nature of the presenting symptom or need.

This means that the distinctiveness of a human service institution is that the human beings they are serving are seen not simply as people with personal specific needs and requirements, but they are also signs and symbols of the society they are in.

As I have argued in Case Study 7 of the Police Service, problems arise if the societal dimension of the constable's presence in symbolically reassuring members of the public about safety is ignored. The police may become more effective in dealing with the presenting issue of crime, whilst paradoxically the public become ever more concerned about their own safety (for example, making more 999 calls about apparently trivial incidents). Similarly, a headteacher needs to be alert to the surrounding culture and not just to presenting the needs of children as individuals (Case Study 8).

One way of understanding the conflict in Case Study 4 is that the management, in seeking to meet the presenting need of the elderly for housing on a larger scale, had lost sight of the societal dimension of the project which was sustaining the involvement of the local community with

INPUTS	CORE TECHNOLOGY	OUTPUTS

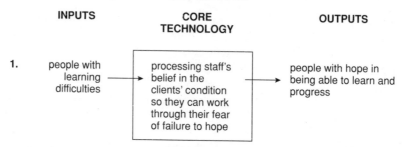

1.   people with learning difficulties → processing staff's belief in the clients' condition so they can work through their fear of failure to hope → people with hope in being able to learn and progress

KEY MANAGEMENT ISSUE: The capability to contain anxiety at the boundary and to interpret staff experience in relation to hostel residents.

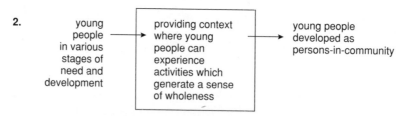

2.   young people in various stages of need and development → providing context where young people can experience activities which generate a sense of wholeness → young people developed as persons-in-community

KEY MANAGEMENT ISSUE: The regulation of changes in context by introducing new activities without displacing the central ethos.

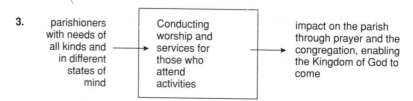

3.   parishioners with needs of all kinds and in different states of mind → Conducting worship and services for those who attend activities → impact on the parish through prayer and the congregation, enabling the Kingdom of God to come

KEY MANAGEMENT ISSUE: Faith that what goes on through worship and prayer goes well beyond the church building.

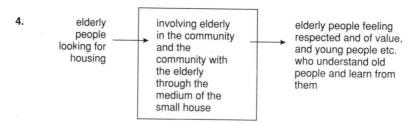

4.   elderly people looking for housing → involving elderly in the community and the community with the elderly through the medium of the small house → elderly people feeling respected and of value, and young people etc. who understand old people and learn from them

KEY MANAGEMENT ISSUE: Understanding how elderly people can give to the community as well as receive from it.

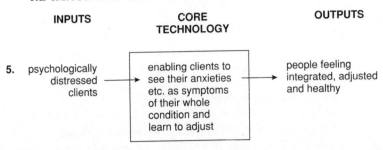

KEY MANAGEMENT ISSUE: Recognising that unless the boundary around the service is held in order to conserve professional values it will be at risk.

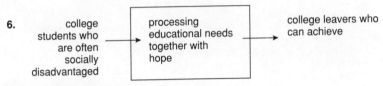

KEY MANAGEMENT ISSUE: Leadership discovering the positive realities in the context and managing the teaching/learning process in harmony.

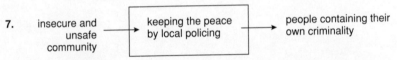

KEY MANAGEMENT ISSUE: Enabling constables to exercise authority on the beat by supportive structures/management.

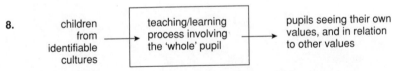

KEY MANAGEMENT ISSUE: Accepting cultural realities and managing provision to work with it in the classroom teaching/learning process.

Figure 6.2 The key management issues in eight case studies

its elderly neighbours. Unfortunately, neither the founder nor management were able to re-imagine the institution in a way which allowed expansion to be achieved whilst preserving the societal dimension.

Analysis of the case studies in relation to both core technology and the societal dimension of the context explains the importance of the argument I set out at the beginning of this chapter about the need for management to find space for reflective activity. It is only by reflecting on what is happening in the inner world of their human service institution and the outer world of its context, and re-imagining the organisation of the institution, that managers can identify how to lead and manage effectively.

REFERENCES

Jenkins, Simon (1995) *Accountable to None: The Tory Nationalization of Britain*, London: Hamish Hamilton.

Miller, E. J. and Gwynne, G. V. (1974) *A Life Apart*, London: Tavistock Publications.

7

CAPTAINS AND CRICKET TEAMS: THERAPISTS AND GROUPS[1]

Michael Brearley

This chapter arose from a review by Isabel Menzies Lyth of my book *The Art of Captaincy* (1985). In her article (1986), Menzies Lyth suggests that W. R. Bion's account of group dynamics (1961) would illuminate the workings of a cricket team. In particular she draws attention to his notion of basic-assumption groups, by which he means, roughly, groups under the sway of unconscious, irrational group emotions which undermine the task achievement. She also raises the question, which I consider in the second part of this chapter, of how a cricket captain can handle such states without the group therapist's tool of interpretation.

The first part of the chapter is an attempt to respond to Menzies Lyth's first point, applying the concept of basic-assumption groups to cricket teams. (I have had minimal experience of therapy groups.) I also try to describe such events in more familiar psychoanalytic terms.

Bion spoke of three basic assumptions: dependency, fight-or-flight and pairing. This chapter is mainly about the first two. The group under the sway of the basic-assumption dependency is, Bion says, a group which demands, unconsciously, an omnipotent leader who may or may not be identical with the titular leader of the group. Such behaviour is, naturally, correlated with certain styles of leadership, though I would add it is often hard to know which is the active and which the passive element in these interactions. I compare basic-assumption dependency with mature dependency, and note some overlap between the two. I also describe an alternative 'solution', the illusion of power in teams and individuals, in which need and shortcomings are denied. I discuss the value of and dangers in such responses. Part of what Bion means by his notion of basic-assumption mentality is that it attacks thinking – that is, real, task-orientated thinking, what Bion calls the 'work-group'. I end this part of the chapter by mentioning the obvious fact that thought which is inappropriate through being over-theoretical can be equally irrational or damaging: in *Othello*, Iago calls Cassio 'a great arithmetician ... that never set a squadron in the field ... mere prattle without practice.'

I am aware that not everyone in the psychotherapy world has a working knowledge of cricket. A Swiss analytic colleague, staying in my house and hearing that I had this 'cricket connection', looked into the garden and asked: 'But where do you keep your horse?' So perhaps I should say a few preliminary words about cricket and the captain's job.

Cricket is a game of individual contests in a team context. Each little drama has two protagonists, a batsman and a bowler. Hence there can be severe conflicts between the interests of the individual and those of the team. Cricket is a game of range – in skills, conditions and time. It is probably the only game that can go on for the best part of a week with an outcome in which neither side is much nearer winning or losing than at the start. The captain has, therefore, to hold in mind the game's range over a long period; he has to consider the interests of the whole team and of the individuals.

To add to the complexities of the job, the captain is required to perform the same first-order tasks – batting and fielding, and maybe bowling – as the other ten members of the team. He or she is therefore well placed to empathise with their problems, but may find it hard to oscillate between wholehearted commitment to his or her own play and the detachment required for an overview of the scene. For many other leaders, such as managers, foremen and orchestra conductors, as a rule this problem does not arise. There are, then, two types of activity, exemplified by humpers of bricks and supervisors of brick-humpers. The cricket captain's job includes both. A third type may occur; perhaps the brick-humping operation becomes inefficient because of emotional interactions within the team; then the supervisor may try to understand and alter these interactions.

For the (group) therapist, by contrast, the primary task lies in this third area, so that he or she has licence to concentrate on the interactions within the group. I return to this later.

I should also say something about the aim of cricketers and the task of the team. The aim, or one aim, is to have fun; to enjoy playing, using one's body skilfully and aesthetically, competing and being involved with others. The work-group task in a given match is to win. Therapy, whether group or individual, has different sorts of aim and task.

Before embarking on the following section – cricket teams as basic-assumption groups – I should say that some of my examples lack something of the insidious force of truly unconscious sabotaging of its task by the group. There are two reasons for this. Firstly, basic-assumption phenomena, being unconscious, are not easy to detect and articulate in any context, even the privileged one of group therapy, and it is harder still to do so in the hurly-burly of emotional engagement in practical team activities. Secondly, my examples should be seen as linking events which are unconscious with others which may not be too distant from consciousness.

CRICKET TEAMS AS BASIC-ASSUMPTION GROUPS

Clearly, members of a cricket team depend on their captain and vice versa. The members rely on the captain to be tactically astute; also to refrain from exposing them to unnecessary risks (for example, by wantonly placing them in dangerous fielding positions). The captain depends on the team for performance, loyalty and working together. Also, members of the team depend on each other – to catch catches and not to run each other out.

Such realistic interdependency is not what Bion is talking about when he refers to basic-assumption dependency. This latter is by definition unrealistic and irrational. Let me give an example. A team becomes pessimistic and flat with no creative ideas. The captain feels increasingly frustrated, isolated and responsible. At the same time the captain hates the members of the team and blames them (in his heart) for not performing better. Sometimes the blame erupts in open anger or bitterness, often towards a scapegoat. The team becomes more glutinous, that is, they mutter and share jokes secretly, keeping the captain out. The situation will of course be more complicated; the captain will have those who remain loyal. whether out of respect or sycophancy or fear; but the split of the team into a passive, smouldering workforce and an irascible frustrated leader is recognizable. As in many marriages, one side projects its articulateness and forcefulness into the other. Feeling empty and useless, the 'weaker' half cannot perform at its best, and resents the loss of part of itself. The 'stronger' half, his or her sense of omnipotence enlarged, feels over-responsible, and therefore often impotent. Both lose touch with their humour and playfulness, being dominated by super-ego functioning. The correlative of basic-assumption dependency is the tendency to basic-assumption omnipotence and thus impotence.

As captain, I experienced such vicious circles of thought and feeling. The public nature of the job does not help one to deal with such trains of thought, as the media and public are all too quick to over-praise a captain when things go well and over-blame when they go badly, thus intensifying both inner voices and tending to create further damaging cycles.

Bion points out that the leader of the basic-assumption group need not be the same person as the leader of the work-group, that is, of the tendencies in the group to think productively about the task. Those on whom the group depends, whose standards predominate, and without whom the group cannot function, may even be absentees.

Some years ago, my son played in a club under-11 team. They were successful in their league, having several steady bowlers; their batting was dominated by three players, a powerful opening batsman, his steady partner, and a classy number three. In several consecutive games only these three batted at all. In the next game, both the powerful opener and the number three were unable to play. When the boys discovered this, they were in a panic, dashing here and there, bemoaning the two's absence, asking each other nervously who on earth would score runs for them.

I think it is fair to say that at this point, before any team talk or steadying influence had time to have effect, the panic of the team paralysed each one's potential for run-scoring; the team, unable to appraise realistically its undoubtedly depleted strength, was suffering from a neurotic dependence on absent star performers, a description that applies to many of us as we face ordeals.

Similarly, I remember a Sunday league match at Northampton in 1971. We, Middlesex, had scored only 76 in our 40 overs on the wet pitch. At tea, Jim Stewart, who had recently joined the home side from another county, was strapping on his pads ready to open the innings when he noticed that everyone was looking glum. 'What's the matter?' he asked. The reply came gloomily, 'Who's going to get these runs for us, then?' Northamptonshire were all out for 41 in 36 overs.

This group seemed to suffer from a basic assumption of dependence combined with the belief that they had no one to depend on, least of all themselves.

One form of basic-assumption dependency involves the often unconscious tendency to leave things to others, thus avoiding full responsibility and detracting from the team's performance. It was to counteract such tendencies that I and others felt it appropriate at pre-Test dinners to stress that it is up to each batsman to see the team through as far as he can possibly go, resisting the temptation to be careless and complacent. Geoffrey Boycott, the successful England batsman, characteristically used to ask players to reflect on how easily an imposing score of 180 for one *can* become a modest 200 for four. Conversely, the team that is operating as a work-group does not lose heart when fielding against the score of 180 for one since it holds on to its knowledge that such a score can be transformed in its own favour.

In a healthy team, then, no individual is over-dependent on others, present or absent. Such self-reliance can even be strengthened in what appears to be a paradoxical way; one can sometimes improve a side's batting performance by picking an extra bowler at the expense of a batsman, thus bringing home to each batsman his importance. Over-manning is demoralising, partly because it encourages basic-assumption dependency.

At times a whole team declines into apathy and hopelessness. During the series against Australia in 1974/5, when England had to face the fast bowlers Dennis Lillee and Jeff Thomson, on some all-too-lively pitches, the team, when batting, would reserve a seat near the door for the next batsman in and would call it 'the condemned cell'. This was no longer robust British black humour; it was the expression of a side which had given up; not so much basic-assumption dependency as basic-assumption depression (though here there are signs of a swinging over, in the absence of any dependable object, into basic-assumption flight).

So far, then, I have given examples of one of Bion's types of basic-assumption thinking and behaviour. It involves a hierarchical split between thinkers (or doers) and non-thinkers (non-doers), in which thinking and responsibility are projected onto, and/or grabbed by, the leader(s). The rest of the team become passive and controlled, sometimes obediently, sometimes subtly sabotaging the work of the group. They lose touch with their creativity of thought and action and become helpless in the absence of key figure(s). The group's super-ego, too, is projected onto the leader; its ego ideal is also projected, sometimes onto the leader, but it also may be lodged elsewhere, out of reach, in the opposition or in the past or future. The British class system, as exemplified in the traditional versions of, say, Army and cricket organisations, fostered such basic-assumption dependency.

A patient in analysis once said, contentedly, that she was confident that 'all will be revealed in the fullness of time'; thus expressing a serenely biblical trust in my omniscience. She assumed that I not only knew by magic all that needed to be known, but also that I would know absolutely the appropriate timing of any revelation. Such thinking is defensive against not-knowing and confusion, as well as against anyone having expectations of her.

Healthy teams require potent leadership and recognition of inter-dependency. They are capable of experiencing self-doubt and of displaying caution and discipline. In all teams, healthy and unhealthy versions of dependency and leadership alternate. They also overlap; the dependency needs of mature teams are fuelled by powerful basic-assumption elements.

For example, a player gains strength from the idea that he or she has a leader trusted to return that trust. A child in a skiing class can tackle a difficult slope because he or she takes courage from the teacher's confidence in him or her. The teacher, and the rest of the group, contain some of the child's fear. The child's dependence, including basic-assumption dependence, permits, with help, a gradual movement towards independence. At critical times the mere presence of the dependable leader allows sufficient calm and dilution of panic for the task to be done.

I remember watching Frank Worrell captaining West Indies in the Test at Lord's in 1963, in which Wes Hall, the fast bowler, bowled for four-and-a-half hours without a break on the final day, and England finished six runs short of victory with their last pair at the crease, one of whom, Colin Cowdrey, had his arm in plaster. I have a clear memory of Worrell standing out as a figure of calm in the midst of a frantic whirl of excitement, and of Hall repeatedly being fortified by the sight and proximity of Worrell. I cannot prove it, but my impression is that without the latter the whole West Indian effort would have collapsed like that of a 2-year-old who in strange surroundings is suddenly unable to locate its mother.

We also know that the safe group is one in which members can, to a point, afford to be childish, just as in analysis the patient can come to trust the process and the analyst enough to be able to risk uttering 'ridiculous' ideas, or to express directly his or her inability to trust.

It is, though, clear that groups operating in basic-assumption dependency mode tend to lose touch with certain strengths – with individuality, self-reliance, creativity and confidence. Such phenomena give rise to an interesting question. Is there something irrational in realistic pessimism, something rational in unrealistic optimism? I think there are stages in maturity here. Some players will allow a realistic assessment of their likely defeat to ensure defeat; the prophecy becomes self-fulfilling. Others have a last-ditch mentality that somehow produces optimum effort only when defeat stares them in the face. Yet others can face the 'two imposters',[2] success and failure, with equanimity even as prospects, in advance of the outcome. Much depends on how different individuals (and teams) deal with the guilt of assertiveness, aggression and the infliction of humiliation or defeat on others (a topic which it is not possible to explore in this chapter). Let me first mention two individual cricketers for whom it went against the grain to admit fallibility or the possibility of defeat – Dennis Lillee and the England all-rounder, Brian Close. I will then describe this attitude when it belongs to teams or groups, and consider whether it represents another form of basic-assumption activity.

In sport, as in many other activities, it probably helps to overvalue rather than undervalue oneself and one's group. Rodney Marsh, the Australian wicket-keeper, tells a story of a one-innings match in 1977 between Western Australia and Queensland, at that time the strongest state sides. Western Australia were bowled out for a mere 78. Marsh, their captain, gave a team talk to his disconsolate players. 'Let's at least put up a show for our home crowd,' he said, 'and get two or three of them out.' At this point, Lillee burst in angrily. 'Put up a show? Get two or three of them out?' he said. 'We're going to win!' He then bowled Viv Richards for nought, took four wickets for 19, and Queensland were all out for 61.

One feature of cricket is that performances are so measurable, a fact which makes it hard for players to fool themselves about their ability. However, players are human, and thus do deceive themselves. Brian Close was an example. He was always convinced that his dismissal was a freak of nature, an act of God, perhaps, or the fault of a bystander; never his own fault. Thus, after being bowled for nought he once sincerely blamed the 12th man for 'giving him chewing-gum of t'wrong bloody flavour'.

It would have been pointless, I think, to try to convince Lillee or Close of the illusoriness of their belief-systems. Firstly, they would not have been persuaded; secondly, the advantages of the over-valuation of self and team probably, in these cases, outweighed any disadvantages of the players' cutting themselves off from opportunities to learn from mistakes. (We could compare the dangers of interpreting a child's fantasies of power solely as failures in depressive position reality-thinking.)

Lillee and Close, in these two examples, both spoke as if they believed something untrue: Lillee that it was likely, or even certain, that they would dismiss Queensland for less than 78 runs; Close that the main factor in his failure lay in the flavour of the chewing-gum. Yet it may be that their attitudes helped rather than hindered. Lillee's team suddenly began to believe that they *could* win (which *was* true). His emotional attitude had an inspiring effect on himself, and his attitude, together with his performance, inspired the rest of the team. Close's attitude saved him from possibly inhibiting self-doubt.

It is clear that in these examples illusion and truth are hard to disentangle. The same is true of group illusions. Team members, when things go well, may come to think, unconsciously, that they are infallible, that they have only to turn up al the ground to win.

In 1980, Middlesex started the season really well. As captain I had to be jolted out of some complacency; the previous season we finished 13th out of the 17 teams in the championship table, and I might have continued to shrug my shoulders and attribute our decline to outside forces, had it not been for a delay in my reappointment while the committee quizzed me about how I intended to change things for the better in 1980.

Thus stirred, I decided to play a more active and authoritarian role in the pre-season practice, and took a tougher line with regard to such things as dates of return from abroad, punctuality and so on. Whatever the effect of this, we had a strong team, and for several weeks we won every match that was not interfered with by rain. After 11 consecutive wins in one-day matches, things started to go wrong, and we lost four such games on the trot. After talking individually with all the players, I called a team meeting. The most persuasive remarks came from Roland Butcher. He said that we had got into a frame of mind in which we were not really concentrating on the matter in hand. He reminded us how much the conversation had become dominated by jokes, bets and arguments about the number of trophies we would win (there were four to be played for). He said that he thought we all had mental images of rows of replica trophies on our mantelpieces at home. Instead of going into games keyed up for each ball, each over, each session, we had half our minds on the long-term outcome.

I think that what Butcher was describing was a group illusion in a flight group; an illusion of invincibility and of magical achievement, in which, as a group, we had lost touch with our work-group mentality.

Another example: pre-Test dinners are occasions whose aim is to foster team-spirit. Collingwood (1938) wrote that 'The tribe which dances a war-dance before going out to fight its neighbours is working up its war-like emotions'. Such ceremonies achieve their aim partly by encouraging a simultaneous group illusion. I say this on the basis of the rather manic atmosphere that prevailed at these dinners, no doubt partly as a denial of anxiety, in which there would be a dramatic exaggeration of the team's ability in relation to the opponents'. For example, we would go through the Australians' batting line-up, discussing their weaknesses. We would then do the same with their bowling. Someone would joke: 'Right, we've bowled them out for 85; now we've just scored a quick 450'.

In short- and long-term ways, the group can serve as a home or nest for its members. To some extent this is a reflection of individuals' insecurity (to some extent it is a natural human need). One solution for the person who lacks good internal objects is the idealisation of the group and the discovery or achievement of an identity, however shallow or precarious, by means of the group.

A young woman who had always hated her home, and particularly her mother, and had wanted to get away, found living in college rooms idyllic. She said that it felt like home, the home she'd never had, a home in which she never had to be alone. She wrote many of her essays in other students' rooms. She belonged to the campus and spent much of her holidays there. However, after leaving university and moving to London she fell apart, feeling 'unreal, a nothing'. For this woman, the university and her fellow students were a source of external maternal holding, but when this exo-skeleton disappeared she felt empty and without substance and identity.

Somewhat similarly, a batsman may long for the muzzy warmth of the dressing-room nest, and be unconsciously keen to get out so as to return to it. Here, the anonymity and safety of the group's sanctum militates against the need for individuals to act with initiative and determination on their own as batsmen.

Group elation which runs counter to the work task can also occur when the group concurs in the breaking of a taboo or the retaliation against an enemy felt to be dishonest or evil. When, admittedly after intense provocation, Mike Gatting, the England captain, jabbed his finger at a Pakistani umpire in Faisalabad, the team and management, entrenched in an attitude of self-righteous solidarity, became unable to extricate themselves and get on with the job of winning the match, which they were well placed to do.

Some groups insist, more or less, on such derelictions of personal standards and jettisoning of misgivings as criteria for membership. Some sporting teams approximate to totalitarian parties.

In these examples (Lillee, Close, Middlesex 1980, pre-Test dinners, muzzy nests, the siege mentality in Pakistan), the common feature is the split between us and them, such that we are felt to possess all strength and the others are weak; though it can be that we possess all moral goodness or security and the outside world is evil or unreliable. I think that what I am describing is Bion's second basic assumption – fight-or-flight. In all these cases, the team loves itself and members of the team love each other (at least on the surface). There is a manic denial of difficulty, failings, internal conflict and depression. The team identifies with their ego-ideal. The interaction with the leader tends towards collusive grandiosity.

As with the dependent team, the fight-or-flight team's basic-assumption mentality overlaps with healthy functioning. After all, fighting spirit and combativeness are essential. Teams need to have self-regard; and good teams have well-earned high opinions of themselves. They have their own myths and a tradition of success. It is regarded as an honour to be admitted or selected. However argumentative within, they tend to support each other and the team in the face of outside criticism. Such teams may not be over-accommodating to newcomers; they may be suspicious of change and resentful at the loss of an old member, and their *esprit de corps* may partly express itself in a degree of contempt for the upcoming generation. They, in their turn, are proud to be part of the set-up. Len Hutton (later to become England's first professional captain), was asked why, sitting in a corner of the dressing room before his first match for Yorkshire at the age of 17, he was smiling. He replied, 'Fancy *me*, playing for Yorkshire'. Those who do prove themselves in the team's eyes are accepted, first as apprentices, later as fully-fledged members; learning in a hard school toughens those who have what it takes. Such teams, as I say, may have good cause for their high self-regard, and that self-regard contributes to their continuing excellence.

I remember occasions on which a cricket team played, as we say, above itself. In the field they perform brilliantly. Each player dives to make improbable stops. Each plays a full part in urging on the others. Each feels a love for the whole team. Lillee helped achieve such a tigerishness in the match I described above. We all know such heightened states of mind and body, which we are inclined to call inspired. We breathe in the perfection and unity of the group, and, breathing it out, we inspire each other.

Such experiences of shared intensity have much in common with both love and infatuation. Marion Milner writes that:

> though it is an illusion when one thinks one has found the exact embodiment of goodness in the external world ... yet such moments are the vital illusions by which we live ... Moments which can perhaps be most often experienced in physical love combined with in-loveness ... but which can be imaginatively experienced in an infinite variety of contacts with the world.
>
> (Milner 1950: 29)

At certain moments the individuals feel thus about their team, and the team about the individuals. From such roots arises the inclination, only recently permitted, for the members of a team to hug each other at moments of shared heightened experience (a goal is scored; a wicket taken). Such experiences are instances of group illusion or primitive emotion bound together by shared phantasies, and none the worse for that. Rational self-regard of, and within, the group is fuelled by powerful emotion.

It may be harder to see the drawback for a cricket team in basic-assumption fight-or-flight. Is it not pleasurable, stimulating and performance-enhancing? Not necessarily. One weakness in such attitudes is the distortion of truth, as in any idealisation. This may not, of course, worry those who are in this state, at least not on the surface. Such a team will not, however, be able to maintain performance, which is liable to be short-lived. The more the team's euphoria about itself is a product of illusion and of infectious mutual idealisation, and the less it is a matter of solidly grounded ability, tactics, preparedness and achievement, the more likely it is to evaporate at the first setback. As such, it is similar to transference cure, dependent on a fixed set of conditions. (One might compare the phenomenon of teams that only play well at home; or away.) Moreover, hostility within the group can only temporarily, or at a price, be dealt with by projection of unwanted aspects of the group onto the opposition or other aspects of the world outside (selectors, crowds, alien cultures, the press and so on). In fact, not everyone feels comfortable with a strenuously macho attitude and though this, and other sources of conflict, may remain suppressed or repressed, the lack of freedom and independence for individuals is likely to result in a stilted and uncreative atmosphere. Group illusion of this sort can militate against full individuality. I have known teams which are so averse to hostility or conflict within that they operate at a level of mutual flattery and falseness. Another unproductive outcome is the expulsion, scapegoating, or withdrawal of players who do not fit in with the group ethos.

Bion's main emphasis is on the ways in which group phantasies block rational functioning. He is not so much concerned to describe the universality of unconscious phantasy or its contribution to the work group. However, Anzieu (1984: 134) is mistaken when he writes 'Bion seems to think that a group functions rationally when its phantasies, once formulated, disappear'. Bion did not believe this. For example, he writes 'Work group activity is obstructed, diverted, *and on occasion assisted*, by certain other mental activities that have in common the attribute of powerful emotional drives' (1961: 146). In fact, both Anzieu and Bion maintain, I think, that, in Anzieu's words, 'where there is a group there are phantasies that circulate among its members; these bind group members together both in their activities and their anxieties' (1984: 134).

Both would agree, too, that much of what passes for thinking is really pseudo-thinking, or an evasion of proper thought. A group which operates in this way at the expense of a real grappling with the practical and emotional task is arid; one could say that such a group has a basic assumption that intellect will solve all its problems. It may well be opposing, and opposed by, the equally anti-work attitude, namely, that thought is bound to be beside the point. The two attitudes may coexist and alternate within the same team, feeding off each other.

While many cricketers veer towards the latter end of the spectrum, denigrating all attempts at thought, others theorise and lack common sense. The former know from experience the importance, in the short term, of chance and the unpredictable, and may well have been exposed to captains – often university graduates – whose approach is over-theoretical (they represent the pseudo-thinking group).

For example, in 1971, my first year as captain of Middlesex, we played a Sunday League game against Glamorgan at Ebbw Vale. The match had been reduced by rain from 40 overs each side to 10. As we fetched our bags from the cars shortly before the start, I said, excitedly and nervously, 'We'll have to think about this!' The senior players found my remark hilarious. 'Think about it?! About a 10-over match! About a sheer slog?'

I can see their point. In those days I had too much confidence in the power of thought in controlling events. I remember, for example, in that same season referring to Wisden's *Cricketing Almanac* to discover which types of bowler had been most successful the year before against each of the counties we played. I soon came to think this was a fatuous exercise; current conditions and the make-up of one's own team are far more relevant as guides to action than the patterns of a year before. However, I also believe that there are no activities on which thought, properly and appropriately carried out, cannot be a help; a captain and a team do need to think about their approach to a 10-over match and about how it might differ from a 40-over encounter.

RESOURCES

In this second section of my chapter I want to discuss the following questions. When basic-assumption phenomena occur, and particularly when they occur in destructive ways, what tools does a captain (leader, manager) have for dealing with them, for lessening them, or for transforming them so that they work towards rather than against the task of the group? And how do these tools differ from those available to the therapist?

I start with a caricature of the two situations to make a contrast. It may be said that the task of the therapist is to provide insight and interpretation, that of the captain, to provide tactical knowledge and persuasive decision-making. Such a statement stresses the undoubted differences in the two roles and mental sets, but unless we look carefully at what is in fact involved in each, we may be tempted to portray the contrast in an artificially stark way, and overlook areas of overlap between the two. For captains may make constructive use of something approaching interpretation, and therapists are in a sense out to persuade.

Interpretation

Bion's interpretations in *Experiences in Groups* characteristically have three features. They make conscious what had previously been unconscious; they refer to the group as an entity; and they refer to current feelings, many of which are about the therapist. An example:

> I say that I think my interpretations are disturbing the group ... No doubt attempts are being made (by the group) to consider that they (the interpretations) are in some way descriptive of the life of the group, but such attempts are overshadowed by a suspicion that my interpretations, when interpreted, throw more light on myself than on anything else, and that what is then revealed is in marked contrast with any expectations that members of the group had before they came.
>
> (Bion 1961: 36)

They expected, Bion goes on to say, an expert who would provide agendas, rules of procedure, leadership. Bion's restricting himself to trying to describe the tensions within the group disappointed the group's unconscious expectations.

By contrast, we may safely say that giving instructions is an essential part of a captain's job. He or she may or may not consult, individually or with the whole team, but in the end the captain tells people what to do. In carrying out this task, he or she will at various times exhort, advise, criticise, congratulate and reassure. In doing so he or she will constantly be conveying judgements about what is good for the team. The captain moreover is under no obligation to study the tensions in the group, except possibly when they obtrude themselves and hinder the performance of the practical task. Indeed, the players have made no contract, explicit or implicit, which would give the captain licence or mandate to make interpretations about their feelings. Bion's group may have had reason to complain that, as he put it, 'no one had ever explained to them what it meant to be in a group in which he was present' but, nevertheless, by entering a therapeutic group with him, they had implicitly granted him this right. Cricketers may justly feel intruded upon by a captain who too cavalierly takes on such a role.

However, there are circumstances in which a captain, or someone, is justified in making interventions which approximate closely to interpretations. Butcher's comment about the team's day-dreaming of trophies had at least two features of the typical Bion interpretation: firstly, it referred to the mental set of the group as a whole; and secondly, this set was not fully conscious. Though the comments were not made by the titular leader of the group (me), they might have been.

Another example, this time from rugby. A captain notices that many of the players are trying to play other roles besides their own. He says to them: 'You are all trying to be prima donnas'.

To repeat, interpretation is not part of the captain's primary task. My point is that it can on occasion be a helpful means of unblocking the work-group by making conscious basic-assumption mentality.

Judgement

Is there a sense in which therapists, who try to avoid advising, cajoling or reassuring their patients, judge them? Captains, of course, do so openly; in the rugby example, the remark about prima donnas was followed by an instruction to the players to restrict themselves to their own more modest roles.

Once again, though, we should beware of caricature. It is true that the therapist refrains from imposing his or her personal values on patients. Nevertheless, analytic therapy, whether group or individual, is not morally neutral. Regarding psychopathology as growing out of an inability to own what one knows or is in a position to know, it presupposes the value of opening oneself up to painful truths. The therapist is obliged, therefore, constantly to assess and evaluate whether the responses of the patients are or are not geared towards such knowledge. These judgements, though not, we hope, made in a moralising spirit, are in a deep sense moral, and they inform interpretations.

So far, I have pointed to areas of overlap between the two. I am aware that on both counts – interpreting and judging – the differences are more striking than the similarities. In my experience, the mental sets of therapist and captain are in these aspects wide apart. However, my third point of comparison is, I think, more compelling. Captains and therapists are both in important ways responsible for the provision of an environment that facilitates the task in hand. This is true in humdrum respects and, as we shall see, in more subtle and far-reaching ways.

Facilitation

On a basic level, the therapist must provide a setting which is reasonably quiet, reliable and constant. The captain should pay attention to the players' facilities – changing-rooms, nets, food, contracts and salaries – and work to improve them where possible. A patient was helped by the evidence of my improving the sound-proofing in my consulting room. The

Middlesex second-team players appreciated my negotiating free lunches for them when they were at Lord's for practice during first-team matches.

More subtly, the captain/therapist is him- or herself a part of the team's/patient's environment. Indeed, even in the mundane examples given above, more important than the material advantage provided was the evidence of thought and effort on my part. True, the main value added by the captain/therapist results from the exercise of what we might call technical skills. The therapist whose interpretations are off the mark won't do much for those in his or her charge, and nor will the captain who has no clue about tactics. Conversely, a player's skills and willingness to sacrifice some degree of self-interest to that of the team are likely to be enhanced if the player has confidence in the captain's use of him or her, in the field placing and so on. A patient or group is similarly deeply reassured by a sense of conviction about the therapist's insight (though other parts of self and/or group may hate it).

However, neither tactical skill nor accurate interpretations are enough. This is easier to see in the practical activity, where the distinction between technical skill and interpersonal facilitation is less artificial. There really are captains whose 'word doesn't count for sixpence, despite his excellent tactics', as G.O. Allen, who captained England in the 1930s, described a pre-war contemporary. Thirty years later, Ted Dexter's swift grasp of the tactical revolution required for one-day cricket was largely responsible for his team's winning the first two Gillette Cup competitions in the 1960s. But in longer matches he invariably became bored when his ideas stopped working or the going got hard, hiding himself away behind the square-leg umpire and practising his golf-swing. One could feel the team's collective shoulders droop. A captain needs to concentrate doggedly on the matter in hand even, or perhaps especially, when inventiveness is unlikely to make a particular difference. Similarly, a captain may inhibit both supportiveness and performance by conveying to the team the expectation that their point of view will be stupid. Or he or she may leave too little space for players' creativity or flair, perhaps, as in the failure during Graham Gooch's captaincy to select the class batsman, David Gower, for England, a failure arising out of an over-zealous emphasis on training. Again, a captain may be either too dogmatic or too indecisive in plans or policies. In short it is clear that in a multitude of ways a captain can either sabotage or enhance the effects of his or her own tactical acumen.

More positively, the captain may actively work towards the creation of an environment tailored for a particular player. Two brief examples.

When a temperamental bowler joined Middlesex, we realized quickly that when things were not going well for him he would play the Court Jester, falling over in the field, presenting himself as an appalling fielder, making provocative and odd remarks. We made a conscious decision to take him seriously. I made a point of consulting him frequently about his bowling and about tactics. A productive rivalry sprang up between him and another bowler. We laughed at him less, and he had less need to gain attention in this way. Thus we refused to enter into a destructive spiral of, on the one hand collusion, and, on the other, impatience.

If this is a case of refusing to take a player at his own lightweight estimate of himself, my second example involves refusing to take someone – Geoffrey Boycott – too seriously. (These details are already in the public domain – I am not breaching confidentiality.)

Here it was the England team whose attitudes and behaviour provided a setting in which Boycott could be less damaging in his effect on team morale than had been the case elsewhere. We were well aware of his capacity for contempt. Playing for his county, Yorkshire, he embodied the aspirations of millions of Yorkshiremen in whose eyes he could do no wrong. This tended to increase his superiority and separateness from the rest of the county team, where he became the object of clusters of strong ambivalent feeling. The England players were able to treat him differently, with a productive humour. They mimicked and teased him, refusing to let him levitate towards his Yorkshire pedestal. This in turn brought out in Boycott his own capacity for humour and comradeliness. We also of course had a healthy respect for his enormous skill and courage. Thus a work-group mentality tended to predominate rather than a basic-assumption mode, in which fight-or-flight and dependency might have alternated, with Boycott a god alternately revered and defiled.

I think these remarks show clearly that the requirements for a captain are both more diverse and more personal than the possession of a shrewd cricketing brain. The captain needs to be able to enlist, preferably sensitively and naturally, the task-orientated elements in the team, to create benign rather than vicious cycles of interaction. The captain's own personality and example are crucial in these complex interchanges and in their outcomes. The captain's skin needs to be thin enough to allow in the projections and desires of the team, and thick enough not to be overwhelmed by them. Ideally, he or she mentally chews over their projections and his or her own counter-transference, while at the same time never ceasing to think constructively about the practical task, giving instructions where appropriate, not omitting to perform well as batsman, fielder and (sometimes) bowler.

In therapy it is harder, conceptually, to separate off insight (technical skill) from relationship as elements in psychic change. I am aware, of course, that much has been written on this topic. The single point I wish to make here is that the patient is influenced not only by the content of interpretations but also by the attitudes in the therapist which they express. These include attitudes towards the patient, towards psychic pain and its vicissitudes, towards the conscious and the unconscious; the therapist also betrays him- or herself in his or her courage, doggedness, capacity to survive, willingness to let patients discover things for them-selves, and his or her ability to struggle with human tendencies that may be all too familiar to the patient. Such qualities, and their lack, are inter-nalised by the patient, in however distorted a form, and affect the progress, or stasis, of the treatment.

In short, both captain and therapist have their own tendencies to fit in with basic-assumption modes which may be in conflict or in tune with work-group mentality.

CONCLUSION

There is a gulf between the mental set of a captain and that of a thera-pist. However, they share this fate: that in all their first-order interactions with team, group or patient – whether changing the bowling or inter-preting conflict – they both convey, willy-nilly, attitudes which have an impact on the others. And although it is not part of a captain's primary task to study the tensions within the team (wherever they originate from), it becomes part of his or her task to do so whenever the primary task is blocked or threatened; which presumably means – almost always.

NOTES

1 This chapter first appeared in the journal *Group Analysis* (vol. 27, 1994) and is reproduced by permission of Sage.

2   If you can meet with Triumph and Disaster
      And treat those two imposters just the same ...
            (Rudyard Kipling *If –* : 1910)

REFERENCES AND FURTHER READING

Anzieu, D. (1984) *The Group and the Unconscious*. London: Routledge and Kegan Paul.
Bion, W. R. (1961) *Experiences in Groups*. London: Tavistock.
Brearley, M. (1985) *The Art of Captaincy*. London: Hodder and Stoughton.
Collingwood, R. C. (1938) *The Principles of Art*. Oxford: Oxford University Press.
Menzies Lyth, I. (1986) 'Psychoanalysis in Non-Clinical Contexts: On The Art of Captaincy', *Free Associations*. 5.
Milner, M. (1950) *On Not Being Able to Paint*. London: Heinemann.

8

WORKING WITH ABUSED CLIENTS IN AN INSTITUTIONAL SETTING

Holding hope amidst despair

Moira Walker

'Getting back to my clients was a real relief. The meeting was appalling. I thought I'd go mad if anyone mentioned a mission statement again.'

'Really, my clients aren't the problem. Generally, I feel at least reasonably competent. It's the advisory committees that are so awful. It takes me weeks to recover from them. They not only deskill me but they are really quite abusive in a subtle sort of way.'

'I'm scared that I'm burning out. I'm so worn down by all the institutional machinations and game playing that I feel completely drained. My clinical work is suffering. I can't be creative; I can only play safe; I'm aware of steering the process away from difficult ground, particularly if it involves negatives. I can't cope with those clinically because there are too many to cope with institutionally. The best I can say is that I'm not doing any harm.'

'I'm getting out whilst there is still some of me left. I'm going freelance – which I have never wanted to do as I have a great commitment to working in the public sector – but it's the lesser of the evils.'

'My clients often feel the sanest thing in a world that appears to have gone completely mad.'

These comments have all been made to me within a supervisory context. They are all from people working within the public sector. They include a university setting, a voluntary organisation and the health service. All came from experienced clinicians with a particular expertise and interest in working with abuse survivors. Another strand that draws the speakers together is that they straddle, uncomfortably, the worlds of clinical practice and service management and accountability. Achieving a satisfactory balance between these aspects is not straightforward. On the one hand, they attempt to act as an effective buffer protecting other staff from aspects of management and policy decisions that do not always enable and facilitate their clinical work. On the other, they are themselves working with a demanding clinical workload, whilst also keeping an overall eye on the effectiveness of the service itself. And this all within the current wider context of personnel at all levels struggling with the effects of policy changes and financial restrictions. No wonder that such stress and discontent filter through, and are experienced at all levels in institutions and agencies.

In reading these comments readers will react variously, depending in part on their own roles and experiences. For many they will ring a bell of recognition – you will have had or uttered similar thoughts yourselves. It may therefore be reassuring to know that others feel the same. Managers who are not clinicians could feel some indignation: questioning whether these people really have cause for complaint. You may feel they are being unduly precious, refusing to enter the real world, especially if you yourself work under pressure. Or you may therefore recognise some truth in their words, knowing that at a managerial level there are also few choices and that staff at these levels can feel similarly misused and worn down.

Others may draw on a different understanding from a psychological perspective. From this angle, these comments could be understood as examples of projection: of counsellors and therapists who are using the wider institution or advisory committees or the government as some sort of psychological dustbin for unwanted and difficult parts of their selves and their work. However, many who are running services within a large institution would argue the opposite: that it is they and their services who act as a receptacle for the parts others want tidied away. My own sense is that the latter is a more accurate understanding, particularly where the main purpose and function of the institution is not of a therapeutic nature. However, clinicians must always guard against denying personal, clinical or managerial difficulties by neatly placing them elsewhere. But, of course, aspects of both – real institutional difficulties and projections – can be present.

The statements quoted could also be understood as examples of splitting: those over there (the management) are bad, and we are good. Our clients, particularly our abused clients, will also create splits. Part of our job is to help them integrate these splits, to assist them towards a more reasonable and realistic understanding of their experiences, and perhaps we ourselves must guard against creating too simplistically an enemy out there. The flipside of this is another dynamic commonly experienced by abuse survivors which, as I will illustrate, also resonates in those working in this field. Victims of abuse have frequently been told in childhood:

100

'It was your fault'; 'You could have stopped it if you wished to'; 'You asked for it' and so on. This brainwashing of the child (or even the adult) into believing they were responsible, accompanied by the underlying implicit assumption that they thereby had some power, when in fact they had none, is extremely effective. The abuser's denial of responsibility is inherent in this and the innocent victim is reframed as the actual protagonist. This dynamic can cause a further twist in the story for the adult survivor. As a child, they may have been brainwashed into believing the abuser's version of events; as an adult, acknowledging its essential falsehood can be extremely painful, and experienced as yet another loss. This is best explained through the words of an abuse survivor I worked with, who told me that:

> Feeling responsible for the abuse has been a most terrible burden to carry, but letting go of that has been extraordinarily difficult and complex. At least if I had been responsible I could in some way believe I could have done something about it: that there was some choice; that it didn't have to be like that. What I've had to face is that that wasn't true; that there wasn't a damn thing I could do about it. That I was small, completely powerless physically and psychologically; that I was totally vulnerable. I have fought facing that one because I had to face my own total powerlessness and the fact that my abuser lied, denied and exploited me and – I now know – others.

Working with this client to acknowledge and work through yet another loss – of recognising her lack of power as a child – enabled her to move on in her adult life and recover some power for herself. This takes me back to the parallel process that can exist for counsellors: tired and disillusioned counsellors may also sometimes fall into feeling responsible for what is not theirs. Taking time to distinguish, acknowledge and work through areas where the lack of power is a personal and political reality is hard when you are struggling under pressure. However, it is time worth taking; it can free you to recover and utilise autonomy and control where you are able.

To demonstrate how the strands can be unravelled with counsellors I will return to the example of the counsellor who feared burn-out. In supervision she explored the organisational dynamics she was caught up in: identifying and clarifying the various issues; noting the different levels these operated on; examining the negative effects of these upon her, both personally and professionally. Some she could do nothing about, but others she could. Having separated the issues one from another she was able to organise and implement various strategies. Adult abuse survivors easily get caught into a generalised feeling that everything is beyond their control, as it was in their childhood, whereas in adulthood some things are not. Counsellors and therapists in this field can also all too easily be

101

overwhelmed by that same sense of helplessness and thereby become enmeshed in the same powerful dynamic. This will be recognised by all practitioners and supervisors who work with abuse, but they will also recognise that this dynamic is further intensified if the practitioner feels sandwiched between the needs of the client and the demands of the institution. In an ideal world, these two should constitute a reasonably close match. Sadly, this is often not the case today.

If counsellors and therapists are helped to deal with these structural issues, they are then freer to address their clinical work. Otherwise, as with this counsellor, a situation is created whereby the counsellor cannot work effectively and, ultimately, clients who have already suffered enough can suffer further. Helping counsellors to deal effectively with their anger and frustration and to understand its basis is essential. This is not always straightforward, and to unravel this it is necessary to understand the complexity of motivations of those entering the caring professions. The theme of counsellors and therapists being unconsciously motivated is not new, whether by a desire to seek both reparation and revenge, or as a reflection of their repression of aggressive drives. These themes are explored both by Prodgers in his article 'On Hating the Patient' and by Jacobs in his paper on the therapist's revenge. Prodgers notes that:

> It can be seen that any resistance or attack on the therapeutic alliance may reverberate with internal frustrations of an infantile origin increasing the sense of frustration. Resistance is therefore hatred to which therapists respond by hatred as it resonates with their own bad internal objects who hate them and they therefore hate back.
>
> (Prodgers 1991: 149)

What I am suggesting here is that counsellors and therapists can experience the interventions and policies of institutions as an attack on the therapeutic alliance, and can thereby 'hate' or attack the institution as an act of revenge in response to this intrusion. However, this can be carried out in a deeply counter-productive way, in turn further harming both the therapist and the therapeutic alliance with the client. As Jacobs notes: 'Acting out revenge risks turning constructive revenge into revenge which is equally destructive of the avenger' (Jacobs 1991: 6).

To expand on this point, I return to my example of the counsellor who was frightened of burning out. Her anger towards her agency was being in part unhelpfully acted out: there was an aspect of what Jacobs refers to as 'destructive revenge' as well as a further element of genuine and justifiable despair and frustration. This was reflected in the feeling which she expressed as: 'Why should I put anything into this when no one supports me? Why should I work well when I'm being so badly treated?' This left her feeling utterly deskilled, thereby further intensifying the downward spiral of hopelessness and paralysing her ability to be clinically effective. By being helped to address these issues in supervision she recognised that if she were able to work better it would energise her rather than exhaust her further. By identifying and understanding that her albeit unconscious attempt to punish the institution by withdrawing her skills was not at any level working, she was enabled to move from such a stuck and potentially self-destructive position. She became able to reclaim her clinical skills and to assess more realistically how best to respond to agency difficulties that were indeed restrictive and unhelpful.

Those who work with abuse survivors know well the strength of their internal pull towards self-destructive acts. However, it may be more difficult for counsellors and therapists to recognise when the same dynamic is at work in themselves, although it is a significant and powerful force. The opposite is also powerful – that is, the desire to be an especially good counsellor or therapist. Paradoxically this can be another means of seeking revenge or reparation. Recognising these various pitfalls – feeling responsible for what is not yours; feeling that you have no power or control; the unhelpful projection of anger and vengeful feelings; too great a desire to get things right – can help enormously in dealing with what, by its very nature, is demanding work. When this work is being carried out within an agency or institutional context yet another layer is present, and both practitioners and supervisors need to be aware of how the context itself becomes enmeshed in the therapeutic work, particularly when agency or institutional objectives clash with therapeutic objectives.

Holding on to hope in working with abuse survivors is not straightforward; practitioners daily hear stories of horror and torture of children. A particular difficulty in remaining hopeful in abuse work in institutional settings in the current climate is that patterns tend to be repeated. Clients express feelings and experiences of having been ignored, disregarded, marginalised and having their realities denied. Counsellors and therapists can sometimes feel much the same, and although these feelings might for a time produce a fighting spirit, in which they feel energised, enthusiastic and active, there is a danger that depression, despair and a sense of alienation from self can result – especially if the underlying issues are not actively tackled.

An example will clarify this point: a counsellor in a sexual abuse project produced a report on the progress of the project and its future needs. The report described the work undertaken and the extent of the problem being uncovered. Some detailed clinical examples were given to show the need for continued funding and for longer-term work. The response she met was not one she expected – although those of us who have worked longer in this particular field may not be surprised. Clearly, the committee she was addressing had great difficulty in hearing what she was saying. There was considerable hostility and scepticism and it was suggested that she

103

must be exaggerating. This was accompanied by annoyance from some of those present that they should be exposed to hearing details of abuse. The counsellor was left demoralised and distressed, questioning her own skills and competence and wondering if she really had got it wrong. However, it was possible in supervision, after detailed discussion with her, to decide on a future strategy for these meetings that she felt hopeful would work. She had not been prepared either psychologically or practically for the strength of the reaction she had encountered, and was consequently left without a voice, as of course happens to abused children and adults. In fact, her description of the meeting was reminiscent of the experience of so many abuse survivors when they try to tell what has happened to them. We should perhaps not be too surprised by this. We need instead to understand the level of resistance and denial that inevitably occurs in this area. Cox notes that:

> The therapist is not only confronted by his patient's violence in fact or fantasy, but ipso facto, simultaneously exposed to his own violence. In other words, the therapist's inner world is always at risk because his patient may arouse ego-dystonic feelings.
>
> (Cox 1974: 2)

If the therapist or counsellor, who is trained to work with distressing and disturbing aspects of the human psyche, can experience ego-dystonic feelings in this way, it is hardly surprising that lay people encounter such difficulty and thereby bring their own defensive strategies into operation. As we work with survivors in terms of understanding the process and exploring unconscious strategies, we may need to understand the responses of others similarly. In that way we can more effectively prepare ourselves for hostile and defensive responses. Understanding responses in process terms creates the possibility of dealing more effectively with them, rather than simply feeling personally attacked. We have to remember that the whole history of the acknowledgement of abuse is marked by resistance and denial: it continually faces humanity with what is not humane and what is deeply uncomfortable. As Alice Miller asks:

> Why is it so difficult to describe the real, the factual, the true situation of a small child? Whenever I try to do this I am confronted with arguments that all serve the same purpose: that of not having to acknowledge the situation, of rendering it invisible, or, at best of describing it as purely 'subjective'.
>
> (Miller 1991: 96)

To return to my example of this advisory committee: it was more complex than an understandable psychological reaction to distressing material. There were other resistances in this agency to this project: they were unconvinced of the need for it. You may then wonder why it was accepted as

· part of their work. The answer is financial: in the words of the counsellor, quoting a committee member, 'it was a nice little earner'. In that area at that time, money was available for abuse work and the agency was desperate for funds and so bid competitively. The counsellors had the skills, but the agency lacked the real concern, knowledge and interest that were necessary for offering effective back-up. So those on the committee were faced with realities and worlds they would rather not see or hear about. They did what so many do, including abusers: they denied the reality. In many ways, those of us working in institutions are perpetually caught up in this dynamic; we remind others of what they would prefer not to know or are trying to deny. Abuse is a highly charged subject for many people and, when we speak on the subject, some of those we address will be abuse survivors. But a less palatable truth is that we also address abusers. Working in this field you inevitably upset people for a variety of reasons.

However, this example is useful in that it demonstrates the need both to differentiate the structural and political issues from the psychological, and simultaneously to understand both their interrelatedness and the consequences that thereby arise from this connection. In the same way as we need to understand the therapeutic process in order to avoid becoming overwhelmed by it, particularly by its negative aspects, so we need to understand social and political processes in order to understand their effect on us as people, without taking it all personally. The present political climate certainly mitigates against an easy holding of hope: any concepts of a universal right to education and services related to need are rapidly and dangerously becoming eroded in the face of cost-cutting, profit-making and the market economy. This, combined with the ongoing and deeply embedded societal resistance to accepting the nature and extent of abuse, does create real and major obstacles both to holding out hope to abuse survivors and retaining optimism ourselves, although both are essential to the work.

All this points to the necessity of clinical work being carried out in the context of acknowledging and understanding both structural and political systems and the psychological dynamics, and their effects on the client, the counsellor and the working environment. However, this is not always the case. The degree to which counsellors and therapists regard clinical work as an individual activity devoted to the internal world, or how much they explore the complex relationship between inner experiences and external realities makes for a fraught and active debate. This relationship has always been regarded as central by the feminist therapists. Maye Taylor (1995) in her chapter in *Peta: a Feminist's Problem with Men* states this position clearly:

> Feminist therapy carries the extra dimension of recognising that for women, at least, transforming their lives is not simply a matter of

their individual strengths and efforts, for the values and mental health of women are so inextricably tied up with the social structure.

(Taylor 1995: 94)

Others are steadily moving away from the traditional purist view. Many would now agree that to separate politics from psychotherapy supports a false and unhelpful split. Andrew Samuels argues that:

to refer to the political development of the person is to challenge the boundary that is conventionally accepted to exist between public and private. If we follow the challenge through, then we will have to consider how psychopathology, usually a discipline confined to the private and interior realms (though often measured by visible behaviour), also refers to the public and political realms.

(Samuels 1993: 55)

Others would disagree and hold the distinction as necessary and essential to the therapeutic task. An analyst said recently to me, in a somewhat heated interchange we had on this subject, that 'analysis is not permeable', arguing strongly that its task was solely to explore the internal world: politics did not have a place in therapy. For any counsellor or therapist working in the public sector who holds this view, these modern times must be very difficult, although denial is a useful defence against inconvenient impingements. But nowadays, working in the public sector makes denial of the significance of external worlds extremely problematic. These worlds have rudely crashed through the privacy of the consulting room door. A few years ago one might have had to argue 'ignore it at your peril'. Now, even the most determined ostrich's head has been dragged from the sand.

Nowadays, counsellors and therapists working in agencies, particularly where a managerial role is combined with the clinical, are called upon to have skills in negotiation, financial management, and whatever the therapeutic equivalent is of creative accounting – possibly writing mission statements and producing statistics. It can seem that trying to match client need to available resources and to agency demands is a thankless task.

The growing emphasis on short-term work in some agencies exemplifies the problem. Short-term work is a potent model in its own right but it is not a universal panacea. It is often highly inappropriate for abuse survivors, where speed can seem intrusive, or even abusive, and where the complexities of the abusive experience and its effects cannot be easily and quickly identified and worked with. Trust is of the essence in any therapeutic encounter. Where it has been so effectively demolished by abuse it requires time, patience and tenacity to begin to re-create it. Yet some agencies are leaping into short-term work in an almost evangelically zealous fashion. Short-term work is not a miracle cure, and those who are working with abuse survivors know it is not. They also know it can be damaging: there is time to begin to expose a sea of pain yet no time to work with it properly. No wonder then that practitioners in these agencies, as they try to fight for their clients, can experience the agency as hostile and not comprehending – again so often reflecting the experience of their abused clients. It is also important to note that not all agencies operate in this manner: some, including those where therapeutic services are peripheral to its central objective, are supportive and trust the professional judgement of the staff in terms of deciding and offering the most appropriate help. In such agencies morale tends to be high and the mood hopeful, even when the service is under pressure and when the material being presented by clients is difficult and demanding.

But many practitioner/managers of services know nowadays that presenting the correct image is often vital. Some counsellors and therapists enjoy being turned into impromptu politicians and learn to play clever tactical games. Others do not: it interferes with their work, and it feels dishonest and too like some of the awful manipulations their clients have suffered from – again, particularly those who have suffered abuse. Dislike of such tactics may even have been one factor that attracted practitioners in the first place to the apparently more apolitical world of counselling and therapy.

In this context, holding on to hope may be emerging as an increasingly problematic concept. However, what is being argued here does not destroy hope. Rather, it argues that for hope to have real substance it has to take place within a framework that faces, acknowledges and works with realities, rather than existing in a vacuum of the fantasy of a perfect or pure therapeutic world which is unsullied by politics and social structures.

So let me reiterate: firstly, the world we are in has to be acknowledged and its effects worked with. This is true for both our work with clients and our relationship with the institutions we work in. Secondly, recognising negatives, as well as understanding and placing them in the right context is essential. As they do not go away for our clients, so they do not go away for us either. We help our abused clients to work with these aspects of themselves and their experiences, and we have to do the same within our own structural contexts. Thirdly, we help our abused clients to differentiate between their real powerlessness and their projections of this. Fourthly, we help them to recognise their anger and deal with this appropriately, and we assist them to learn how to contain their murderous parts or to use them creatively without acting them out destructively. We also need to do the same for ourselves. Finally, we also help clients to work through and then let go of some of their experiences, whilst clarifying and identifying other aspects that may need to be more actively struggled with. Perhaps within our institutions we also need to recognise what must be grieved for and let go; and where we stand our ground, what we fight for and how we do it. As with our clients, we too have to accept that the world we are having to live in nowadays is often not as we would like. Our disappointment and the sense of betrayal that can exist has to be acknowledged if we are not to be overwhelmed.

As previously noted we, like our clients, find it hard at times to have a voice. We, like them, can easily feel marginalised and misunderstood. Amidst this, we have to maintain our faith in what we do. We have to hold on to hope, and we have to retain this at times for ourselves and for our clients:

> It is crucial that the therapist does not fall into the same pit of despair as the client. When clients feel no hope, and feel they are drowning in a sea of pain, the therapist must stay afloat. It is hard for a therapist to carry hope for someone who feels none, at a time when the therapist's own sense of hope is under challenge. Carrying hope for both is further complicated by the parallel necessity to help carry the pain and the agony. It is not straightforward balancing these two requirements.
>
> (Walker 1992: 152)

It is relevant to return to the comments made by counsellors that I quoted at the beginning of this chapter. As you perceived, a feeling was often expressed that working with clients could come as a welcome relief after dealing with agencies and institutions. In terms of holding on to hope in what often feels like an alien and alienating world, in which money matters and people become marginalised as units, clients are indeed important. They do matter; the work is valuable; and maintaining a high therapeutic standard in circumstances that often seem to mitigate against this is extremely commendable. I would add that there is frequently a very high standard of clinical work in very hard-pressed services and that some employing institutions do not always recognise this. However, it is equally important to acknowledge those that do actively and positively support these endeavours, and those others that are quietly content for services to work without managerial interference.

As for the client, it is he or she who is the most important, and it is that belief that is possibly most significant in maintaining optimism. But they must not become too important if both their and their helper's emotional well-being is to be safeguarded. There may be a danger that tired and disillusioned counsellors and therapists look to their clients to provide the sustenance and the hope that is lacking externally. I am not suggesting that this is a conscious or simple choice or strategy but, that if you are having to deal with and respond to conflicts and negatives imposed from the institution – which often in turn reflect what the insti-tution is experiencing as a direct result of government policy – it can be too great a relief to return to clinical work.

Abuse survivors in their own history have often had to develop extremely sensitive emotional antennae to help them survive or minimise abuse. Many will have unconsciously developed strategies aimed at appeasing their abuser. They will have little trust in the ability of people to be consistently available to them, or in others as able to be responsible for their own emotional needs. The abuse survivor is quite used to meeting the emotional needs of others whilst their own are entirely disregarded. They are accustomed to being used as fodder for the uncontained and unacknowledged needs and demands of their abuser. All these dynamics can all too easily be repeated within the therapeutic relationship. It is similarly possible for the counsellor and the abused client to collusively enter a relationship in which the enemy for both of them is firmly placed out there, whilst all in here is well and negatives are denied. There is a parallel here to the pattern of abusive families who not only deny the abuse but instil their children with a sense of the external world as being a dangerous place. The danger and viciousness that actually lie within the home are projected outwards, and any risk of the child speaking is thereby effectively minimised. Counsellors and therapists must continually monitor themselves and their own practice, especially when they are under stress, if they are to work with these dynamics rather than repeat them.

So we may prefer working with our clients to struggling with the policies and politics of our institutions. After all, as I noted earlier, it is what we are trained to do and what we thought we were employed to do. Many of those working in the caring professions nowadays feel as if management interferes rather than facilitates, and that it criticises or ignores rather than validates. Yet good work is done and we must somehow hold to that reality whilst not denying other real issues. In order to work well with abuse survivors we have to hold on to hope. In the same way as we must not be overwhelmed by institutional pressures, we must not be overwhelmed by the pressure of difficult and disturbing material. In working with clients who have been abused, details of violent and depraved behaviour against children are regularly encountered – details that still, I suspect, most people do not want to know about or believe in.

In order to maintain hope when working with these appalling situations it is essential to have and hold on to a belief in what you are doing. This does not mean being falsely optimistic, refusing to see negatives or believing that you can offer cures – that is a false therapeutic evangelism that is dangerous and unrealistic. But faith in therapeutic process based on knowledge and skill, combined with an ability to make contact at a deep level with people in great pain, can achieve a considerable amount for many clients. This may need to be accompanied by patient determination to see the process through; a belief in your own ability to survive emotionally, and a sense of resilience that is communicated

109

to your client. She or he needs to know that however great the internal struggles, however much negative and destructive feelings may threaten to swamp them, you will remain intact; that you can contain the feelings and that you will hold carefully to appropriate therapeutic boundaries. As Sheila Youngson points out in an article relating to ritual abuse but equally relevant here:

> To be clear about the extent and limitations of one's role, and the boundaries of the task and acceptable behaviour for both client and helper, provides the safety and security that allows and nurtures positive growth and change.
>
> (Youngson 1994: 298)

Equally, maintaining a balance of involvement and distance is crucial, as I have written elsewhere:

> Helpers have to try and find a position that represents the ideal interface between objective distance and personal involvement, if they are on the one hand to convince the client that they will be with them, will believe in them and will fight for them: and on the other are not to collapse with them.
>
> (Walker 1992: 197)

I would add that this balance between objective distancing and more active involvement also needs to be achieved within the agency or institution. It is partly linked to knowing when it is helpful both politically and clinically to do nothing. There are some issues that are best ignored: silence can be an effective response in some situations. As Andrew Samuels points out in *The Political Psyche*:

> Drawing on clinical experience, an analyst can offer the men and women of action – though the most brilliant of them know it already – a trained sense of timing: when to speak and act and when to keep silent and do nothing.
>
> (Samuels 1993: 77)

It is also essential to refer to some of the work we have undertaken because here we see the most heartening and the most significant reason for hope. We see in our clients their bravery in facing and dealing with the horrors they have encountered. Not all our work will have concluded as we and the client would have wished, and sometimes we will not know at the time if progress has been made. One client with a long history of abuse was seen in therapy without much obvious benefit. At the time it had been just a drop in the ocean. But afterwards it became clear that it had been a very crucial experience for her. It was the first occasion she had told anyone of her abuse, and it had been deeply significant for her. In her words:

110

It was both being believed and that you listened calmly and didn't collapse and that nothing terrible happened as a result that meant so much. But I couldn't have acknowledged that at the time. I wasn't ready to. But it's meant that I've now been able to decide to see someone else and I feel very optimistic. I know it will be painful but I really have faith that it will be worth it.

Another client was abused physically by her mother and sexually by a teacher. She had been self-abusive, unable to maintain relationships and unable to allow herself to succeed: all good things had to be destroyed in the same way as so much in her childhood had been destroyed for her. She had tried to destroy the therapeutic relationship too, and there had been many tempestuous and difficult times with her. Now she is in a relationship that is very strong, in a job she enjoys, and she is hoping to have her own child, an option she had believed for many years would never be open to her.

Other outcomes are not so obviously clear cut but, nevertheless, progress has been made: for instance, the client who overdosed and cut herself regularly and who is now able to deal with difficult feelings without hurting herself; or the woman who at the age of 40 was finally able to leave her abusive father. In both these instances much remains to be done, but such changes should not be minimised and should be celebrated. In this work we are continuously seeing distressed people, and it is sometimes hard to recall those who have moved on, having had a good enough experience, in which they have been given enough, and have been able to take enough, to cope more comfortably with life.

The question remains: what do counsellors and therapists need in order to hold on to hope in this very demanding work, that is taking place currently in the context of a country in which disillusion seems to be the order of the day? Some factors have already been mentioned. Supervision is indeed a professional necessity, and my experience from both ends of the process suggests that if you work in an institution it is particularly helpful to have a supervisor who has both clinical skills and an understanding of institutional dynamics. If you work therapeutically in a way that attempts to understand the interaction between inner and outer worlds, a supervisor who thinks similarly and who has a matching knowledge-base can offer a very particular form of support. The ability to stand back both from therapeutic and institutional processes, to observe them and make sense of them, may be hard to achieve but it is worth striving for.

To have other things and other people in your life is vital: to allow yourself to have fun and enjoy yourself without guilt is important for all of us. A clinical involvement in very demanding work needs to be balanced by involvement in other worlds – and you have a right to them. A very liberating point for abuse survivors comes when they are able to put the abuse on one side – not to deny it but to give themselves a break from it. The recognition that it need not be their only identity is a crucial one. Similarly, counsellors and therapists need to allow themselves to put it down, to leave it in their consulting room, as we sometimes invite clients to do. Being clear of our own limitations is central; of course we need to be resilient, but fantasies of being a saviour need to be firmly addressed. We need to be realistic about our own needs, and value and care for ourselves. If we care for clients, we must also care for ourselves. A desire to heal others has to be matched by our own self-knowledge and self-awareness. As we encourage clients to be self-protective, so must we be.

Working with abuse survivors is a complex process for both the counsellor and the client. It is rendered even more complex if the counsellor is working in a setting that is problematic and unsupportive. Working with abuse faces counsellors and therapists with believing the unbelievable, thinking the unthinkable, and working with heartrending and tragic consequences. If it is hard for us to hear these things, it perhaps indicates how very problematic it is for those who run institutions or agencies to comprehend the nature of the work. As a counsellor or therapist you enter a different world, that many do not really want to know about; or if they do, they will struggle to understand. Resistance and denial are common. Difficult feelings are encountered which may sometimes seem impossible – which is of course just how abuse survivors can feel. You will also be impressed and amazed by the tenacity of the human spirit and the will to survive, as well as the inevitability of encountering and facing themes of death and destruction. It is no wonder this work can drain you as well as inspire you.

An abuse survivor I know said to me that her biggest triumph in life was bringing up her own daughter, and knowing that she would not be abused within the family, that the cycle of abuse had been broken in this generation. She was proud of herself and proud of her daughter. In a very important sense her revenge against her abuser was to reach a point where against many odds she could allow herself to be a successful parent and a fulfilled adult. She had overcome her abuse, and she could allow herself to live well and to celebrate that. She knew that there would be difficulties and problems but that, essentially, she would remain intact and overcome difficulties. Perhaps the best revenge for counsellors and therapists against policies and structures that are problematic is that against many odds we can allow ourselves to retain high clinical standards, remain hopeful and work well in an atmosphere that often seems aimed at mitigating against this.

REFERENCES

Cox, M. (1974) 'The Psychotherapist's Anxiety: Liability or Asset?', *British Journal of Criminology* 14, 1: 1–17.

Jacobs, M. (1991) 'The Law of Talion as a Motive for Caring', *Contact: Interdisciplinary Journal of Pastoral Studies* 2, 105: 2–11.

Miller, A. (1991) *Banished Knowledge*, London, Virago Press.

Prodgers, A. (1991) 'On Hating the Patient', *British Journal of Psychotherapy* 8, 2: 144–54.

Samuels, A. (1993) *The Political Psyche*, London: Routledge.

Taylor, M. (1995) 'Feminist Psychotherapy' in Walker, M. (ed.) *Peta: A Feminist's Problem With Men – In Search of a Therapist*, Buckingham: Open University Press, pp. 94–110.

Walker, M. (1992) *Surviving Secrets: the Experience of Abuse for the Child, the Adult and the Helper*, Buckingham: Open University Press.

Youngson, S. (1994) 'Ritual Abuse: the Personal and Professional Costs for Workers' in Sinason, V. (ed.) *Treating Survivors of Satanic Abuse*, London: Routledge, pp. 292–302.

9

HUMAN RESPONSES TO DESTRUCTIVE REGIMES

Paul Hoggett

What choices are available to an individual who belongs to an organisation or society which is increasingly experienced as destructive? This question seems highly pertinent to our times. Working with individuals within the public services I find a new phenomenon emerging in the 1990s. People can point to it and name it without hesitation. It seems to be pervasive. Front-line staff, professionals and managers I have encountered in local government, the health service and the education service have all spoken to me about it. In the 1980s the experience that such people mentioned most frequently was uncertainty. In the 1990s, however, it is fear. At the root of the phenomenon is undoubtedly fear for one's job, but this root has provided the condition for the establishment of a culture of fear within such institutions. People seem increasingly afraid to speak out, perhaps particularly in the NHS where a number of widely publicised recent incidents (British Medical Journal 1994) have demonstrated the danger of 'whistle-blowing'.[1] As the post-1987 government reforms threaten to undermine the principle of social justice upon which, however inadequately, the welfare state was based, so workers in it feel increasingly trapped within a regime which is abandoning the principles which drew many of them to work there. They also find themselves subject to a massive intensification of work, greater job insecurity and increased surveillance and monitoring (Hoggett 1996). No wonder stress levels within the public sector workforce are at a record high (British Medical Association 1992; Bogg and Cooper 1995; Cooper and Kelly 1993).

Many of the dilemmas faced by workers within such institutions parallel those they face as citizens in the wider society. The triumph of the market in Britain seems so complete that effective political responses are at times virtually impossible to construct. Outside the direct action campaigns around environmental issues we search hard for any 'victories' of even an ambiguous nature which have been achieved by either the labour or wider social movements during the last decade and a half. Many people feel angry or frustrated, some have withdrawn into cynicism or despair or

114

gone into a prolonged hibernation which waits upon the spring of a non-Conservative government, whilst others have made their peace with the 'new reality' and, if they are lucky, pursue their material interests within the embers of the enterprise culture. The choices we make and the roles we assume when faced with destructive regimes at work or in the wider world have not been extensively documented. This is the purpose of this chapter.

'CHAMPIONS OF CHANGE'

In a number of articles on the rise of the new public management in the UK I have tried to investigate the displacement of the public service ethic by what might be called the public enterprise ethic (Hoggett 1991; 1994; 1996). A number of other commentators such as Stephen Ball (1993) have noted how the new discourse of management is one that both liberates and enslaves; indeed, we now find some of the foremost proponents of the new management incorporating the very language of liberation in their rhetoric (Peters 1993). Perhaps the most striking feature of this discourse is its embrace of change. Most of contemporary management theory is devoted to describing the process of organisational change and prescribing strategies for accomplishing it (Kanter 1985; Peters 1989; Belasco 1990). The language is profoundly normative and, in a way, quite transparent. It hates bureaucracy, inflexibility, tradition, resistance to change, caution, complacency, and so on. One is reminded here of Giddens' (1991) comments on modernity as a restless process of making and remaking the given. The contemporary trends towards globalisation (Ohmae 1990), permanent innovation (Morris Suzuki 1986) and constant adaptability are revered by this tradition. Belasco (1990) cites approvingly the editors of a British management journal:

> We are moving from the set piece trench warfare of Flanders in 1914–18 toward the quick response jungle war of Vietnam. Seventy years ago great armies moved on detailed instructions of supreme commanders and their general staffs. Today we need the flexibility of response seen in a well-led fighting patrol, harnessed within the vision that ensures a victorious campaign.
>
> (Belasco, 1990: 174)

Change is a self-evident good, resistance to change is obviously bad. Change towards what and for what? These are distracting questions. Belasco, without a hint of self-consciousness, states:

> Management is about "how". Management is about process. Become obsessed with "what" and you forget "how" ... This is particularly true about change. Change is a process, not a destination. It never

115

ends. Regardless of how successful you are this year, there is always next year.

(Belasco 1990: 243)

The role which seems to exemplify this lemming-like infatuation with change in modern management is the 'champion'. Change needs its fired-up individuals to champion the new policy, the new technique or the new flavour. Peters and Waterman (1982), the inspiration of the new management, revere 'product champions', etc. Reflecting upon the apparent chaos of the innovation process in today's big firms they note, 'all the activity and apparent confusion we were observing revolves around fired-up "champions" and around making sure that the potential innovator, or champion, comes forward, grows, and flourishes – even to the extent of indulging in a little madness' (Peters and Waterman 1982: 202). They point out that excellent companies 'are structured to create champions' (211). Moreover, they suggest that one 'trick' which is often adopted is to make managers 'believe they are would-be champions, yet at the same time maintain very substantial control where it counts' (213).

For some, to be a champion pushing at the frontiers of change is positively intoxicating. Here is Belasco again:

It's exciting to think about a new vision, particularly when you're the creator/driver of it. You see the need clearly. You feel the urgency in your stomach. You're motivated to change. You see the fire with your own eyes. You smell the smoke in your nostrils. The tent is on fire. You have to change.

Why are others in the organisation so lackadaisical? Don't they smell the smoke? Don't they see the fire? Don't they feel the urgency to change?

(Belasco, 1990: 219)

For managers embedded in this kind of culture, one constantly reinforced by business and professional journals, by colleagues returning from MBA programmes, by conferences, consultants and commercials, it is easy to leap upon the next wave which comes surging across the quiet waters of the public services and embrace the change that it offers without asking where is this leading, for what purpose and to suit whose ends.

Indeed, the rhetoric of 'excellence' and 'total quality' has proved profoundly seductive to many managers in the public sector. These kinds of texts have constituted a critique of bureaucracy at the very time when, at a deeper level, a new paradigm of the organisation of production, sometimes referred to as post-Fordist, was emerging (Burrows and Loader 1994). In the context of the UK this was also a period when the idea of 'bureaucracy' was also the target of a sustained political attack by central government. And, whilst in one sense this attack was legitimate (the welfare state had become profoundly bureaucratic and unresponsive), in another sense it concealed and legitimatised an attack on the very notion of a democratic public sphere as an area of life with a rationale which was different from that of the market economy. It was, for example, as if the complexity of organising forms of care and support for those in need could be reduced to the simple calculus of potato-chip production. If one reads these management texts, there are no irresolvable tensions between contradictory objectives, no conflict between human values and organisational imperatives, no indication that some organisations may be asked by society to undertake a wellnigh impossible task which they cannot help but fail to accomplish, no realisation that those organisations whose task it is to care for the sick and dying, the emotionally distressed or the socially excluded will inevitably have to contain the hopes and anxieties of the society for whom this work is performed. And therefore there is no sense of human complexity, ambivalence and perversity. It is as if much of this contemporary management, as a body of ideas and set of practices, has been imported into the public sphere as a way of protecting managers from the pain of thought (Lousada 1993). It is as if it is enough for managers to accumulate an armoury of facts and techniques via the acquisition of a set of competences: heaven forbid that they should need to develop their capacity for thoughtfulness!

As a consequence, for the past 15 years there has existed a collective crisis of confidence throughout the UK public sector, a crisis for which public managers have been made to feel particularly responsible. The pursuit of excellence and total quality and the symbolic festivals and rituals which have been enacted in their name can be seen as a means by which beleaguered public managers sought to find hope and reassurance. Many public institutions in Britain today are deeply damaged, their body is stretched and torn, and those in the front line of service delivery (and for many staff it does indeed feel like a 'front line') are often preoccupied with material and psychological survival. Contemporary managerial rhetoric has drawn a veil over this reality, ensnaring many senior public service executives in a delusional system and reinforcing the cynicism and despair of ordinary workers and managers. The ideology of business management, stressing the managers' right to manage, has eschewed practices of consensus building, consultation and dialogue as inefficient. As Obholzer notes, 'it has become a top-down model, with dialogue and cooperation between the different sectors seen as old-fashioned ... this style of management could be described as "paranoid-schizoid by choice", fragmenting and splitting up systems instead of promoting collaboration' (Obholzer 1994: 173).

Moreover, behind much of the brouhaha of change, excellence, total quality and entrepreneurialism one can nevertheless discern the familiar struggle for executive survival. Speaking of the large number of corporate survival guides issuing from the United States in the late 1970s and early 1980s, Lasch notes the emphasis upon being streetwise, ironically detached and maintaining a quality of healthy paranoia, a strategy for survival 'based on watchfulness, suspicion and distrust' (Lasch 1984: 69). Even the champions of change are potentially its victims.

EXPERIENCING DESTRUCTIVE REGIMES

How are people responding to the new management culture emerging within the public sphere? The cameo that follows is of a public organisation driven by one of the new change masters and his all-male board. The local authority had nearly always been Conservative-controlled but during the past few years it had been taken over by the new breed of Conservatives, Thatcherites rather than 'one-nation' Tories. This local authority was into privatising everything, encouraging management buyouts and schools to opt out and was ahead of government legislation when it came to submitting services to competitive tendering. The authority naturally had its mission statement which committed it, among other things, to 'excellence in the service of its customers' and to valuing its staff. The latter seemed somewhat surprising given that during the last two years it had managed to make almost a thousand staff redundant.

I was working with ten senior managers, the next tier down from the chief executive and board that ran the organisation on their political masters' behalf. I had been asked to do some work on 'cultural change' with this group of managers, for it seemed that they were not embracing the new spirit of entrepreneurialism in quite the style that someone had hoped. I took the job out of curiosity. I had rarely worked with Conservative-controlled parts of the public sector, this organisation had a reputation for being at the 'cutting edge' of the Municipal Right (Ridley 1988) and I wanted to know what it was like to work for it.

I will begin with my encounter with Julia, the senior personnel manager in this organisation. As such, Julia was responsible for managing the redundancy process. She was clearly very ambivalent about her position. On the one hand, she was resigned to the fact that this was one of the duties she had to perform given her professional role; on the other hand, she was outraged by the absence of any redundancy policy which reflected the values the organisation said it was committed to (i.e. valuing your staff) – there was no redundancy counselling, no programme of retraining, and so on. Julia felt that the board tended to manifest a mixture of blindness and viciousness; in her hopeful moments she preferred to think it was the former. Although perhaps a bit naive Julia, nevertheless, did not lack courage. She hoped that other senior managers would combine with her to confront the board with the reality of working for the organisation. Julia's professionalism irritated many of her colleagues. They saw her as a 'hatchet woman' who bleated about her job. Nevertheless, many of them were being placed in a similar position given the direction the organisation was going in; indeed, they were the ones who were having to make the redundancies, Julia simply performed the operation once the victim had been chosen. Without exception, this group of nine managers expressed negative feelings about the organisation they worked for which ranged from discomfort to outright loathing.

What follows is an extract from the notes I made when reflecting on the work I did with this group. First, I will recount my initial reaction on meeting Julia before the pair of us went to meet the board who had called for a presentation regarding the work Julia had commissioned me to undertake.

> There used to be a children's programme on TV called the Krankies – it was a brother and sister act, the woman played the part of a young schoolboy who was always getting into trouble. Well, this woman we'll call Julia reminded me of the schoolboy, she'd even adopted some of the mannerisms. Like she appeared to hitch up her skirt before she went into battle, and she swayed backwards and forwards and rocked on her heels like a copper addressing a crowd of miscreant youths – all five foot of her. She was a mixture of 'gung ho' and simple terror. The terror came from the place where she worked and particularly 'the Board', a group of eleven men who ran the place. Some of them were plugged into the Party that ran Whitehall. Their ambition was for their organisation to become a household name, like Wandsworth or Westminster.

The next set of reflections were made after working with Julia and the other nine managers for a week in a hotel in the country. A technique I sometimes use to help managers get beyond the constraints of language is to invite them to draw or paint the organisation in which they work. Some of what follows refers to my reflections on the picture Julia drew of the organisation she worked for, a macabre picture of death above which Julia drew herself as a parachutist. Some refer to an incident, right at the end of the week when there was too little time to repair the damage, when the group suddenly turned on Julia who had been encouraging them for most of the week to stop moaning and unite with her in taking on the board. The pretext for the attack was their annoyance at the constant phone calls for Julia sent by the organisation to the hotel during our stay. Julia was considerably shaken by the attack and temporarily withdrew from the programme of work which we had designed together as a group for the coming months. Anyway, here are my reflections, starting with the picture:

She was suspended on a parachute somewhere above the civic centre, floating freely and swinging backwards and forwards, but not coming down. Above the civic centre there was a large cloud, called the Board, which pissed on the crowd below and occasionally sent down thunderbolts which killed groups of tiny people who could be seen milling about on the ground.

She spent the week with a number of the most powerful members of the crowd who didn't know what to do either. Some were happy with their lot, some wanted to get out, some spoke of fighting. They were perplexed because many of them had friends on the board and yet it pissed on them. Like decent people they wanted to believe in the best of others, they wanted to believe that it would all blow away. Throughout the week the group waited for Julia to come down to earth but somehow she conveyed the impression that she wanted to stay a cut above them. So on the last day they shot her.

It was suggested by one that Julia wished to create 'a little impression' by receiving messages from the board at the hotel where they were staying. This behaviour caused intense irritation to the group. The comment about 'a little impression' was the first arrow that they fired, several others followed in quick succession. It was done so swiftly and so quietly that it was difficult to appreciate at the moment that it had happened. Indeed, afterwards, the archers angrily proclaimed that they could not see 'what all the fuss was about'. As far as they could see, nothing had happened, some comments had been made and she should have taken them professionally not personally. I was puzzled and afraid. I thought I knew this group pretty well. Perhaps they hadn't realised that the parachutist was so thin-skinned, so easily pierced. And I hadn't understood how thick-skinned some of the group could be.

There was another twist to this tale. The two key players, the parachutist and the one who fired the first arrow, were both women: indeed, the only women discernible on this organisational landscape. The cloud, the crowd leaders and most of the crowd were men. I had developed the impression that to have any power in this land you had to be a man, even if you were a woman. Julia, as we have seen, has become a caricature-man, hitching up her skirts, tightening her holster – a small man in drag who resembled a schoolboy. The other woman was without any obvious feminine qualities – she presented herself as a non-woman rather than as a man; although in her forties she continued to live at home with her parents; she was diligent and reliable. From the outset I had been worried about how she would cope with the work we were going to do together. I had assumed that although she was an incredibly 'defended' person she was quite harmless. Of course I was wrong.

120

After finishing my work with this group I have followed their fortunes from a distance. I know that one was placed on indefinite sick-leave, another left, Julia herself had a long period away from work as a result of a stress-related illness. Towards the end of my work with them I hoped as much as I dared that they would unite, link with others, and make a stand. But they didn't. If there was fighting to be done, so it seemed, they would choose each other as victims.

I hope the cameo conveys something of the fear that was about in this organisation. The people I was working with were on large salaries, many were responsible for multi-million pound budgets and for managing hundreds of staff. Big people, all of them, yet they felt real terror of the board and the chief executive in particular. I heard from elsewhere that the latter occasionally had 'tantrums' when he would scream and rant at his senior managers. His public persona was quite different. He was quite well known as a champion of the new management in the chief executive networks in which he operated. He presented himself as a thoroughly modern and responsible man, a well-known speaker at conferences and the writer of brief but humorous pieces in the local government press.

LOYALTY IN THE GREY ZONE

In 1970 Albert Hirschman wrote a book called *Exit, Voice and Loyalty: Responses to Decline in Firms, Organisations, and States.* Hirschman construed 'decline' primarily in terms of deteriorating economic performance rather than in a normative sense. His point was that Exit (for example, withdrawal of custom or staff turnover) and Voice (for example, complaints by customers or workers, lobbying or campaigning for change) were the two primary mechanisms whereby signals could be sent to the organisation concerning its deteriorating performance. Loyalty referred to the situation in which customers or employees were prepared to bide their time, to tolerate temporary periods of decline without resort to Voice or Exit because of their commitment to the organisation. Hirschman's analysis has had an important impact upon public policy in recent years. His advocacy of Voice, which he made particularly clear in a number of subsequent publications (Hirschman 1973), has provided a redoubt behind which those who seek to defend the principle of democratic accountability have been able to rally in the face of the trend towards the marketisation and privatisation of public services (Hambleton and Hoggett 1993). However, Hirschman's notion of 'loyalty' requires further thought. He tends to assume that loyalty is something which is voluntarily given, whereas in the organisation described above 'loyalty' simply described the strategy that was left in a situation from which there was very little chance of immediate Exit (the labour market in that area and in Britain as a whole at that time was collapsing) and considerable risk in exercising

Voice. This situation, at one time only common to a few 'cutting-edge' Conservative local authorities, now seems to be the norm for much of the public services in the mid-1990s.

By focusing on the experience of one person, Julia, in this kind of organisational setting, I hope to have indicated that a variety of responses is possible when an individual finds herself caught within a destructive regime. Julia was both a collaborator with the regime (the hatchet woman) but also someone who sought to take a stand. Because of her professionalism she refused to adopt the role of sullen resistance, a strategy much preferred by some of her colleagues. Finally, she ended up being a victim, shot down by her fellows both because of her naivety and her professionalism – a quality she was then accused of lacking because of her inability to take their attack 'on the chin'. In Figure 9.1 I illustrate the various roles we tend to adopt when we find ourselves trapped within destructive regimes.

The vast majority of organisational participants are not the agents of change: rather, they feel like its victims. But the concept of the victim is a profoundly ambiguous one. The boundary between the victim, the collaborator, the survivor and the resistor is not hard and fast but blurred. Primo Levi refers to 'the space which separates (and not only in Nazi Lagers) the victims from the persecutors' (1988b: 25) as the 'Grey Zone'. It is to an analysis of this area that we now turn.

The area of life we are concerned with here is familiar to us all, for we are all at some time or another the objects of changes wrought within either the organisations in which we work or the society in which we live. In what follows I shall therefore draw upon material from the survivors of total institutions, participants in ordinary work organisations and our broader experience as citizens within democratic or repressive societies.

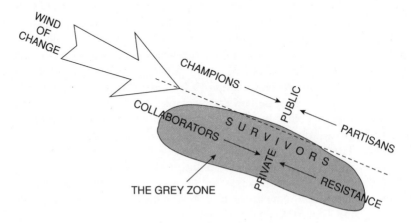

Figure 9.1 The dynamics of change

122

THE VICTIM

I have no information ... I feel like I'm a bit of flotsam about to go down the drain ... after a while it will stop hurting – they'll go and beat up somebody else.

(Two health service managers talking)

First, we must clear out of the way those instances in which an individual or group may for strategic purposes adopt the role of the victim. Within organisations the process whereby participants disavow the positional power which they actually possess is common enough. Such forms of feigned powerlessness are often assumed as a way of dealing with the fear of taking action in pursuit of one's beliefs, a tactic which was employed often enough by the managers who faced Julia's exhortations. Within the sphere of civil society a number of commentators have noted the tendency for different groups to compete, on the basis of their victimhood, for scarce public resources. Speaking of this experience in the USA Lasch notes 'as they vie for the privileged status of victims, they appeal not to the universal rights of citizenship but to a special experience of persecution' (1984: 67). In such cases, the identity of being 'a victim' may enable some groups to obtain competitive advantage over others but at the expense of the fragmentation of common struggle (Cain and Yuval-Davis 1990; Sivanandan 1990).

The status of victimhood may also be claimed as a means of denying one's own power to help or oppress. This issue is familiar enough within the women's movement today (Pheterson 1990). Much contemporary social theory has been anxious to avoid 'objectivist' accounts of social behaviour through which the subject is seen simply as the object of assumed forces beyond her control. As Giddens puts it, 'power presumes regularised relations of autonomy and dependence ... all forms of dependence offer some resources whereby those who are subordinate can influence the activities of their superiors' (1984: 16). Clearly then, failure to mobilise such resources is equivalent to acquiescence in one's dependence. Later, Giddens suggests that individuals very rarely experience compulsion where they are wholly incapable of resisting. Such occurrences tend to be momentary, as when one person is physically rendered helpless by another: 'all other sanctions, no matter how oppressive and comprehensive they may be, demand some kind of acquiescence from those subject to them' (175).

It is vital, however, to be able to sustain a perspective which on the one hand gives emphasis to human responsibility without on the other conceding ground to those who would otherwise be only too happy to 'blame the victim'. As Levi notes, 'the oppressor remains what he is, and so does the victim' (1988b: 13); they are not interchangeable. Examples of regimes which sustain compulsion over time are rare, but the extermination camps perfected the art as Levi's testimony so eloquently shows. He speaks of the camps as 'a condition of pure survival', a daily struggle 'in which the room for choices (especially moral choices) was reduced to zero' (33). His book, *If This is a Man*, recounts the experience of the victims, the Muselmanner, the drowned:

> On their entry into the camp, through basic incapacity, or by misfortune, or through some banal incident, they are overcome before they can adapt themselves; they are beaten by time, they do not begin to learn German, to disentangle the infernal knot of laws and prohibitions until their body is already in decay, and nothing can save them from selections or from death by exhaustion . . . an anonymous mass, continuously renewed and always identical, of non-men who march and labour in silence, the divine spark dead within them, already too empty to really suffer.
>
> (Levi 1988a: 96)

The victim is always alone, always in the dark, always one step behind.

THE SURVIVOR

> We're all in it, all the people around me . . . keep your head down . . . comply only when you have to . . . build a wall around your area – your little bit of influence and power and hang on . . . we'll still be here when they've gone.
>
> (A local government manager and a worker in higher education)

As Lasch notes, the experience of those in the camps has become a key metaphor for our modern times. He argues, 'everyday life begins to take on some of the more undesirable and ominous characteristics of behaviour in extreme situations: restriction of perspective to the immediate demands of survival; ironic self-observation; protean selfhood; emotional anaesthesia' (1984: 94). The art of survivalism has now become one of the most recurrent themes in modern literature and social theory. It is as if Weber's 'iron cage', made invisible, has become a synonym for reality itself, or, as Cohen and Taylor (1992) put it, reality has become an open prison from which we ceaselessly construct escape attempts. Surviving is about enduring, getting by, maintaining detachment, mentally distancing oneself and, just occasionally, making out. The myriad little pathways and pursuits through which survival is achieved, methods first charted in detail by Goffman in his analysis of everyday life (Goffman 1959), is a testimony both to our creativity and to our fear of freedom. For ultimately the survivor is one who has found ways of accommodating to, and therefore colluding with, the regime which oppresses him, but without openly collaborating with it. Above all, the survivor is one who does not 'make a stand' nor go to the rescue of others. The survivor survives but at the cost of his status as a moral being; the survivor is a demoralised person (Havel 1987: 62). Primo Levi knew this well, it was a knowledge which haunted him along with all the other survivors. As he put it:

> The 'saved' of the Lager were not the best, those predestined to do good; the bearers of a message. What I had seen and lived through proved the exact contrary. Preferably the worst survived, the selfish, the violent, the insensitive, the collaborators of the 'grey zones', the spies. It was not a certain rule ... but it was, nevertheless, a rule.
>
> (Levi 1988b: 62–3)

But what are the arts of survival? Clearly, there are many and they vary according to the context in which one is engaged. The first and most vital art is to know the rules. Within organisations, as in the camps, the starting point is a detailed understanding of the rules which govern behaviour in a given place. Survivors break rules but their knowledge is such that they know how to break them without being seen, or to bend them in such a way that their intent becomes corrupted, or to follow them slavishly and to the letter so that they become unworkable in the manner of the Good Soldier Svejk (Hasek 1990). Lasch describes this in terms of the ability to adopt 'the protective colouration of one's immediate surroundings' (1984: 97). Robert Jackall, in his study of managers at work, provides a detailed account of organisational survival. Methods employed included the ability to move so quickly that one's mistakes never caught one up; the ability to provide 'plausible' explanations rather than ones which were in some way honest; 'covering up' and 'covering your back'; alertness to expediency; 'flexibility' (how many management texts have there been which sing the praises of the flexible manager – i.e. one who is not set in his ways?), and so on. Jackall (1988: 130) also notes 'the virtues of stead-fast silence', a theme which brings us back to the starting point of this chapter, i.e. the importance of voice and the risk of using it.

A second essential art of survivalism is to immerse yourself in routine. Cohen and Taylor (1992) suggest three primary techniques of managing routine. 'Unreflective accommodation' refers to the more or less auto-matic and unreflective process of getting on with things. It is important to keep in mind the possibility that, for many professional, scientific and managerial workers, the daily routine is in fact one with great variety. Indeed, as Mintzberg's (1989) research on the manager's day revealed, the reality of the day is not at all the ordered and planned phenomenon of the time-management manual. The day is in fact quite chaotic, one with constant interruptions, accidents, unforeseen events and so on. Yet, taken over time, it remains routinised, the same kind of stuff over and over again, but at such a pace. One of the striking things about the public sector in the UK has been the gradual process of 'speed up' (Hoggett 1996), referred to by apologists of the current changes as 'getting more for less'. At the beginning of this chapter I noted the toll this has taken in terms of morale and stress but for some managers and professionals such hyper-activity can become perversely intoxicating – it is sometimes fondly referred to in terms of 'getting high on getting by'. The point about routinisation, and one made consistently by Giddens, is that whilst we may feel trapped within it we also feel safe. In this sense, routines become a way of containing anxiety, a way of not having to think except in the most focused and immediate fashion – hence, no doubt, the longstanding practice of giving routinised work tasks to psychiatric patients in so-called 'occupational therapy'.

Both Cohen and Taylor (1992) and Lasch (1984) note that 'distancing' is a crucial method of coping with the routinisation which is so often such an integral part of survivalism. Cohen and Taylor describe this as 'a mental way of effecting an escape from some of the terrors of patterned living', a technique whereby 'we "play at" or "act against" roles and rou-tines'(1992: 53). Distancing can assume many forms. It includes mental escape into fantasy, emotional detachment, 'going through the motions' and the use of irony and sarcasm. Lasch notes that it involves the trick of observing oneself as if events were happening to someone else rather than to you. Crucially, in organisational life, it involves the withdrawal of commitment, the refusal to be drawn in or taken in.

A third element of survivalism concerns the narrowing of time, space and social horizons. Lasch (1984: 95) speaks of the need for survivors to adopt 'narrow, clearly defined objectives and the dangers of dwelling on the past or looking too far into the future'. People live from day to day and travel lightly. Because the future seems so uncertain both within the organisational life-world and in the wider society, it is best not to have too many plans, or at least if you have them don't become too attached . . . just in case. To travel lightly it is best not to have too many emotional ties, not to care too much for others. What organisation rewards caring for others these days? There is no time for me to worry about you, organ-isations can no longer afford to carry 'passengers' we are told. Again Levi shows where this mentality ultimately leads to:

> The demand for solidarity, for a human word, advice, even only a listening ear, was permanent and universal but rarely satisfied. There was no time, space, privacy, patience, strength; most often, the person to whom the request was addressed in turn found himself in a state of need, in credit.
>
> (Levi 1988b: 59)

The processes of 'distancing' and individualisation have become an essential element of our modern culture. Paradoxically, however, today's organisation members find that in order to survive in the corporate jungle it is also necessary to identify with the organisation and not be too obviously preoccupied with self. Increasingly, organisations endeavour to engineer our active commitment – the manipulation of organisational culture being crucial to this task (Ray 1986). The task of eliciting commitment is both more urgent and more difficult within organisations which are engaged in activities which have little or no social value. The danger is of course that this is the direction public organisations are pushed as they are exhorted and seduced into seeing themselves simply as a business. But how can cynicism be harnessed to organisational commitment? Don't these pull in opposite directions? I have argued elsewhere (Hoggett 1992) that this contradiction is only apparent. The commitment that is sought by post-bureaucratic regimes is a commitment to what I have called the simulated moral community. The new regimes have not abandoned rational planning; rather, the focus of rationality shifts from systems and procedures to human relations themselves. The classic text on the subject is quite open and unselfconscious about this. Peters and Waterman (1982) argue that the task of contemporary management is not to create winners and empowered employees but to make people feel as if they are these things. This is management by illusion. As I put it (Hoggett 1992: 128) 'here, then, we find the art of simulation taken to the highest degree: the simulation of teamwork, the simulation of enthusiasm, the simulation of caring (hoop la!) and the simulation of values'. Within this world there is no contradiction between cynicism and commitment: in fact, the one requires the other.

Many years ago Gouldner (1970) offered a sustained critique of forms of sociological analysis, such as Goffman's (1959), which appeared content simply to describe the many tactics of self-presentation in modern life. But the idea that the sociologist might take a normative stance when examining such behaviour appears to be lost on some contemporary writers (Gergen 1991; Tseelon 1992). Instead, by arguing that the very notions of sincerity and integrity somehow belong to a bygone era, they appear to be content to act as apologists for current forms of superficiality. Ironic detachment and cynicism have become a pervasive but diffuse element of the way of being, particularly of the 'educated middle classes'. Sloterdijk (1984) refers to the unhappy consciousness which makes its peace with the world, despite its own better knowledge of the collective predicament that we are now all in. He has in mind a class which knows enough to be aware of the global and local inequalities upon which its own comfort is based and that the machine upon which it rides has no driver and appears to be rushing towards a fatal collision with the ecological fabric upon which it feeds. It is a class which may also be aware of the strategic importance it now plays in the reproduction of a system which delivers and destroys in equal part. But, if this class were to become the locus of transformation towards a better world, it must first come to terms with its own cynicism, and then with its deep despair. There are many within the intelligentsia who appear to give counsel to this despair, who have come to view the very idea of commitment to a value position as an indication of naivety or stupidity. They not only describe but appear to celebrate the demoralisation of life and the abandonment of even the most modest visions of a better world. As such, they constitute a pernicious conservative element in modern life. Such people are not simply survivors: they have become collaborators with the very system they observe.

THE COLLABORATOR

Although the boundary is a fine one, there is value in drawing a distinction between the passive forms of collusion which we engage in to get by and the active doing of another's will which is a form of collaboration. Levi wisely advises against a rush to judgement within the grey zone. The motivations for collaboration are many and varied. In extreme situations such as the camps, complicity was often imposed. As Levi notes, the awfulness of Nazism lay in its refusal to allow the Jew even to be a victim. The man who screamed at you as you got off the transit train in the camp and the one who cleared up your remains after you had been gassed was a fellow Jew. In this way, Nazism sought to transfer its own guilt and shame onto its victims: 'you are no longer the other race, the anti-race, the prime enemy of the millennial Reich . . . we have embraced you, corrupted you, dragged you to the bottom with us' (Levi 1988b: 38).

In less extreme situations collaboration cannot be compelled: it is always based upon some form of fear or desire. But even as such it may not be the result of ill intent. In Julia's organisation what struck me was the way in which a number of her fellow managers had been drawn into a position of active collaboration because of the care that they still had for their own staff. Their hope was that they could use their power to implement the policies of the elite which controlled the organisation in such a way that their staff would be saved or, if not saved, then at least the number of victims might be less than if another was allowed to take control. To cite one manager from this group, 'It's as if I've been placed in charge of a boat whose rations are being continuously reduced; we can only survive by chucking people over'. The tragedy is that those who collaborate in this way receive little thanks from either workers or voters. Even those who communicate their predicament effectively still run the risk of being seen as responsible when the bodies go overboard. Furthermore, the potential opposition becomes disoriented and divided, the movement towards resistance and partisanship is harder precisely because one has become caught in the game, albeit as a reluctant player. In Clegg's (1989) terms, an outflanking move is hard when one has become complicit in a game which progressively disempowers those who might otherwise resist.

But more usually collaboration has a less noble basis. As Levi notes, besides fear there is seduction, servile imitation and the desire for any kind of power whatsoever. For the most cynical and amoral, collaboration requires no self-justification, but these people are exceptional. For most of us collaboration is not easy to perform in good conscience. But the problem of self-justification, of bad faith, is inherent to the condition of the survivor also. In one of the most moving passages of *If This is a Man* Levi reflects upon the shame he and his Auschwitz comrades felt upon being forced to witness the hanging of a survivor of an attempted rebellion at Birkenau. Even in that desperate situation, Levi and his friend Alberto were crushed by the knowledge that they could have acted differently and by the realisation that passivity was itself a form of human agency.

Havel's famous essay 'The Power of the Powerless' (Havel 1987) derives its strength from Havel's insistence that ideology (in his case, the ideology of the last years of Eastern European communism) draws its support from the very human subjects that it oppresses. For Havel, ideology offers a 'bridge of excuses' for making one's peace with the world. Even though he was writing in 1978, well before liberalisation had begun, Havel insists that it was not fear of the state that primarily accounted for the absence of dissent but 'the general unwillingness of consumption-oriented people to sacrifice some material certainties for the sake of their own spiritual and moral integrity' (54). In other words, even in Eastern Europe, the moment of consent was stronger than coercion. For Havel, the system depends upon and deepens its subject's demoralisation, their having no sense of responsibility for anything higher than personal survival. Repeatedly, he insists that everyone in his or her own way 'is both a victim and a supporter of the system'. The hegemony of the system is maintained because it finds something in us that responds to it: 'human beings are compelled to live within a lie, but they can be compelled to do so only because they are in fact capable of living in this way'. In this sense the system relates to humanity 'as a degenerate image of its own degeneration, as a record of people's own failure as individuals' (53–4). The power of such passages lies in Havel's courage to accuse us all. There is no dry sociological analysis here, nor any attempt to explain away people's passivity in terms of false consciousness. Rather, he calls the subject back in, he insists upon its accountability, upon its capacity to do differently.

It is often argued by the political right that sociological accounts of things such as family breakdown are dangerous because of the way in which they undermine the importance of human responsibility. Clearly, this is often no more than crude political rhetoric behind which lies the attempt to blame the victim, i.e. single mothers or errant fathers. The problem for both the left and for critical social theory is that because they have not taken the subject seriously they have abandoned the terrain of moral argument, the terrain of truth and the lie. In short, their language and mode of being has become both dehumanised and demoralised. The left in particular seems terrified of calling the powerless to account, of drawing attention to the ways in which workers, women or black people reproduce their own oppression in their relations with others. Only a few, such as Lasch (1984), have been prepared to point to the ways in which we in the West, secure in the enjoyment of our material comforts yet obsessed by thoughts of disaster, are complicit in maintaining the uneasy order we seek deliverance from. Havel speaks of the many justifications put about for the way things are:

> Individuals need not believe in these mystifications, but they must behave as though they did, or they must at least tolerate them in silence, or get along well with those who work with them. For this reason, however, they must live within a lie. They need not accept the lie. It is enough for them to have accepted their life with it and in it. For, by this very fact, individuals confirm the system, fulfil the system, make the system, are the system.
>
> (Havel 1987: 45)

From this perspective the question of hegemony and ideology can be restated. The question is not 'How are we lied to?' but how does the other's desire to mislead connect to my own fear of the truth? The question is not 'How does the state or the organisation dupe us?' but how does this external 'establishment' connect to the one inside us? The true idea, as opposed to the fact, is one full of personal meaning. The lie, on the other hand, refers to an experience or event which is stripped of its significance. Perhaps this enables us to reconstrue the problem of ideology in the modern world. The issue was always posed in terms of the problem of 'false consciousness', i.e. the way in which people appeared to be misled by misrepresentations of the world. But perhaps today this is not the real problem. For, whether as employees or citizens, we often know that the situation we are in stinks and yet we do little about it because we have destroyed the emotional significance of our experience. In this sense, the knowledge remains abstract and dissociated; it is not personal knowledge but disembodied knowledge, it is knowledge without understanding. This is what Havel means by 'living within the lie'.

THE RESISTANCE

Resistance begins when individuals, even in small ways, stop colluding. In a paradoxical way resistance begins by the process of distancing oneself from the life one is otherwise embroiled in. Cohen and Taylor (1992: 56) note that sociologists have long realised that such forms of distancing can be the prelude to radical change but they have failed to see how distancing more frequently leads to escape attempts concerned with survival. Let us not forget our infinite capacity for kidding ourselves. Organisations are full of griping individuals who can (and do) go on *ad nauseam* about how awful things are and yet are superbly adept at never actually placing themselves in a position which could be compromising.

Such forms of cynicism and detachment which, as we have seen, are so much the basis of survivalism nevertheless can have a constructive effect in creating a latent climate of resistance to oppressive regimes. The cynical outlook is universal in its scope and, as such, is corrosive towards all forms of power. For the cynic there just isn't any good out there. Everyone is either incompetent, self-seeking, untrustworthy or malicious, except for (or even including) the cynic and his or her group. The cynic is hateful in equal measure towards the establishment and those, like Julia, who seek to challenge it.

Resistance proper begins with a commitment to agency in a situation where there is some risk (Jesmier, Knights and Nord 1994). For this reason, more often than not, the initial moment of resistance is covert, private rather than public, hidden rather than visible. Typically, the starting point of resistance lies in inaction for here the element of risk is at its lowest. We are creative people. Companies and institutions throughout the century have been dogged by manifestations of private resistance – the spanner in the works, the defaced mission statement (about six years ago I noticed that the house motto of the then Conservative-controlled London Borough of Kingston had been altered by some wag from 'Kingston Bright and Clean' to 'Kingston Tight and Mean'). These and countless other examples are well known and, in most organisations, much loved by those employees whose task is otherwise to endure. Foot-dragging, lead-swinging, passivity, non-compliance or compliance with the letter but not the spirit of an edict or instruction, the cheerful adoption of the latest organisational rhetoric (but only when the boss is present), the manipulation of data in order to comply with the latest performance standards, working to standard (the professional equivalent of working to rule) – indeed, all the arts of performance management can be called upon to present an inertial force in the face of change.

One searches hard to find a single management text which has something good to say about resistance to change in organisations. Given, as I have argued, that management discourse assumes change to be a self-evident good, it follows that it construes resistance to change as a self-evident bad (Kotter and Schlesinger 1979). Whilst more enlightened texts seek to understand resistance rather than to condemn it – pointing to the way in which change brings about the experience of loss (Marris 1986) or anxiety (Obholzer 1994) which can have a grave impact upon

131

morale if not recognised and responded to – the idea that change itself may be contestable, that it may be regressive rather than progressive, is rarely considered.

As the saying goes, 'You can't stand in the way of progress'! Indeed, we seem to live in a world in which change has assumed the status of a force of destiny. I offer two examples to illustrate the point. The first extract comes from an excursion into the popular press by one of Britain's leading theorists of globalisation:

> Continuity, community, social repair – these are undoubtedly themes with a strong appeal to the erstwhile Tory strongholds. Yet we now live in a global economic order in which, middle class or not, everyone *must* compete. Global economic competition *demands* a dynamic attitude towards the world, not a static or 'conservative' one; and it brings in its train disruptive consequences which *no* political party can do more than somewhat mute.
>
> (Giddens 1995, my emphases)

The second comes from the Borrie Commission on Social Justice which undertook a major review of the future of welfare for the British Labour Party:

> Far from making the welfare state redundant, social and economic change creates a new and even more vital need for the security which the welfare state was designed to provide. Frightened people cannot welcome change; they can only resist it or be defeated by it. It takes secure people – secure in their abilities, their finances and their communities – to cope with change at the workplace or in the home.
>
> (Report of the Commission for Social Justice 1994: 222)

Change is. Everything changes. Yes, this has always been true. We are born, we die, we fall ill, the seasons come and go, friends fall in and out, dreams disturb us. Yes, everything changes, everything has always changed. But now change has been pulled out from the flow of life. It is no longer something which just happens, now it can be made to happen – willed, crafted, implemented, shaped. You can't stand in the way of progress, for if we don't change our competitors will, economic development demands it, the market insists.

Change no longer just is, for it has become a good: indeed, it is *the* good. If it is new it must be good. New technologies, new ideas, new forms of art, new musics, new commodities. 'The spectacle presents itself as something enormously positive, indisputable and inaccessible. It says nothing more than "that which appears is good, that which is good appears"' (Debord 1983: para. 12). Hey friend, what's new?!

But it is just possible that we are becoming tired of this relentless, fetishised mantra of change. A new character can be seen upon the stage, one who realises the value of the past and of the timeless, recurring, cyclical time of the pre-modern. Suddenly, radicals, particularly those influenced by ecological ideas, are getting excited about tradition (Gross 1992; Telos Collective 1992–3; Blackwell and Seabrook 1993). Out on the margins of politics, resistance to change is becoming radical and the wisdom of tradition is becoming appreciated.

The point about resistance to change is that it slows things down: that's why corporate managers hate it. This is the essence of resistance, its inertial quality. But most examples of resistance are an illustration of negative power, that is, the power to hinder or stop. They are not yet forms of organised resistance nor public resistance: they are in this sense prepolitical. The task is to move from private and individual resistance, to collective resistance, to openly organised public opposition, i.e. to partisanship. Only then can the conditions for what Blackwell and Seabrook call the revolt against change be assembled in order to provide 'the roots of an energising and transforming radicalism' (Blackwell and Seabrook, 1993: 14).

THE PARTISAN

The partisan is someone who goes beyond acts of private resistance by making his or her position/opposition public. Within repressive organisational or social regimes this can be a risky process as a succession of whistle-blowers in the UK have discovered to their cost. For this reason, as we have seen, the initial moment of resistance is necessarily covert, private rather than public, hidden rather than visible.

An American study (Soeken and Soeken 1987) reported that the majority of private sector and half of public sector whistle-blowers lost their jobs as a result of the action undertaken. Jackall's (1988) research on whistle-blowers indicates the external risks involved. Individuals may be engaged not just in defying their organisation but also their professional association: 'professionals of any sort are reluctant to have their masks of consistency stripped away, particularly by one in a position to know intimately the inconsistencies necessarily generated by the tensions between monopolised privilege and ideologies of public service' (Jackall 1988: 146). Several recent examples in the UK, such as the Helen Zeitlin and Graham Pink cases, indicate that the whistle-blower is likely to receive little if any support from their immediate colleagues. As Ball (1993) notes, the introduction of markets within the public sector has so deepened workers' sense of vulnerability that the pressure to collude with one's own management in order to ensure that one's own organisation survives is intense.

It probably requires a particular kind of person, 'made of another metal than us' (Levi 1988a: 156), to take a stand in this way. But beside the strength of one's moral and political beliefs there are other factors which can motivate people to act. For example, the partisan may be propelled by a sense of self-righteousness or even martyrdom, which makes it impossible for her[2] to act in concert with others. Jackall's (1988) case studies of organisational dissidents revealed the variety of motivations which may underlie taking a stand. In the case of 'Wilson', for example, there was a clear clash between the organisation's valuing of expediency and Wilson's meticulous pursuit of proper procedures – Wilson's public concern for the quality and safety of the product had become entangled with the obsessional elements of his character.

Even where personality plays an important role, a stand will nevertheless also be taken on the basis of a set of political and social values. Moreover, these are values in the real sense, that is, values which lead to engagement with the world rather than values which are maintained as a form of consolation as one distances oneself from a world which seems unjust. The partisan not only recovers the sense of her own truth but she then acts upon it, counterposing this truth to the reality which has become 'normalised' within the regime of the group, organisation or society in which she finds herself. In this manner the partisan offers a different vision of 'the real', by asserting her right to speak and to act she confronts reality not as a given to be accepted but as a dynamic system in which to intervene. The partisan is therefore a revolutionary, not in the sense of subscribing to a particular kind of political ideology but because she refuses any longer to play the game in which, until that point in time, she has been a willing or unwilling player. For this reason she will be hated, not only by her opponents but also by those friends and colleagues who are committed to the continuation of the game. Through her refusal to continue she reveals their bad faith and arouses their shame. As Graham Pink noted, 'telling the truth of what I witnessed and was unwillingly party to has been a wretched, distressing and costly business' (Pink 1994: 1700).

This presents the partisan with a dilemma, for in taking a stand she inevitably must resort to some kind of splitting. To act decisively one must have some sense of being right. But to act effectively the temptation to be righteous must also be foregone; a benign attitude must be maintained, one which insists that 'those who are not against me must be with me'. In other words, the partisan has to believe in the best in people despite the weaknesses that they demonstrate. What the partisan possesses is 'intolerable knowledge' – the living realisation of the routinised injustice of the family, group, organisation or society to which she belongs. It is this kind of knowledge that Graham Pink speaks of when describing the reality of providing nursing care on the night shift of a desperately understaffed ward for chronically ill and dying elderly people:

As I tried to prevent Mr B from climbing out of his urine-soaked bed and falling to the floor, another patient called out ... Once Mr B had quietened, I hurried round the partition to find Mr V, a quiet and gentle man, lying on the floor in a pool of urine, sobbing ... As I lifted the emaciated man I seemed to carry a much greater burden: a sense of shame that I, a registered nurse, should be forced to witness, nay inflict, such outrageous neglect on a dying man.

(Pink 1994: 1701)

Such knowledge is intolerable because the understanding that flows from it is one which brooks no compromise with life. And yet we know that if we are to live as reasonably sane beings who derive some contentment from life then we must make compromises with the very systems which not only disempower us but, on occasions, threaten to destroy us as emotional or physical beings. Faced with this kind of personal contradiction it is easiest to survive by choosing one polarity or another – either we disavow our own better knowledge and make our peace with the system or we renounce our need of others and take the cold and impersonal path of the implacable oppositionist. What is really hard is to live this personal contradiction, to contain the tension without resort to splitting and work with it in our own imperfect fashion.

NOTES

1 A survey by the trade union the MSF in 1993 (*Guardian*, 22 February) found that nurses working for the newly created hospital trusts were less likely to speak to journalists than those still employed directly by local health authorities. Today, three years on, virtually all nurses within the NHS are employed by hospital trusts.
2 References to 'she' and 'her' apply equally to men and women.

REFERENCES

Ball, S. (1993) 'Education Policy, Power Relations and Teachers' Work', *British Journal of Educational Studies*, 41, 2: 106–21.
Belasco, J. (1990) *Teaching the Elephant to Dance: Empowering Change in Your Organisation*, London: Hutchinson Business Books.
Blackwell, T. and Seabrook, J. (1993) *The Revolt Against Change*, London: Vintage.
Bogg, J. and Cooper, C. (1995) 'Job Satisfaction, Mental Health, and Occupational Stress among Senior Civil Servants', *Human Relations* 48, 3: 327–41.
British Medical Association (1992) *Stress and the Medical Profession*, London: BMA.
British Medical Journal (1994) *The Rise of Stalinism in the NHS*, 309: 1640–5.
Burrows, R. and Loader, B. (eds) (1994) *Towards a Post-Fordist Welfare State?* London: Routledge.
Cain, H. and Yuval-Davis, N. (1990) 'The Equal Opportunities Community and the Anti-racist Struggle', *Critical Social Policy*, 29: 5–26.

Clegg, S. (1989) *Frameworks of Power*, London: Sage.

Cohen, S. and Taylor, L. (1992) *Escape Attempts: The Theory and Practice of Resistance to Everyday Life*, London: Routledge.

Cooper, C. and Kelly, M. (1993) 'Occupational Stress in Headteachers: a National UK Study', *British Journal of Educational Psychology* 63: 130–43.

Cummins, A-M. and Hoggett, P. (1995) 'Counselling and the Enterprise Culture', *British Journal of Counselling and Guidance* 23, 3: 301–12.

Debord, G. (1983) *Society of the Spectacle*, Detroit: Black and Red.

Gergen, K. (1991) *The Saturated Self: Dilemmas of Identity in Contemporary Life*, New York: Basic Books.

Giddens, A. (1984) *The Constitution of Society*, Cambridge: Polity Press.

Giddens, A. (1991) *Modernity and Self-identity: Self and Society in the Late Modern Age*, Cambridge: Polity Press.

Giddens, A. (1995) 'Middle England and Global Capitalism', *Guardian*, 27 February.

Goffman, E. (1959) *The Presentation of Self in Everyday Life*, New York: Anchor Books.

Gouldner, A. (1970) *The Coming Crisis in Western Sociology*, New York: Basic Books.

Gross, D. (1992) *The Past in Ruins: Tradition and the Critique of Modernity*, Amherst: University of Massachusetts Press.

Hambleton, R. and Hoggett, P. (1993) 'Rethinking Consumerism in Public Services', *Consumer Policy Review* 3, 2: 103–11.

Hasek, J. (1990) *Good Soldier Svejk*, London: Penguin.

Havel, V. (1987) *Living in Truth*, London: Faber and Faber.

Hirschman, A. (1970) *Exit, Voice and Loyalty: Responses to Decline in Firms, Organisations and States*, Cambridge, Mass.: Harvard University Press.

Hirschman, A. (1973) '"Exit, Voice and Loyalty": Further Reflections and a Survey of Recent Contributions', *Social Science Information* 13, 1: 7–26.

Hoggett, P. (1991) 'A New Management in the Public Sector?', *Policy and Politics* 19, 4: 143–56.

Hoggett, P. (1992) *Partisans in an Uncertain World: The Psychoanalysis of Engagement*, London: Free Association Books.

Hoggett, P. (1994) 'The Politics of the Modernisation of the UK Welfare State', in Burrows, R. and Loader, B. (eds) *Towards a Post-Fordist Welfare State?* London: Routledge.

Hoggett, P. (1996) 'New Modes of Control in the Public Services', *Public Administration*, 74, 1: 9–32.

Jackall, R. (1988) *Moral Mazes: The World of Corporate Managers*, New York: Oxford University Press.

Jesmier, J., Knights, D. and Nord, W. (eds) (1994) *Resistance and Power in Organisations*, London: Routledge.

Kanter, R. (1985) *The Change Masters: Corporate Entrepreneurs at Work*, London: Unwin.

Kotter, J. and Schlesinger, L. (1979) 'Choosing Strategies for Change', *Harvard Business Review* March/April: 106–14.

Lasch, C. (1984) *The Minimal Self: Psychic Survival in Troubled Times*, London: Picador.

Levi, P. (1988a) *If This is a Man*, London: Abacus.

Levi, P. (1988b) *The Drowned and the Saved*, London: Michael Joseph.

Lousada, J. (1993) 'Self-defence is No Offence', *Journal of Social Work Practice* 7, 2: 103–113.

Marris, P. (1986) *Loss and Change*, London: Routledge.

Mintzberg, H. (1989) *Mintzberg on Management: Inside Our Strange World of Organisations*, New York: Free Press.

Morris Suzuki, T. (1986) 'Capitalism in the Computer Age', *New Left Review* 160: 81–91.

Ohmae, K. (1990) *The Borderless World: Power and Strategy in the Interlinked Economy*, London: Collins.

Obholzer, A. (1994) 'Managing Social Anxieties in Public Sector Organisations', in Obholzer, A. and Roberts, V. Z. (eds) *The Unconscious at Work*, London: Routledge.

Peters, T. (1989) *Thriving on Chaos: Handbook for a Management Revolution*, London: Pan.

Peters, T. (1993) *Liberation Management: Necessary Disorganisation for the Nanosecond Nineties*, London: Pan.

Peters, T. and Waterman, R. (1982) *In Search of Excellence: Lessons from America's Best-Run Companies*, New York: Harper & Row.

Pheterson, G. (1990) 'Alliances between Women: Overcoming Internalised Oppression and Internalised Domination', in Albreacht, L. and Brewer, R. (eds) *Bridges of Power: Women's Multicultural Initiatives*, Philadelphia: New Society.

Pink, G. (1994) 'The Price of Truth', *British Medical Journal* 309: 1700–5.

Ray, C. (1986) 'Corporate Culture: the Last Frontier of Control', *Journal of Management Studies* 23, 3: 287–97.

Report of the Commission on Social Justice (1994) *Social Justice: Strategies for National Renewal*, London: Vintage.

Ridley, N. (1988) *The Local Right: Enabling not Providing*, London: Centre for Policy Studies.

Sivanandan, A. (1990) 'All that Melts into Air is Solid: the Hokum of New Times', *Race and Class* 31, 3: 1–31.

Sloterdijk, P. (1984) 'Cynicism – the Twilight of False Consciousness', *New German Critique* 33: 190–206.

Soeken, K. and Soeken, D. (1987) *A Survey of Whistle Blowers: Their Stressors and Coping Strategies*, Laurel, Maryland: Association of Mental Health Specialities.

Telos Collective (1992–3) *Special Issue on Traditions* 94, Winter.

Tseelon, E. (1992) 'Is the Presented Self Sincere? Goffman, Impression Management and the Postmodern Self', *Theory, Culture and Society* 9: 115–28.

10

A STRUGGLE TOWARDS HEALTH IN HEALTH SERVICE POLICY-MAKING

Jean White

This chapter is an attempt to locate the recent changes in National Health Service structure and the thrust of its new management and service delivery policies within a national and global economic context. I will look at the cost of some of these policies in terms of the quality of public health care, and at the psychological effects both on those who are involved in creating the policies and on those employed by the NHS. I will then explore a number of creative possibilities that we may be able to develop within the market system, and that could remain if the management system of the NHS were changed to a more satisfactory one. I will look in particular at the transformative potential of an expanded paradigm of health. Finally I will call for a review of current management structures from the perspective of the healthier policy-making options I have described.

As many economists have documented – probably most clearly and cogently Will Hutton (1995) – the 1980s witnessed an international disenchantment with Keynesian principles of economic management. Some of the arguments and the effective thrust of the policies within this are explored in more detail in Chapter 11: 'Internal Space and the Market'. Here, suffice to say that in the 1980s the USA, Sweden, France, Germany, Spain, Canada, New Zealand, Russia, Eastern Europe and East Asia minimised controls on national financial regulation and entered into fierce competition for multinational investment and a stake in the global financial market. Britain implemented the most aggressive privatisation programme and the most comprehensive attack on the welfare system of any advanced state. As part of this, the NHS was reinvented as a market (or a 'quasi-market', as social policy theorists argue) based on the USA model, with no prior testing of these ideas or introduction of institutions or agencies that could mediate or regulate the 'reforms'.

Two entirely distinct and separate issues have been conflated and fudged by the Conservative government with the introduction of market mechanisms into the health service in Britain. Whilst few (although a very few still *do*) dispute the need for review, reform and modernisation of the

NHS to make it more user-friendly, and to expand and improve the models of health in operation and make them more accessible and equitable, the argument for such change has been confused with the introduction of the market 'reforms' at great political convenience to the government. Although, as a nation, we remain rightly proud of our ability to deliver free health care to all and extremely healthily resistant to changing that cardinal human right, the 'old-style' NHS did incur financial and human wastage through an overemphasis on somatisation as the only legitimate expression of distress, and therefore much unnecessary expenditure on drugs and high-tech surgical interventions. There was discomfort in many quarters with the hegemony of the medical profession in deciding what were appropriate treatments and, indeed, in setting the ground rules or the paradigm within which human well-being could be thought about. It is arguable that we were operating a 'sickness' model of health in this country until very recently, and that relatively little attention had been given to the multiple and complex factors that determine health. And although the traditional Western medical model has achieved supreme success in the prevention of infectious and contagious diseases, and is usually the treatment of choice in acute or advanced conditions which require radical chemical or surgical intervention, it is probably fair to say that its theoretical location within a mechanistic Newtonian biological prototype greatly limits its application. The need for expansion into a more holistic model of health, and one that could take social, political and psychological factors into the equation was long overdue.

Many on the Left (for example, Hall 1988: 271–83) have advanced similar arguments. As Stuart Hall says, 'We cannot simply defend the NHS as it is, as if nothing has happened since it was first introduced in 1947' (276). His arguments centre round the need for increased choice for patients – for which GP is to be consulted, for having a wider range of therapies available at health centres, and for recognition of the role of consumers of health care in defining needs and how they are met. He sees all of these as issues of democratisation, rights and the expansion of social citizenship. He argues too for

> the greater involvement of mothers in the hospital care of children; the social movements for a healthier diet, for better care of the body [and, I (White) would add, inseparably, the mind], for greater control by women over their fertility and reproduction; for a less unequal relationship between patients and the medical profession; for more preventive medicine, a healthier environment, a programme of health education that is not at the mercy of the industrial lobbies, the pharmaceutical companies or the homophobic and anti-abortionist bigots of the 'moral minority'.
>
> (Hall 1988: 281–2)

These arguments are quite separate from the changes in management structure and health care delivery introduced by the market reforms. I will use them, though, along with others that I introduce myself, as benchmarks for what could be envisaged as a 'healthier' health service. We cannot turn the clock back to 1947. It is therefore necessary to distinguish between the harm that has resulted from the market reforms and the improvements that have resulted or that could result from them, or even in despite of them! It may then be useful to evaluate the changes in management structure in the NHS from the point of view of how the service *could* be improved and modernised.

As a result of 'marketisation', all sectors of the health service have now been split into either 'purchasers' which commission services, or 'providers' which deliver them, so that internal market mechanisms can operate. It is arguable, and at the date of writing (November, 1995) looks increasingly likely, that this restructuring of the NHS into a business enterprise opens the possibility for private health care corporations to tender their services in competition with the NHS provider units and for the health insurance companies or even private individuals to purchase services within the same 'playing field'. In other words, 'a mixed economy of care', much like the one in operation in the USA, is one potential outcome of the marketisation of the NHS, but whether this will, in effect, be the shape of the future depends upon political developments in this country and remains to be seen. For the moment, although the market remains predominantly internal, the re-structuring of the NHS has had a profound impact upon the delivery of health care in this country.

THE COST OF THE 'REFORMS'

At the moment, the major 'provider' units are hospitals, of which at the date of writing about 450 are run by Trust Boards, which are independent of any direct health authority control and are predominantly composed of representatives of the large corporations and the Conservative party. The District and Family Health Services Authorities are combining to form 'health commissions' which 'purchase' the services that the provider units tender at competitive rates. General practices have been offered financial inducements to become 'fundholders' and, to date, about 2,000 practices have taken up this option, although there are extremely mixed views amongst GPs about the consequences of fundholding for patient care. Fundholding practices function as business enterprises and also purchase the treatment of the hospital providers, although primary care is less amenable to the purchaser/provider split because GPs continue to provide frontline services for their patients, whether or not they are also purchasing services from other providers. A very recent development is the changing of the management structure of various locality-based provider services, such as non-acute mental health and maternity services, into 'community trusts' which, like the hospital trusts, can be independent of direct health authority control.

Whether or not the gains in efficiency claimed to be effected by these changes are accurate is hard to measure, owing to the inadequacy and blatant massaging of government statistics. However, certain consequences, most markedly in London but also to varying extents nationwide, have become inescapably observable and the most immediately apparent of these is the severe reduction in availability of hospital services. The theoretical justification for these cuts was provided by a well-intentioned report produced in 1992 in response to a commission from the King's Fund (Tomlinson 1992). This, *The Tomlinson Report*, argued that in the capital there was an over-concentration of resource in acute and specialist services and that the indigenous population could benefit from a redistribution of funding from some of these 'centres of excellence' to primary care. However well-principled in intention, the application of the recommendations of *The Tomlinson Report* has resulted in a dramatic reduction in funding for hospital services *before* suitable alternatives could be set up elsewhere and a therefore inescapable increase in human suffering.

Long waiting lists, especially for cardiac interventions, have already resulted in preventable deaths. The difficulty in gaining admission to hospital for 'non-emergency' treatment has caused unnecessary pain, suffering and long-term damage to thousands of people's health. And yet it is argued that waiting lists are an effective control mechanism or form of 'rationing' for demand despite, or because of, their stated consequences of 'Risk that the patient is lost to the system (*death*, spontaneous recovery [!], patient withdraws, loss of contract, private/other treatment).' (Bagust 1994 – my emphasis.) Hospital beds often lie empty, in increasing numbers towards the end of the financial year, for lack of budgetary resources. The total number of hospital beds available, whether or not used, has decreased by 33 per cent since 1979, and 30,000 beds were closed in 1994 alone (Labour Party NHS Audit 1995: 5). Many hospitals, principally in London but also in varying degrees throughout the country, have been closed completely. One in five hospitals overall has been closed since 1979 (ibid.). The argument that these closures will enable a redistribution of investment into primary and community care holds *some* validity and is resulting in some partial improvements. However, analysis of the actual sums of money involved (for example, a cut in overall spending on health of £7.5 million by 1999/2000 in East London and the City alone) clearly demonstrates that the predominant outcome is and, without a change in funding policy will continue to be, a categorical reduction of services available. Other factors that contribute to the overall cut in patient services must include the massive investment in the increased management costs

141

(now effectively over 20 per cent) of making the marketisation process possible, and the enormously high salaries paid to NHS executives today.

Inevitably, this situation places many people working within the NHS at the moment in a difficult and often severely morally compromised position. Those working at the 'coalface', the clinicians, struggle to maintain adequate levels of care and treatment in situations which are frequently both under-resourced and under-staffed. Often working long hours at low levels of pay, they may have to face the additional stress of dealing with angry patients who may not always realise that the delay or failure of service delivery is not the responsibility of the doctors, nurses, radiologists, etc. with whom they are in immediate contact. Working under these conditions is extremely demoralising: it means that the staff involved are having to manage pressure and anxiety that can result in their own sickness, and they can sometimes be faced with choices and quandaries that *do* place them in an ethical dilemma. But, in my view, the burden of ethical accountability rests squarely with the executives, managers, and members of the Trust Boards, health authorities and commissions whose job it is to implement government policy. These latter, for purposes of brevity, I will dub 'the policy-makers'.

The policy-makers are doubly compromised. They are answerable for cuts in services which may result in lives being lost, or permanent or serious damage to the health of the public. The constant 'restructuring' of both management and service delivery means that they are also responsible for effecting redundancies which can at best result in relocation, often to another part of the country, for an entire family, and at worst in a broken career, financial hardship and waste of precious experience and skills. Even when the decisions made may have less obviously destructive results, the 'change fatigue' induced by constant and much too rapid restructuring makes it much harder for everyone involved to remain reflective and sensitised to possible consequences and outcomes, and therefore to plan for the future in a rational and sensible way. The policy-makers have a range of options as to how they deal with or don't deal with these moral dilemmas.

The fact that many, if not most, policy-makers may not see themselves as working in a compromised or even untenable ethical situation is evidence of the use of the major defence mechanisms of denial or 'turning a blind eye' to the most serious consequences of their decisions. The exercise of these defences may be well-practised in some executives and board members who have been imported from a business background. For those less skilled in this area, the employment of these defences is greatly assisted by the evangelical tone of the language in which NHS reforms are promulgated. It insists on a relentless optimism which permits very little space for thinking critically, oppositionally or even looking at the changes from a different perspective. As George Orwell argued very cogently in 'Politics and the English Language' (1957), the state of health of a political movement, whether it be dubbed to the Right or to the Left within conventional political designations, can be fairly accurately assessed by the nature of the language it deploys. The more there is a use of words which function as euphemisms, jargon, generalisations or blanket terms which serve to obscure or pervert meaning rather than allowing space for thinking in or beyond it, the more corrupt is the political organisation and purpose.

Judged in these terms, the rational basis for the NHS management reforms is dubious in the extreme. A few brief examples should suffice to give the tenor of the current NHS vernacular – to list the terminology in any detail would be to expose the reader to the kind of mind-numbing assault to which those within the NHS today are constantly subject. 'The NHS Management Family' (how could we think that what's going on is anything other than benevolent?) has been 'crisping up' the choice towards fundholding in general practice (i.e. making it harder to gain access to secondary and tertiary services, and creating financial disadvantages for those practices which choose not to take up the fundholding option). 'Rationing dilemmas' does address the fact that there are difficult choices to be made but neatly glosses over the fact that it is people's lives that are at issue. 'Priority overload' is worse in that it subtly displaces the blame for lack of resources onto those people whose health needs are too urgent to be met by budgetary constraints. 'Efficiency savings' usually implies a cut in services, whilst 'opportunity costs' can be used to imply the necessity of expenditure that makes structures within the NHS more amenable to the introduction of market mechanisms and sometimes to privatisation. At the same time, 'no strike deals' and 'confidentiality clauses' within new staffing contracts do spell out pretty clearly that opposition and speaking out from within the ranks are not to be tolerated.

The linguistic context, the constant use of lists, 'bullet points', and 'mission statements', within NHS policy-making all serve to promote a blind and unquestioning faith in the efficacy and rightfulness of the reforms, and to make dissenting or divergent thought and language extremely arduous. It should be a matter of the gravest concern to all interested parties that, on the whole, our national and regional policy-makers are involved in such serious psychological contortions as to render them oblivious to the consequences of their actions. However, a few extremely hard-headed and brave souls within health authorities and trusts do manage to voice their opposition and dissent in reasoned terms to the press, and do lend their support to protest and scrutiny from outside the system. This is of critical importance because it slightly modifies what would otherwise be a very stark 'us and them' scenario, and is one way of preserving some integrity as a policy-maker. It is also a significant strategy because it makes it harder for fellow board members to preserve their defence mechanisms of denial or disowning. *Owning* one's personal responsibility for and part in the damage that is being caused through these NHS 'reforms' is a prerequisite to staying sane within the system. It means that a realistic assessment of the extent of the damage and depressive concern for its consequences can be maintained. Without it, a truly terrifying capacity to continue to inflict more and more harmful cuts without *seeing* the effects in human terms becomes possible, and could lead to the sort of loss of contact with external reality that Christopher Bollas describes in 'The Fascist State of Mind'. In this seminal paper, Bollas describes how in the pursual of extreme states of political persecution, the Fascist mind deals with its own moral vacuum by splitting off its dead core self and projecting it into a victim, who must then be eliminated (Bollas 1993: 203). It may seem a little far-fetched to compare this process with those in existence in NHS policy-making today, but the earlier we become aware of the beginnings of a psychologically vicious circle, the more chance there is of an effective intervention to arrest its development while change is still possible.

SOME CREATIVE POSSIBILITIES THAT REMAIN

There is also, I think, the potential for some genuinely creative and constructive policy-making strategies within this extremely sombre context. But before I go on to outline what some of these might look like in practice, I first of all want to issue a very strong caveat. The fundamentalist tenor of most current NHS policy dicta encourages a mood of manic optimism, possibly as a defence against what might otherwise sometimes be suicidal despair. Like most manic states within groups and organisations, it is extremely difficult to avoid getting caught up with, not least because to do so renders one liable to carrying *all* the depressive pain for the organisation and therefore very vulnerable to scapegoating and elimination by the organisation as a means of ridding itself of unwanted anguish. It is, therefore, crucial to develop a means of differentiating between what could give grounds for reasonable and sober optimism, without losing sight of the ravages that are still being inflicted, and optimism that may be based on inflated enthusiasm which serves to protect oneself from the distress which is a necessary concomitant of a realistic attitude within the NHS today.

Some of the strategies I will outline are embryonic consequences of the thrust of the marketisation process, which has brought some necessary modernisation and improvements in its train. To a large extent, though, the effects of these changes, which I will designate as structural improvements, will depend on how the policies are interpreted and implemented, and therefore whether or not they permit changes of consciousness. The other strategies which I outline, and which I designate theoretical or conceptual shifts in the understanding of health, could be made possible by exploiting the chinks created by the slippage engendered by constant structural change, and the opportunities for rethinking the meanings of health and illness thrown up by reorganisation. It is of paramount significance to remain conscious of whether one is using a possibility opened up by market policy, or whether the opportunity to develop a more enlightened view of an aspect of health is due to the process of change itself, because it will affect the means and the tactics used to implement these strategies and therefore their chances of accomplishment and survival. It may be possible to effect policies now which remain as advances and models of good practice, whatever the political future of the NHS.

There are four major structural alterations, currently in different stages of the process of implementation which *could*, depending on how they are interpreted and used, lead to more enlightened and equitable models of health management and delivery: the putatively enhanced role of consumer consultation and feedback, the shift of some resources from tertiary and secondary to primary care, the increased emphasis on links between primary and community care and on a multidisciplinary approach to health, and the comprehensive computerisation of primary care.

1 Structural changes

Consumer consultation and participation

A significant advance that has been imported from the effective business strategies of the multinational corporations is the notion of the usefulness of consumer consultation and feedback. Now, this can be deployed in a tokenistic, even cynical fashion, as is arguable that it was during the 'consultations' about some of the closures of the major London hospitals, or departments thereof. However, *with careful thought*, it can also open a window onto a very different approach to dealing with the needs of certain groups of people whose particularities might otherwise have been marginalised, belittled or pathologised.

It could be argued that up until now, the fact that some sections of the population did not 'fit in' with the forms of existing provision has been dealt with by displacement of the responsibility for the inadequacy of the services onto those who were not catered for, and sometimes by pathologising the needs of certain marginalised groups. For example, some doctors have refused to register homeless people, implicitly deemed too irresponsible to merit health care, and have therefore also effectively barred their way to hospital treatment, doubtless in case they might be trying to manipulate their way into a bed for a few nights.

The so-called 'section rate' (or incidence of compulsory detainment in psychiatric hospital) for young black men has been documented as about 13 times the rate of the rest of the population. (Harrison *et al.* 1988) In effect, certain common behaviours or forms of expression of Afro-Caribbean males are misconstrued as madness by the medical authorities involved, resulting in a massive over-representation of one section of the population amongst those compulsorily detained in psychiatric hospital, and a needless and debilitating stigmatisation of a large group of people. Several psychotherapeutic practitioners have detailed the psychological processes involved in this sort of mass branding (for example, White, 1989). They generally concur that what is going on is the projective identification of psychotic anxieties belonging to the white population into black men, who are then perceived as a dangerous and violent threat to the stability of society. Put more simply, sometimes we can experience anxieties which feel unmanageable or as if they might be overwhelming. These sorts of anxieties are exacerbated by very rapid social change, loss of large areas of secure employment, and the break-up of long-standing social and residential communities and the sense of continuity they provide. One way in which we can deal with the powerfully disturbing internal sense of disruption and loss of containment caused by massive anxiety is by projecting it into another group of people, who are then locked up for the 'safety' of society. The real issues for young black men in terms of health, employment and social standing remain unaddressed.

Another example of a pathologisation of need is that of HIV/Aids. In some, but by no means all quarters, spectacularly encouraged by the tabloid press, the questions and radical rethinking required by the introduction of a major new disease have been able to be ignored through a process of locating the problem solely as that of gay men. Their behaviour is then held responsible for the disease itself and homosexuality further stigmatised.

The process of projective identification is extremely damaging – obviously for the recipients, perhaps less apparently for those of us who rid ourselves of anxiety by using it. Psychoanalytic theorists (Klein 1946; Bion 1957; and others) have demonstrated how in individual cases the use of this primitive defence mechanism weakens the ego, or the mind's capacity for thoughtful coherence, by splitting and fragmentation. In common parlance, we become less adult, less mature, the more we resort to dealing with our anxieties in this way, and therefore less capable of making reasoned and sensible assessments of external reality. That this is true in individuals is easily observable in those people we might describe as bigots. That it is also true in a health policy-making context is less immediately detectable but is demonstrable by the sorts of nonsenses that it can lead to, like, as I have argued, the mass psychiatric sectioning of young black men.

146

Such insights might be used to facilitate the development of a healthier form of projective identification, in the form of empathy or understanding. This might allow the formulation of more sensible policies, and the new emphasis on consumer consultation and feedback *could* be used to assist this process. For example, at a board seminar held in January 1995 by two Inner London Health Authorities, the issue of an equalities strategy was addressed in detail. They agreed on the necessity to think about the particular health needs of, amongst others, the homeless, refugee communities, ethnic minority communities, travellers, those in psychological distress, lesbians and gay men, and people who are socially and economically disadvantaged. They thought that an integral part of any reformulation of policy should be the setting up of consultation processes that were adequate and available to give previously disenfranchised groups a real voice in terms of addressing their own issues and health needs.

All those attending the seminar felt that the Authorities should make a commitment 'to ensure that the services are relevant, accessible, appropriate and sensitive to the needs of all sections of the community addressing current disadvantage and discrimination' and that they should also 'promote positive action to redress past disadvantage and discrimination to groups/sections whose needs have been identified'. They also thought that it would be advantageous for membership of the board of the ensuing Health Commission to reflect these sections of the local population. However, and indeed whether, concrete, effective and durable policies eventually result from this seminar, it does provide a model of laudable intentions which could have wide-ranging implications and ramifications, not only for those who are consulted and whose needs are addressed by the services provided, but also for the policy-makers themselves.

Now, the policies that may result from this board seminar on 'equalities' in health care could have obvious benefits for the population of the area served by these Health Authorities. But they are also evidence of healthier functioning in the members of the authorities themselves. With regard to these particular issues, the authorities were attempting to *prioritise* as opposed to *pathologise* health needs of particular groupings. This means that they were trying to own their own part in damage that has already been done, as evidenced in the statement about the need to redress past disadvantage and discrimination. The *owning* of previously projected areas of difficulty and distress makes the policy-makers more capable of rational and informed decision-making, with a sound basis in empathy and concern. I would argue that it is a model of good practice which could be adopted on a much more widespread scale, even within the context of current NHS reforms.

The shift of some resources to primary care

To what extent policies like this are amenable to implementation is, of course, dependent on the financial resources made available. As I have already shown, the overall thrust of the restructuring of the NHS is towards a gradual but major reduction in spending. But, in London at least, a proportion of the resources released by cuts in spending on secondary and tertiary services is being redirected into primary care. The manner in which it is being redistributed is extremely unsatisfactory on two counts – it is temporary (all the London Initiative Zone – LIZ – funding for new projects which improve services available at primary care level is limited to a maximum of five years, and is more commonly made available in one-, two- or three-year grants), and it is distributed in such a fashion that policy-makers usually have inadequate time (sometimes as little as two or three weeks) to design programmes or projects to use it effectively. But it does, at least, provide a starting point from which primary care can begin to be rethought in a way that is hopefully more up-to-date, more in tune with the needs of the population, and with more emphasis on early intervention and prevention. It could be used as an opportunity to develop prefigurative forms in primary care which embrace a more holistic understanding of health. By this I mean that what LIZ money can be, and to some extent is being used to set up now, may not be either widespread or long-lasting, but could be used as a exemplar of what is possible at the frontiers of primary care today.

In thinking about health in an overall sense, we need to place people in their contexts – social, political and historical (especially some ethnic groups and refugees). We also need to take into consideration their family background, perhaps sometimes over more than one generation, and their state of mind, without resorting to psychiatric diagnosis but again within the informed understanding of their overall setting. The links that are currently beginning to be made between primary and community care, or what used to be called general practice and social services, make this development more possible. Recent thinking about health care emphasises a multidisciplinary approach with bigger health centres within which many diverse skills (those of psychologists, counsellors, advocates and translators, nurses, physiotherapists, and even sometimes psychotherapists, staff team development consultants, osteopaths and outreach workers) are annexed or shared.

An enhanced role for user feedback

As part of the new emphasis on consultation and consumer feedback, there is also more scope for patient participation in decision-making. The complaints procedures are being reformed to make them less legalistic, except in cases of severe malpractice. Instead, more prominence is being given to conciliation as a means of dealing with complaints. This is a procedure which usually gives both patients and doctors psychological space to work through and resolve a grievance, and it often highlights an area of mispractice or inattention that can be learnt from by the practitioner, without resort to damaging disciplinary proceedings. Taken to its logical conclusion, it would make sense for doctors and other health practitioners to save time and pre-empt some of the need for individual complaints by setting up forums such as, for example, open practice meetings, in which their patients can come and give their views about the effectiveness or otherwise of health centre policy and practices.

Comprehensive computerisation

There has also been much attention given to the necessity for comprehensive computerisation of primary care, which has multiple possible usages and is a double-edged sword. Although, like many of the changes introduced by the market reforms, it can contribute to a mechanised, fragmented, number-crunching approach to patient care, it also has applications that can promote increased understanding of the needs of the patient population and efficiency in addressing them. It can provide instant access to patient records for individual practitioners and the potential for health centres within a locality to share a database and collate statistics about health trends and needs that can be used in preventive strategies. There is, in development, a Europe-wide computer network which enables patient records to be accessed internationally. One ingenious doctor has devised a means of codifying the patient's family history and state of mind in an extremely sympathetic, understanding and non-stigmatising fashion but in computerisable form. Again, this kind of international database *could* be used for purposes of political control, or it could be used to effect unprecedented gains in and understanding of social medicine and patient care. *How* this kind of development is implemented again depends on the kind of understanding that informs and interprets it.

2 Conceptual shifts

All the above are what could be designated as *structural* changes within primary care: they are already in process to varying degrees and could promote shifts in consciousness which make a holistic and less mechanistic approach to health more feasible. There are also, though, much greater theoretical or conceptual shifts which need to be put in train and have been given much less attention and consideration. The changes in consciousness implicit in these latter are probably not amenable to policy-making alone – they also have profound ramifications for medical

149

education, but this chapter cannot address those issues in any detail. Suffice to say at this point that the core question of 'Why is this person ill?' must be opened to other perspectives in addition to a purely biological and mechanistic one.

A more holistic approach to health

The Dutch are way ahead of us in terms of incorporating a psychodynamic understanding of health into their practice (Grol 1983). This means, in effect, that the mind and body are not thought of as separate, independently functioning entities, but as parts of a complex whole organism, interdependent and sensitively interrelating. It does *not* mean that every physical symptom can be explained psychologically – that would be psychological reductionism of a degree that would be likely to create even worse adverse effects than the present somatic reductionism. What it does signify is the critical importance of considering a symptom within the context of a person's life circumstances, background and history.

To give just one brief possible example, a Mrs X was experiencing fainting fits and difficulty in breathing which always took place on the same day of the week and often at the same time on that day. Neurological and respiratory investigations had thrown no light on the problem. But a thoughtful and psychologically minded GP had given sufficient attention and time to discover that a few months previously, Mrs X's mother had died on that day and at that time, and Mrs X had been present. Mrs X had a very close attachment to her mother – she continued to live only a few streets away and saw her almost daily. But it was an ambivalent attachment – to a large extent, she felt suffocated by her and constrained from living her own life as independently as she might otherwise have wished. Mrs X was, in fact, extremely angry with her mother, both about her mother's dependence on her and her own inability to stand up to her and assert her own wishes on occasions. Her latent hostility had interfered with a natural mourning process after her mother's death. Because she felt guilty about her rage, and could not acknowledge it or give it expression, she could not separate from her mother sufficiently internally to let her go, and her continued identification resulted in her replaying her mother's symptoms at the time of her death. Informed by this understanding, the GP was able to refer Mrs X to the psychotherapist (who was shared between two health centres in the locality) so that she could do the necessary psychological work, not only to begin to mourn her mother's death, but to begin to conduct her own life in a way that was more conducive to her wishes. Mrs X, who had frequently suffered from a range of minor physical ailments, demonstrated a considerable improvement in her health and became a much less regular attender at the Health Centre.

This sort of psychodynamic understanding will not obviate the need for specialist hospital referrals, consultations and treatment, but it is likely to have a marked effect on when, how and how frequently GPs refer in this way. Therefore, although costly in terms of the need to provide specialist back-up psychological services, it is conceivable, although not yet demonstrated, that it could save on enormously expensive hospital referrals. It also has profound implications in terms of possible approaches to both mental health and team management and development within the NHS.

Early intervention in psychological care

An area that has begun to be addressed within some health authorities, although not, in my view, to anything like the extent that it could be, is the issue of prevention and early intervention in psychological/psychiatric care. Like the mind/body dualism already mentioned there is still, amongst most policy-makers, an unwavering desire to maintain a split between the 'mentally ill' and the mentally well. This is a difficult split to address on the ground because it threatens all of us with questions and issues about our own mental health, and does not keep the feared arenas of madness, anxiety, depression or other forms of psychological malfunctioning or distress safely 'out there' in others. But it is arguably the most critical issue that we must address if we are to improve our services from the antiquated barbarities still involved in traditional psychiatric in- and out-patient care. There is still an over-reliance on the use of ECT and major and minor tranquillisers, with all their ill effects, and the unnecessary stigma of the acquisition of a psychiatric history can still effectively destroy a person's career, morale, and legal and civil rights.

Very slowly, there is beginning to dawn a realisation in some quarters that such extreme forms of treatment are preventable in many, if not all, cases, although the issues of prevention and early intervention in mental health remain contentious, under-researched and under-funded. The most logical place to start is at birth, possibly even before, with psychologically informed management of ante- and post-natal care. Joan Raphael-Leff has argued persuasively that the mother's state of mind in pregnancy has a significant impact on the later development of the child (Raphael-Leff 1994: 13–39). Research has been undertaken in Italy that demonstrates links between pre- and postnatal behavioural patterns (Piontelli 1992). And slightly later in life, as I have heard one extremely enlightened GP argue, a short psychodynamic intervention with a disturbed four-year-old could save thousands of pounds worth of investment in acute psychiatric or even prison services 20 years later. Such forward thinking is unusual and such services are hard to come by except in the most acute extremes, and often not even then.

What has, laudably, been given more attention is the need for specialist psychological services for adolescents. This is the age at which, as most psychological practitioners recognise (for example, Bollas 1987; Laufer and Laufer 1984; Searles 1965), most first breakdowns occur. The reason why this is so is that during adolescence the defence structures established in early infancy must be renegotiated and partially broken down in order for a transition to adulthood to be possible. The personality is hence subject to such extremes of turbulence that areas of psychotic confusion are most likely to emerge at this point. Meltzer is probably the psycho-analytic practitioner who has documented these processes in the most precise detail.

> the underlying severe confusions at all levels with which the adoles-cent is contending ... with the breakdown of the obsessional, rigid, and exaggerated splitting characteristic of the latency structure, an uncertainty in regard to all differentiations, internal–external, adult–infantile, good–bad, and male–female which was characteristic of the pre-Oedipal development reappears. In addition, perverse tendencies due to confusion of erogenous zones, compounded with confusion between sexual love and sadism, take the field. This is all 'in order', as it were; the group life presents a modulating environ-ment *vis-à-vis* the adult world and distinct from the child-world, well-equipped to bring this seething flux gradually into a more crystallised state – if the more psychotic type of confusion of identity due to massive projective identification does not play too great a role.
>
> (Meltzer 1973: 53)

Whether it be breakdown or other signs of psychological distress or distur-bance, an intervention in adolescence is most likely to have dramatic effects, and often to turn a person's life around for good. This has been recognised quite widely within tertiary education but similar services remain largely unavailable to the rest of the population. Appropriate psychological services for the young might reduce but would not obviate the need for other forms of non-stigmatising help at other critical stages in the life cycle, perhaps especially mid-life and the third age. Long-term planning and preventive thinking in mental health remain, in my view, the greatest challenge left to health service policy-makers today.

CONCLUSION

The gains and possibilities that I have highlighted are by no means a *necessary* consequence of the marketisation of the NHS. Some are the product of long-overdue modernisation. Some are possible ways of turning to good advantage strategies that have proved useful in the business and industrial sectors. Mainly, although the process of change itself has had deleterious and damaging effects, some of which I have documented, it has also opened up a new discussion about the meaning and maintenance of health. This latter opens up fresh and extremely important opportunities for thinking about health care and delivering it, which it is absolutely critical to maintain. I want to emphasise two points as guidelines towards the future in my conclusion.

Firstly, the issue of owning as opposed to projecting areas of difficulty and distress could be one of the fundamental tenets of health service policy-making, and a new emphasis on organisational health could make that possible. The NHS effectively functions as a container for anxieties and forms of guilt that most of us would rather be rid of. I have mentioned the projection of primitive psychotic anxieties which has resulted in the mass psychiatric sectioning of young black men. Similar anxieties about our own fear of madness lead to the maintenance of a rigid, unrealistic and extremely damaging split between those designated as mentally ill and those designated as mentally well within the system. There are also other forms of 'nameless dread' that are held and carried within the health care system. Perhaps most critically, the fear of death and the fear of murderousness may lead most of us to evade critical choices and dilemmas about the fact that some people have to die, an issue that has been, with rare and individual exceptions, increasingly ducked as the advances of high-tech medicine enable us to do. But do we really want to leave this issue to the vagaries of the market or, by default, in the hands of doctors who may then be attacked or penalised for having made decisions that most of us would not choose to own? Surely this is an area best opened up to the widest public and political debate possible. Issues of vulnerability and dependency, and fears of bodily and/or psychological intrusion and violation, also need to be thought about as areas that may be projected into 'the patients' and remain there with the most bizarre consequences unless we can think about the psychodynamics of what is going on within the health-care system. A benchmark question, then, for policy-makers could be: what is the anxiety that is currently being dealt with and in what ways can we own/contain it? A great many abuses of our own or any other system of health care could be better managed if we were to be able to think about some of these issues.

Secondly, and probably as critical, is the matter of whether or not the market system is really the best way to implement better health policy in Britain. I have outlined what some aspects of a 'healthier' NHS might look like – these and/or other benchmarks might be used to assess the new market arrangements. A thoroughgoing scrutiny of the effects and the costs of the new management should have been put in train before implementation. It is not too late now to set up an investigation, and for those interested members of the public and the health service professionals to participate in a management audit aimed at looking at the effectiveness of the health care we deliver from below, from the point of view of the public. In a few years' time, when large sections of the health service may well have been privatised, it *will* be too late. There is no point in maintaining a righteous stance about what 'they' are doing, unless we are prepared to get our hands dirty, and by whatever means still available to us, to join and further the debate.

AUTHOR'S NOTE

From 1992 until 1995 I was a non-executive member of an Inner London Health Authority. Much of what has been written in this chapter therefore derives from my personal experience. Thanks are also due to Drs R. D. Hinshelwood, L. Lyttelton and J. Payne for their comments and suggestions, and, in particular, to Dr Hinshelwood who wrote a long and considered response to this chapter and contributed some of the ideas about the health service as a container for primitive anxieties.

REFERENCES AND FURTHER READING

Bagust, A. (1994): *Contracting for Management of Waiting Lists and Waiting Times*, York Health Economics Consortium: University of York.
Bion, W. (1957) 'Differentiation of the Psychotic from the non-Psychotic Personalities', in Bion, W. *Second Thoughts*, London: Heinemann.
Bollas, C. (1987) *The Shadow of the Object – Psychoanalysis of the Unthought Known*, London: Free Association Books.
Bollas, C. (1993) 'The Fascist State of Mind' in Bollas, C. *Being a Character*, London: Routledge.
East London and the City Health Authority, and City and East London FHSA (1994), *Towards a Strategy for Health in the East End*.
Frankel, S. and Faulkner, A. (1994) *Cutting the Wait*, NHS Executive.
Grol, R. (1983) *To Heal or to Harm*, London: The Royal College of General Practitioners.
Hall, S. (1988) *The Hard Road To Renewal*, London: Verso.
Harrison, G., Holton, A., Neilson, D. and Boot, D. (1988) 'A Prospective Study of Severe Mental Disorder in Afro-Caribbean Patients', *Psychological Medicine*, August.
Hinshelwood, R.D. (1995) 'The Relevance of Psychotherapy', *Psychoanalytic Psychotherapy* 8, 3.
Howland, G. (ed.) (1995) *The Institute of Health Services Management Yearbook*.
Hutton, W. (1995) *The State We're In*, London: Cape.
Klein, M. (1946) 'Notes on Some Schizoid Mechanisms' in Klein, M. *The Writings of Melanie Klein*, London: Hogarth.
Labour Party NHS Audit (1995) *Taking the Temperature*, London: Labour Party.
Laufer, M. and Laufer, M. E. (1984) *Adolescence and Developmental Breakdown: a Psychoanalytic View*, New Haven and London: Yale University Press.
Le Grand, J. and Bartlett, W. (1993) *Quasi-Markets and Social Policy*, London: Macmillan.

Meltzer, D. (1973) 'Identification and Socialisation in Adolescence' in Meltzer, D. *Sexual States of Mind*, London: Clunie.

New Internationalist (1993) *The New Globalism – Multinationals Take Control* 246, August.

NAHAT (National Association of Health Authorities and Trusts) (1993) Briefing, no. 38, January.

NHS Management Executive News (1992) 62, October.

NHS Management Executive News (1992) 63, November.

Orwell, G., (1957) 'Politics and the English Language' in Orwell, G. *Inside the Whale*, London: Penguin.

Piontelli, A. (1992) *From Fetus to Child – An Observational and Psychoanalytic Study*, London: Routledge.

Raphael-Leff, J. (1994) 'Imaginative Bodies of Childbearing' in *The Imaginative Body*, Erskine, A. and Judd, D. (eds), London: Whurr.

Searles, H. (1965) *Collected Papers on Schizophrenia and Related Subjects*, London: Maresfield.

Tomlinson, D. (1992) *Report of the Enquiry into London's Health Service, Medical Education and Research*, London: HMSO.

White, J. (1992) 'Adolescence and Education in the 1990s' in *Idealism, Mastery and Futures*, Conference held by City University 1991, London: City University.

White, J. (1989) 'Racism and Psychosis – Whose Madness is it Anyway?' Unpublished paper.

11

INTERNAL SPACE AND THE MARKET

Jean White

Internal space is our most precious commodity. That this statement is a contradiction in terms and an absurdity of gross dimensions is the subject of this chapter. What do I mean by internal space? Theoretical elaborations and detail will come later – for the moment, I will attempt to give a sense, a flavour, of what it can signify. It might be commonly described in an individual as depth. It certainly implies a capacity for subjectivity, for reflective thought, for imagination. Manifestations in different individuals will be widely divergent but always recognisable by the way in which internal space will enhance the other's capacity to think, to dream, to feel that they have a valid subjective viewpoint which is worth listening to. It may come across as either serious or playful, and its impact may transmit through words, images, ways of seeing or doing which cause the other to pause and reassess. It is always subversive, in the sense that it is never the product of standardised or automatic responses. It is not bound to particular classes or groups of people. Its presence might approximate to what Edward Said means by the 'intellectual', 'the author of a language that tries to speak the truth to power'. (Said 1993: 16) If that sounds as if internal space is the prerogative of a select, highly educated elite, it might as easily be translated into what Paulo Freire, the great third-world educationalist and liberationist, described as a possible concomitant of becoming literate:

> Problematisation, which means both asking questions and calling into question and is therefore a challenging attitude, is, at one and the same time, the beginning of an authentic act of knowing and the beginning of an act of subversion of 'overdetermination', that is, subversion of praxis inverted upon man.
>
> (Freire 1972: 9)

Probably two of the most immediate and obvious examples in recent history of individuals with an unusual capacity for internal space are South Africa's President Mandela and Archbishop Tutu. Both have demonstrated a remarkable (in Mandela's case almost unbelievable) endurance

156

and ability to remain thoughtful in the face of appallingly difficult external circumstances. Both, in the autumn of their lives, retain a sense of play-fulness, even mischievousness, a potential for joyous celebration, and that capacity for surprise that is the outward manifestation of a deeply wrought and sparkling imagination and is truly the stuff of subversion. Probably only Tutu, the man of God, on receipt of the Nobel Peace Prize in 1984 could respond with anecdotes like:

> I once went to a friend's house in England. There I found a charming book of cartoons entitled *My God*. One showed God with appeals and supplications bombarding Him from people below and He saying, 'I wish I could say, "Don't call me, I'll call you."' And another declared 'Create in six days and have eternity to regret it.'
>
> My favourite shows God somewhat disconsolate and saying, 'Oh dear, I think I have lost my copy of the divine plan.' Looking at the state of the world you would be forgiven for wondering if He ever had one and whether He had not really botched things up.
>
> (Tutu 1989: 96)

The notion of internal space also has important ramifications for the concept of democracy. If we agree with Castoriadis that a definition of democracy could be 'a regime of reflectiveness' (Castoriadis 1995: 148) and that 'in the case of politics, one cannot speak of an "end", there will always be debates over common collective objectives and there will always be problems of institution. It is not a question of establishing the once and for all perfect society' (146), then a healthy society becomes one which encourages diversity, subjectivity and participation.

I do not wish to idealise either the post-war period up to and through the 1960s and 1970s or some of the radical philosophies it threw up. However, this era in Britain was not only one of relative economic pros-perity, but one in which a great flowering of consciousness became possible for many people, particularly the young. Multiple questions were opened or reopened about what was 'normal', what was 'true', what was 'reality', and how information was selected and processed to 'reify' certain defin-itions of normalcy and reality as immutable. (See, for example, Ingleby 1972: passim.) The Thatcherite project, whose economic and social impli-cations I will explore shortly, was, in intellectual terms, precisely the reverse of this: an attempt at foreclosure of debate and a movement of all political assumptions to the Right. Andrew Gamble explained: 'The hope of the New Right is that eventually the debate can be shifted onto ground where all the protagonists accept the primacy of market princi-ples, and all other positions are ruled illegitimate' (Gamble 1986: 52). This project has been overwhelmingly successful.

The great misapprehension – consistently applied and greatly exploited by the New Right in all its manifestations – is that to adopt a questioning attitude equates with permissiveness. Although I suppose that this might sometimes be the case, having the freedom to ask difficult questions more often necessitates being able to contemplate difficult answers. As Stuart Hall has argued, it is precisely the failure of the Left in this country to engage with the changes in world patterns of employment, consumption and attitudes, that has allowed the New Right hegemony to reign unchallenged by any really effective political and economic strategy, for which, as he says, 'successive encounters at the dispatch box' are no substitute. But, alas, it is not the purpose of this paper or within the ability of this writer to aim for the articulation of a thoroughgoing challenge of political strategy, but merely to suggest a few ways and means in which we can keep our minds alive, healthy and critical, possible nuclei around which more powerful forces may gather, and maybe enjoy ourselves in a non-consumable form at the same time.

This chapter outlines how our capacity for internal space has been diminished during the last 15 years by our living in a culture increasingly dominated by 'market forces'. I will first of all give a brief account of some of the economic and political changes that have taken place. I will examine in particular their impact upon political liberties, upon the arts and upon education in Britain. I will argue that an overall cultural regression has taken place and show how this impacts upon individual psychology. Lastly, I will suggest some possible cultural acts of freedom which may open both our minds and arenas in society from the stultification induced by the ideological hegemony of the market.

THE CULTURAL REVOLUTION OF THE LAST 15 YEARS

From the post-war period until the mid-1970s, the economic management of this country was dominated by Keynesian principles. These centred on the notion that inflation, and therefore unemployment, could be regulated by public spending, and hence facilitated the social policies of the welfare state. Concern about the human consequences of the depression of the 1930s fuelled both the economic and the social policies of the post-war era. In the latter part of the 1970s, monetarist economic policies began to be introduced in Britain, the USA and Western Europe. The 1980s saw a massive intensification of market policies in all the latter and the deregulation of financial controls in most industrialised nations, including in Eastern Europe and the USSR. As Will Hutton (1995) has argued, Britain launched the most thoroughgoing privatisation programme of its national utilities and introduction of market mechanisms into the welfare sector of any of the 'advanced' nations. Arguments from monetarism and supply-side economics underpinned these changes theoretically, and heralded a revolution in economic, political and social policy, which continues apace. As Andrew Gamble claimed:

The triumph of monetarism in the 1970s, and its widespread adoption as the new orthodoxy, was presented not as a modification of established principles of economic management, but as a decisive shift involving the overthrow of previous conceptions and assumptions. The more this view was taken, the more not just post-war economic management, but the principles of social democracy began to be questioned. Monetarism was the battering ram that made the breach.

(Gamble 1986: 32)

Monetarist economic arguments have now been thoroughly intellectually discredited by both Right and Left as a one-dimensional 'answer-all' to the world's problems, taking no account of the complexities of government or regional tradition and culture. (See, for example, Gray 1993; Wainwright 1994.) Gray, himself a Conservative, but a conservative one as opposed to a 'liberal' free-marketeer, describes the New Right ideology as being a simplistic, utopian and fundamentalist belief in 'the institutions of the market ... as a sort of perpetual motion machine for economic growth, which only the ill-advised interventions of governments could disturb or dislocate' (Gray 1993: 11). Nonetheless, the tenets deriving from the reinvocation of Adam Smith and Hayek (spiritual guru to Pinochet, Thatcher and the free-marketeers of eastern Europe) have proved powerfully persuasive and succeeded in capturing the moral and political ground in this country to an overwhelming extent. It is still argued that to keep the economy buoyant, state interventions in political and social policy must first and foremost protect and guarantee the maximum freedom of circulation of money. Supply-side economics lends the view that people work best when they have the economic incentive to do so, thereby justifying (within this tortuous logic) reductions in the level of taxation for the better-off, and the, by now offensive, idea that the poor will eventually benefit from the 'trickle-down' effect. Therefore, although a theoretical minimalisation of the role of the state has been preached, in practice, many state-economic interventions have been intensified, aiming at a cultural transformation of all institutions, including educational and cultural ones, into agents of 'market forces'. We have now become so accustomed in practice to Andrew Gamble's dictum that 'The price of forcing the market to be free is a strong state' (Gamble 1986: 51), that we may be in danger of forgetting how very much has changed.

There has been a dismantling, in large part, of the welfare state. The argument was that statism, or as Margaret Thatcher liked to call it, 'nannying', promoted dependency, which was portrayed as the enemy of individual initiative. The American Enterprise Institute and Michael Heseltine in this country contended that poverty is as much rooted in

159

personal behaviour as in lack of resources. Even those Conservatives, like John Gray, who still show some concern about the ever-growing numbers of the poor and completely disenfranchised, now draw a distinction between impoverishment which is the result of lack of moral fibre and family breakdown, and poverty occasioned by unfortunate circumstances (Gray 1993: 53–4). Industry, thrift, moral fibre and family stability were therefore to be encouraged in the workforce by policies which supposedly encouraged independence and individual initiative. These included, for example, the replacement of welfare benefits for young people with 'workfare', or benefits which were tied to something that could loosely be described as 'training' or 'work experience' (Hoover and Plant 1989: 72), and resulted in the increased availability of cheap labour and the reduction of the unemployment statistics. The deprivation of the freedoms conferred by decent public provision of housing, transport and health care affects people's capacity to define themselves in any other way than in relation to the market.

At the same time, political liberties have been curtailed, and the personalisation of poverty has provided sordid justification for invasive legislation which further debilitates those already in difficulty or at the margins. Workers' rights and the political power of trade unions were severely reduced by the Employment Acts of 1980 and 1982, the Trade Union Act of 1984, and the Wages Act of 1986. (Jones 1989: 98–100) The abolition of the Wages Council in 1994 made yet another swingeing dent in what minimal protection is left for those in paid employment. Single parents have been scapegoated as morally heinous and financially penalised by the removal of the single parents' allowance in 1995.

Probably everybody reading this chapter could continue to add to this depressing litany. We are all, by now, well familiar with the fact that poverty in Britain has been massively increased. In a report for the European Commission which remains unpublished, the Child Poverty Action Group revealed that poverty in Britain doubled between 1975 and 1985, and it gets worse. The numbers of people with incomes below basic social security benefit rose from 2.1 million in 1979 to 4.4 million in 1989, and those with incomes at or below basic social security level rose from 6.1 million to 11.3 million in the same period. Since that time the government has stopped publishing figures for people with incomes below the level of basic social security benefits. It is estimated that more than 31 million people, over half the population, live without minimal financial security – they say they cannot save £10 a month or insure the contents of their homes, or both. (Wilding, in Jones (ed.) 1994) This level of poverty is the greatest unfreedom and restriction on people's capacity to behave as free and autonomous human beings, as well as being intrinsically demeaning, degrading and damaging. J. K. Galbraith has argued persuasively that there is now a tacit agreement between all of us who have some, however little, and who still constitute the political majority, that to protect our savings and our assets from inflation, we tolerate an unemployed and homeless underclass as a permanent social institution. (Galbraith 1995: 4)

But even if we wanted to protest, political legislation renders us increasingly powerless to take effective action against the thrust of these policies. One of the 'strong state's' most recent legislative coups is the Criminal Justice Act of 1994, which took many of these developments to their logical conclusions. In particular, the increased police powers in relation to 'all trespassory public assemblies' (which are defined by the Act as any proposed assembly which *might* result in serious public disorder, serious damage to property or serious disruption to the life of the community, i.e. almost anything!), create the potential for severe restrictions on those rights to public protest still left to us. The Act also contains many provisions about, for example, the right to silence for those accused and the right to jury trial, secure training orders for 12–15-year-olds, extensions of the trespass laws which seriously affect travellers and gypsies and have potential implications for all of our freedoms of movement, and expansion of police stop and search powers. These all curtail civil liberties and make possible a greater infiltration and control of our everyday lives. The prison population now stands at an all-time high of 52,000.

The effects of these economic and legislative changes have been further intensified by their impact upon the arts and media in this country. Publishing, the media and the cinema have become increasingly dominated by what is 'marketable' in its lowest common denominator. As the small publishing houses get gobbled up by the megaliths, massive advances are paid to those who produce 'blockbusters' whilst there is decreased opportunity for the publication of unknown writers who may be more independent, critical or original in their thinking. With the reduction in real terms of Arts Council funding, a similar polarisation is being produced in cinema and theatre. Eric Hobsbawm has argued that the consistently conservative content of most British newspapers, especially the blatant racism, sexism and chauvinism of the tabloids, has trickled irrevocably through working-class culture. (Hobsbawm 1988 quoted in Jones 1994: 67) The impact on the educational sector is equally thoroughgoing and needs to be documented in more detail in order to understand the particularities of its implications.

In the early 1980s, the free-marketeers, led by the Institute of Economic Affairs and Keith Joseph, were interested in a scheme whereby parents would be given cash in the form of vouchers which could be redeemed only in education, and would enable schools to be privatised and run like educational firms (Brown 1989: 39), in a way not dissimilar to the purchaser/provider system now in operation in the Health Service. This idea proved to be too much for the traditional Conservatives, though, and

161

has been replaced by various mechanisms to increase the role of parents and central government in education, to decrease the power of the local authorities, and most recently to provide financial inducements to encourage 'opt out' or independent schools. The left-wing authorities, in particular, were blamed for the decline in educational standards since 1983. In the words of the Hillgate Group in 1987:

> the teaching of facts has given way to the inculcation of opinion; education has been confounded with indoctrination; and in many places there is a serious risk of disciplined study being entirely swamped by an amorphous tide of easy-going discussion and idle play.
>
> (Brown 1989: 34–5)

In place of this allegedly over-liberal state of affairs a National Curriculum has been introduced and the formal testing and assessment of pupils at the age of 7, 11, 14 and 16. The core curriculum restricts the choice available to all except those who are able to pay for their children's education and limits the exercise of imagination and the pursuit of special interests at those critical ages, particularly in adolescence, when such freedoms are most needed. It could be argued that the constriction of educational possibility is likely to be a material factor in teenage unrest and delinquency. The Education Reform Act of 1988 gave the Secretary of State over 175 new powers.

This Act also had four provisions which directly affected the funding of higher education and effectively made its provision more accountable financially both to the Secretary of State and to the private sector through the operation of market and quasi-market mechanisms. In the words of Professor Gareth Williams of the Institute of Education:

> All institutions are experiencing a considerable increase in the influence of market forces and they are now responding to the purchasing power of a wide variety of client, for example, overseas students and their sponsors, the Training Agency, local authorities who have increased powers over teacher-training budgets, private industrial and commercial enterprises, government departments other than the DES (especially the Department of Trade and Industry), research councils and charitable foundations. These various 'customers' of higher education now account for nearly half the income of universities, compared with about a quarter in the early 1970s. It is a reasonable forecast that before the end of the century the figure will have risen to about two thirds.
>
> (Williams 1989: 112)

It would probably be a mistake to view all of these changes in black and white terms. The new provision has, for example, led to an expanded role for the new universities (ex-polytechnics) and colleges of further education, and a reduction in the elitist power of the traditional universities. It is argued that it will also improve access for students from class and ethnic backgrounds who would not previously have had the opportunity for further education. Nonetheless, it is undeniable that the concept of education is taking on a different meaning, and is effectively much more closely tied to industrial, commercial and vocational training. To quote Williams again: 'the main danger of market financing is that it will become progressively more difficult to teach broadly cultural subjects or to teach other subjects in ways that do not promise an immediate economic return' (116). One has only to look at the degree courses being offered by universities in 1995 to see the truth of this argument. Without going into mind-numbing detail, the prevalence of such narrowly vocationally oriented options as Agricultural Food Production and Marketing; Business Property Management; Consumer Studies; Leisure Management, and even 'Licensed House Management' (!) clearly demonstrate that the notion of a broadly based tertiary education which encourages the capacity to think independently is rapidly becoming replaced by market-oriented 'vocational' courses. The latter permit very little space for freedom of thought and promote the acquisition of skills and knowledge within a very narrow remit of application which is likely to be superseded rapidly as the international market changes.

The question of more open access to higher education is vexed by the shift in funding of individual students from grants to loans, which ties the notion of further education yet more closely to that of training for a specific career. The continued supremacy of Oxbridge and the 'top' league of universities as passports to the higher echelons of the Civil Service and national policy-making bodies, and the fact that entrance to these universities is still heavily weighted toward applicants from public schools and the independent sector in secondary education, makes the 'equity' argument even more dubious.

It is therefore not difficult to see that within politics, the arts and education, space for thinking critically or independently, space for imaginative re-elaboration, has been dramatically reduced. Moreover, this development has taken place as part and parcel of a culture that has arguably regressed or gone into decline. According to free-market ideology, we should now be experiencing our lives in more adult, dynamic and entrepreneurial forms. But if we take a closer look at the society we live in, there is more evidence of stifling of individuality, of increased conformism, of more infantile levels of functioning, than of enhanced maturity.

For example, the rapidly widening gap between rich and poor, those enfranchised and those marginalised by the market, encourages the use of splitting and projective mechanisms in thinking about our fellow human beings. The divisions created and intensified between North and South, employed and unemployed, housed and homeless, amongst others, make it more likely that we will project onto the 'others' disowned and unwanted parts of ourselves, like the needy, the malnourished, the thriftless, the dirty and the helpless. It has become much more acceptable to demonstrate overt contempt for those in less comfortable circumstances than our own (for example, the occasion on which Margaret Thatcher castigated those who 'drool and drivel' about caring for those in need, in an interview with David Dimbleby (Jones 1989: 3), and, even more outrageously, when in the summer of 1995, Jack Straw, as Shadow Home Secretary, called for a clampdown on graffiti artists, 'winos and addicts', aggressive beggars and windscreen 'squeegee merchants').

One of the most overt acknowledgements that we feel more at ease with having puerile needs pandered to than with demonstrating adult concern and responsibility is the level at which advertisements woo us to buy. Their tactics can veer between babyish images and jingles which indulge a sanitised, infantilised sense of ourselves, and the sort of shock tactics, used originally in the Benetton advertisements and now becoming more widespread, which exploit the extremes of human suffering and distress, blurring the distinction between glamour and degradation, and hence our own connection with or human response to those who are degraded. We tolerate a tabloid press in which pornographic images and sensationalist scandal pass for 'news'.

Truth is tending to become a word used in the media to engender what Walter Lippman called 'the manufacture of consent'. A Home Office study stated: 'Economic analysis tends to view broadcasting as an economic commodity – a service from which consumers derive satisfaction much as they might from a kitchen appliance and whose value to society should be assessed accordingly' (quoted in Pilger, 1990). The distinction between information and entertainment is becoming fudged, and language suffers correspondingly. Freedom and democracy are used as blanket terms to mask processes which often tend in the opposite direction. We are therefore being asked to suspend our rational and critical faculties in a blind act of belief. Margaret Thatcher was the most forthright exponent of this tendency. She announced as early as 1979: 'The Old Testament prophets did not say "I want a consensus." They said: "This is my faith, this is what I passionately believe. If you believe it too, then come with me" (quoted in Gamble 1988, Preface). By now, it has become such common practice that we are expected to believe government assertions on matters that are patently untrue that we hardly notice it. This is not only bad for our minds; it serves a totalitarian political purpose. The consequences are extreme rigidity and stultification of the imagination.

All of these phenomena – the unquestioning acceptance of an attitude or set of ideas as being the only tenable view, the perversion of language so that it loses its symbolic function and meaning and comes instead to be used as a form of action or a subtle form of coercion, and the extreme hostility and anxiety with which new, questioning or oppositional ideas are greeted – are characteristics of what Wilfred Bion called a basic-assumption group (Bion 1961: passim). This term was always intended to apply to social and organisational processes as much as to therapeutic groups. The regressive cultural manifestations I described earlier are symptomatic of basic assumption mentality, whose hallmark is the loss of critical and rational faculties and the capacity to preserve concern and respect for others as separate individuals, and the maintenance of a prevailing unconscious attitude which is extremely difficult to change, challenge or think independently within. Bion described three different kinds of basic-assumption functioning – the one that seems to correspond most closely with present-day processes is that of the basic assumption of dependency (BAd), identifiable by 'a belief in the omnipotence or omniscience of some one member of the group', but which can equally be a thralldom to an ideology. The irony, of course, is that whilst the welfare state was described as a dependency culture by its opponents and dismantlers, it is much more psychologically accurate to designate free-market culture as that of dependency because it makes it so much more difficult for individuals to remain independent, separate and mature, with all the emotional and subjective qualities that those words imply.

THE IMPACT ON INDIVIDUAL PSYCHOLOGY

There has indeed been a corresponding change in the forms of distress and personality structure manifest in those who present themselves to clinical services for psychological help. Many clinicians have chronicled the increased presentation of what could be broadly described as narcissistic personality disorders within the last decade. (Lasch 1980; Bollas 1987; Hewitt 1988; White 1992; Wilson 1992; and others) As early as 1980, Christopher Lasch, writing from the United States (as always somewhat ahead of us in these matters), described the emergence of a personality type characterised by

> dependence on the vicarious warmth provided by others combined with a fear of dependence, a sense of inner emptiness ... pseudo self-insight, calculating seductiveness ... These patients, though often ingratiating, tend to cultivate a protective shallowness in emotional relations. They lack the capacity to get along or to mourn, and are therefore often sexually promiscuous rather than repressed, although they find it difficult to elaborate the sexual impulse or to approach sex in a spirit of play.
>
> (Lasch 1980: 74–81)

Hewitt (1988), Wilson (1992) and White (1992) have more recently described the increased incidence of this kind of presentation in adolescents, and particularly within an educational setting. In the cases they refer to, the student has attempted to turn him- or herself into a marketable commodity at enormous cost to their inner world. Bollas coined a new term 'normotic illness' to define 'a particular drive to be normal, one that is typified by a numbing and eventual erasure of subjectivity in favour of a self that is conceived as a material object among other man-made products in the object world' (Bollas 1987: 135). These clinicians are recounting various stages or degrees of severity of a major shift in the internal structure of the self becoming prevalent in contemporary society.

Two brief examples from my own clinical experience, in these cases in a tertiary educational setting in the late 1980s, may serve to illustrate this shift. My own impression was that, although the picture was by no means a uniform one, there was indeed an increasing and very sad emergence of young people whose main goal in life was a material one and who often wanted a quick 'fix-me-up' in a behavioural or chemical form in order to help them attain a readymade image of who they thought they should be. X was an 18-year-old who just happened to take 'accidental' mini-overdoses, but otherwise protested vehemently his 'ordinariness' and that of his family, in which, he said, 'nothing ever changes'. After each overdose he would adopt a completely different but recognisably stereotypical image. In rapid succession, he moved from a quiffed-hair, denim jacket 'Cliff Richard' look to, during a briefly religious episode, a black rollneck, short back and sides, folded hands, young priest look, to the then fashionable round-spectacled, white shirt and braces, young executive look. It seemed that with each small overdose he was endeavouring to 'kill off' a part of himself that was causing him pain or conflict, and replace it with a ready-to-wear external image which he then strove to live up to. It seemed to me that this process expressed a deeper level of despair about his internal world than ordinary adolescent experimentation with often outrageous images. It seemed to resemble a mechanism more akin to that of adhesive identification (Meltzer 1975; Bick 1986), in which the mimicry represents and replaces, indeed becomes, the experience because of an absent sense of internal space. It therefore demonstrated his hopelessness about finding his identity through more dynamic interpersonal and intrapsychic means.

Y was a woman in her mid-20s, a mature undergraduate student, who, once we had got beyond her initial protestations about the happiness and normality of her life, disclosed that she had gone through a briefly stormy and 'difficult' period in adolescence, which she had then 'cured' herself of by marrying very young. She married a man who worked for the kind of corporation, common in the United States and rapidly becoming more common in this country, which not only expects very long hours of work from its employees with fitting financial remuneration, but also expects that large portions of its executives' lives should take place under corporation auspices, with correspondingly attractive offers of sponsored holidays and other kinds of social events. She too strove desperately to maintain an appearance of a self appropriate to her husband's needs in their very public lives. Her degree was intended to enhance her ability to do this, but being with a group of people younger than herself had stirred up yearnings and uncomfortable feelings about the part of herself that she had tried to close down completely. She was worried about spending her time daydreaming instead of studying, and what she was asking me for was something to stop her daydreaming. When it came to a choice between exploring the parts of herself expressed in the daydreams or ignoring them and continuing to strive for the readymade identity she had opted for, she chose the latter.

I have already argued in detail the way in which the emergence of this type of personality structure is related to the foreclosure of the ordinarily turbulent processes of adolescence (White 1992: 7–9). Questions also remain about the early experiences of these patients and their family backgrounds, which are not within the remit of this chapter to explore. Instead, I have tried to look at how the increased presentation of this kind of personality in clinical settings reflects contemporary changes in social structure and prevailing culture. A superficial, one-dimensional society inevitably begins to produce people who resemble it, with tragic human consequences in terms of the depletion of internal space, capacity for growth and change, and ability to make a creative and original contribution to that society. What possible remedies do we have to begin to address this truly terrifying phenomenon? Certainly *not* psychotherapy for all, although this may on occasions be necessary and useful.

CULTURAL ACTION FOR FREEDOM

What I *would* like to suggest are possible political, artistic and educational forms which may enhance our subjectivity, enlarge our internal space and help us maintain thoughtful depth and therefore the ability to 'speak the truth to power'. They may also enhance our zest for life and therefore the energy to make a challenging attitude possible in innovative and imaginative forms. And something to bring a little injection of necessary disorder and dissent, a little grit, in order to inject some life and health into a society that is becoming stale, flat and one-dimensional. This idea will be familiar to all those who have seen the biological consequences of an over-tidy garden, or observed the phenomenal fertility of something previously tilled left to 'the wild' for a while. Or observed the tremendous toll taken on women's sense of ourselves and restrictive effect on the power of our sexuality by the mechanisation of obstetrics. There are analogies within contemporary post-Einsteinian physics, especially the central tenet of complexity theory:

the edge of chaos ... is where the components of a system never quite lock into place, and yet never quite dissolve into turbulence, either. The edge of chaos is where life has enough stability to sustain itself and enough creativity to deserve the name of life. The edge of chaos is where new ideas and innovative genotypes are forever nibbling away at the edges of the status quo, and where even the most entrenched old guard will eventually be overthrown ... The edge of chaos is the constantly shifting battle zone between stagnation and anarchy, the one place where a complex system can be spontaneous, adaptive and alive.

(Mitchell Waldrop 1992: 12)

Complexity theory is a recently developed scientific paradigm and is used, *inter alia*, to describe the conditions which made the beginnings of what we call life possible in biochemical terms. I am arguing that injections of creative disorder and dissent are also necessary to the health and life of our society and the people who live in it.

Psychoanalytic theorists have tended to focus on the creative impulse as a derivative of the reparative capacity and therefore an elaboration of or means of working back to the depressive position (Riviere 1955; Segal 1955; and others). Put more simply, in the process of creation, the artist, writer and, I would argue, sometimes the activist is striving to make good damage that has been perpetrated internally by the hating and destructive parts of the personality. By recognising and working through an internal scenario that is common to all of us in struggling to deal with the effects of our sadism, the 'artist/creator' produces a work of great emotional power and beauty that helps us, the audience, the readers, the witnesses, to recognise and share in similarly reparative processes in ourselves. The artist/creator is always working on the edge of and in the knowledge of their destructive impulses, without allowing these to become dominant. The Greeks also held a moral position on the function of drama in society – Aristotle claimed that pride and want of 'commiseration' were the most predominant vices of mankind, and that Tragedy, a profoundly social event within the City State, could cure us of these two by working on the corrective virtues of fear and pity. Although these ideas hold great truth and importance, something further needs to be added.

My thesis is that in order for individuals to maintain and develop internal space, mature concern and thoughtfulness, there need to be cultural forms into which parts of the self can be temporarily projected. In this way, both contemporary and age-old conflictual dilemmas can be worked through and re-introjected in modified form, with a corresponding enrichment of the personality. Not only can this give the individual greater depth and sense of meaning in life, but also a healthy detachment from and perspective on prevailing trends which then enhance that person's capacity to make a creative contribution to their society. At the edge of order and chaos lies complexity, life and health. We have to be able on occasions to at least partially disintegrate in order to remain fluid as personalities, to re-merge into our psychologically primal undifferentiated state, and to re-emerge fresh, revived and re-invigorated intellectually and emotionally from the experience.

Some psychoanalytic theorists have advanced similar arguments and I will touch on a couple of these briefly. Winnicott emphasised the need for what he called a 'transitional space' or an 'area of creativity' between self and other, internal and external reality. Marion Milner pointed up the critical role of the arts in society in providing an arena in which inner self and outer world can be psychologically re-merged 'by the recurrent providing of a framed space and time and a pliable medium' (Milner 1955: 102). The partial disintegration of the personality thus enabled and held or contained by the artistic form is necessary for growth of the person-ality and change. Both Winnicott and Milner argue the need for the environment to be 'in-giving' in this sense, and this cultural capacity is becoming increasingly rare with the market's saturation of almost every aspect of life with a bombardment of stimuli intended to coerce us to buy consumer products, which then serve as compensation for a richness of experience that is being eroded.

But these cultural spaces are something that we can consciously strive to create and maintain in the full awareness that they may be merely drops in the ocean of commercialism, but nonetheless produce significant and perhaps sometimes cumulative effects on ourselves and others. I think we have to hold onto this notion in the coming years as an antidote to what may otherwise become a bleak mentality of survivalism, because realistically we may not be witness to massive cultural changes in our lifetimes. Let us examine what these forms might look like in practice. The following are tiny examples of the sorts of possibilities that *do* exist and are intended as a spur to remembering and imagining many others.

Politically, the forms of direct action exemplified par excellence by Greenpeace both wake us up and give us pause for thought, as well as sometimes having dramatic results in terms of preventing another piece of gross destructiveness to the planet. One example from 1995 could be their prevention of the dismantling into the North Sea of the Brent Spar oil rig by Shell, by keeping two people who had been helicoptered onto the rig permanently in place and a ship circling the rig to diminish Shell's capacity to send in further reinforcements. These actions are impor-tant because they are both bold and imaginative. They take us outside the usual channels we have come to rely on for protest and, because the participants are often involved in great personal risk, they serve as a model antidote to the emphasis on personal comfort and material security encouraged by the market. Direct action of this kind can be seen as a sort of street theatre on a global scale – but with a purpose and usually with a result. They provide us with examples of heroism, an old-fashioned concept, but one that is necessary if we are to stick our heads above the parapet and risk standing out against what often seem to be implacable forces. By the identifications that direct action enables, they also help us to find within ourselves the strength and personal authority to take bolder steps ourselves in relation to smaller matters in the workplace, in our local environments and in our personal lives and interaction with others.

Experimental drama and films that will usually by definition be low-budget can play a critical role in enabling us to *re-vision* our lives in such a way that may result in less reactive and more original responses to common contemporary dilemmas. I will choose one example from 1989, Spike Lee's 'Do the Right Thing'. With deceptive simplicity, Lee takes us through the 'ordinary' events of a long hot day in midsummer Brooklyn. We follow playful and serious interactions on the streets, through the rounds of a takeaway pizza deliverer, played by Lee himself, from the only Italian pizza and ice-cream parlour in a predominantly black neighbourhood. Relationships, everyday tensions with long roots in political history, old and originally insignificant feuds, gradually (and the film enables us to see how understandably), pile up in the course of this one long day, and erupt with the heat into a mass violent attack on the pizza parlour, precipitated by a minuscule piece of irritation. Someone (black) is killed. The neighbourhood, we understand implicitly, will never be the same again. We empathise with both 'sides', their reactions are entirely comprehensible and forgivable in the political circumstances; at the same time, they are tragic and irredeemable. Preventable? We are left with that question, as with many others. For we do not realise until we are presented with the black and white stills at the end of the film that we have witnessed a so cleverly articulated dialogue between the contrasting philosophies of Malcolm X and Martin Luther King and we did not even notice that we were enabled to think through the contradictory approaches in a very calm, low-key way. At the same time, because the whole sequence of events is so entirely human and recognisable, the identifications and the enhanced understanding produced by this film do make it much less possible to react with the minor irritations displayed with such humanity and humour. It is also conceivable that this film could make violent eruptions less likely, precisely because it is undogmatic and uncoercive. Our own violent and unthinking responses have been modified by our involvement with the characters in and the events of the film, and we redigest the difficulties and conflicts with fresh insight, in a way not that dissimilar to the Greek notion of catharsis.

And in education? It will be clear from the preceding analysis that we are swimming against the current. Perhaps it might be useful to bear constantly in mind Meltzer's inimitable precis of the learning and developmental needs of the 17–25-year-old age group:

> When the pubertal groupings begin to peel off into adolescent coupling, ambition begins to replace rebelliousness and the creative urge to rise in place of the more anarchic drive. Methodological guidance is therefore more in order rather than formal teaching. The firing of imagination, the freedom to pursue interests to the limit, inspiration by contact with figures of outstanding accomplishment, all favour mobilisation of talents, while rigidity of syllabus, mechanisation of examination and promotion of rivalry conduce to continuation of the pubertal pattern or a relapse, in the early twenties into latency sterility and narrowness.
>
> (Meltzer 1973: 164)

It may not be a popular idea for already overworked and harassed lecturers to set up provision for alternative workshops in which figures of outstanding accomplishment can inspire what is possible amongst the young and energetic. Reduction in resources also makes it harder for the young themselves to set up these kinds of arenas, although the Greenpeace example does extend the imaginative boundaries of what is possible. Some alternative intellectual spaces *have* to be created if there is to be any hope of extending the possibilities of broad-based and multidisciplinary learning outside the confines of narrow vocational syllabuses. Figures of outstanding accomplishment may need to be immodest about their achievements and inspirational potential and offer their services for free or for very little. For the late adolescent, even a tiny input can inspirit, motivate and serve as a model, and set in train an urge to learn independently. Workshops on broadly based political, philosophical, scientific and artistic issues, which are 'in-giving', in which the young can pursue their learning needs actively, could also provide the kind of cultural island in which the development of internal space is made possible.

Well, I still haven't answered my introductory question – what is internal space? We can consider it as an amplification of the concept of subjectivity, Ogden defines this as 'a reflection of the differentiation of symbol, symbolised and interpreting subject' (Ogden 1985: 131). He adds, 'Meaning accrues from difference. There can be no meaning in a completely homogeneous field.' I would say therefore that internal space is *an inner derivative of the differences between people*. It begins to develop very early on in life from what Winnicott designated 'potential space', somewhere between self and other, baby and mother, in which play becomes possible and, within that, the development of imagination or a layering of symbolic meanings. It prevents a collapse into either fantasy (or psychosis, loss of contact with external reality) or into normosis (loss of contact with internal reality and foreclosure of imagination). Experiences within potential space

171

have to be sustained and repeated throughout a lifetime to maintain the continued development of an internal space that is alive and the source of an authentic subjectivity. My ideas about remedial cultural forms echo what Winnicott called the third area (that is, neither wholly internal nor wholly external), the area of creativity and the location of cultural experience: 'something that is in the common pool of humanity, into which individuals or groups of people may contribute, and from which we may all draw *if we have somewhere to put what we find*' (Winnicott 1971: 116 – his emphases).

Within this cultural dialectic, the individual's capacity for alpha function is augmented. Alpha function is Bion's concept of original and authentic thought that is the product of a profound transformation of emotional experience, through dreams, through symbols. It is the antithesis of what Bion designated beta elements, which are unthinking automatic responses, and effectively discharge affect as opposed to processing it. My argument is that the evacuation of beta elements and the foreclosure of internal space are encouraged by a consumer-oriented, market-led society. Alpha function is that which makes internal space and the capacity to dream creatively possible. Without cultural arenas which facilitate the development of these qualities, it is much harder for us to begin to 'speak the truth to power' or to think independently and originally.

The connection between New Right ideology and the favouring of order (and a strong state to protect that order) over creativity has also been observed by others (see, for example, Wainwright 1994: 5). Meltzer has interesting comments to make about the psychological roots of the corresponding mentality:

> Conservatism is the state of mind resulting from regression to latency mechanisms in the face of adult responsibility ... Its longing for stability at any price inclines it to sacrifice growth and development just as it sacrifices sexual passion to comfort ... The belief in omnipotent control and balancing techniques inclines it to bargaining and compromise, while impaired symbol formation and constricted imagination render it at once materialistic, acquisitive and prone to confuse social roles with whole people.
>
> (Meltzer 1973: 154–5)

Toynbee noted the loss of flexibility, uniformity and lack of inventiveness during the decline of civilisations. Fritjof Capra comments about our own:

> Although the cultural mainstream has become petrified by clinging to fixed ideas and rigid patterns of behaviour, creative minorities will appear on the scene and carry on the process of challenge

172

and response. The dominant social institutions will refuse to hand over their leading roles to these new cultural forces, but they will eventually go on to decline and disintegrate, and the creative minorities may be able to transform some of the old elements into a new configuration.

(Capra 1983: 10)

In other words, despair not – hope may lie in the interstices! But perhaps there is a also a message in this way of thinking for the mainstream. If, by the time this book is published, we have, or may be about to have, a new Labour government in Britain, international market forces will severely restrict the extent of its powers to change our political institutions, and it may already have adopted much of the ideology of the New Right. *But* the arguments that I have advanced about the roles of certain kinds of political activism, the arts and educational arenas are worth considering and taking on board as a means of preserving or reinjecting health and vitality into our cultural institutions. We have no means of knowing where they could take us or what further possibilities they might open up. Let us therefore take heart and the courage to act boldly, remembering always that it has been intrepid leaps of the imagination that have made scientific progress, changes in society and transformations of attitude possible. 'Exuberance is Beauty' (Blake 1793: 151).

REFERENCES AND FURTHER READING

Ball, C. and Eggins, H. (eds) (1989) *Higher Education into the 1990s – New Dimensions*, Buckingham: Open University Press.

Bick, E. (1986) 'Further Considerations of the Function of the Skin in Early Object Relations', *British Journal of Psychotherapy* 2: 292–9.

Bion, W.R. (1961) *Experiences in Groups*, London: Tavistock.

Bion, W.R. (1962) *Learning from Experience*, London: Maresfield.

Blake, W. (1793) 'The Marriage of Heaven and Hell' in Keynes, G. (ed.) (1969) *Blake: Complete Writings*, Oxford: Oxford University Press.

Bollas, C. (1987) 'Normotic Illness' in Bollas, C. *The Shadow of the Object – Psychoanalysis of the Unthought Known*, London: Free Association Books.

Brown, P. (1989) 'Education' in Brown, P. and Sparks, R. (eds) *Beyond Thatcherism – Social Policy, Politics and Society*, Buckingham: Open University Press.

Brown, P. and Sparks, R. (eds) (1989) *Beyond Thatcherism – Social Policy, Politics and Society*, Buckingham: Open University Press.

Campbell, L. (1930) *Shakespeare's Tragic Heroes*, London: Methuen.

Capra, F. (1983) *The Turning Point – Science, Society and the Rising Culture*, London: Flamingo.

Castoriadis, C. (1995) 'From the Monad to Autonomy' in *Free Associations*, 5, 2, no. 34.

Freire, P. (1972) *Cultural Action for Freedom*, London: Penguin.

Galbraith, J.K. (1995) 'To Have and Have Not' *Observer*, 29 October.

Gamble, A. (1986) 'The Political Economy of Freedom' in Levitas, R. (ed.) *The Ideology of the New Right*, London: Polity Press.

Gamble A. (1988) *The Free Economy and the Strong State*, London: Macmillan.

Gray, J. (1993) *Beyond the New Right – Markets, Government and the Common Environment*, London: Routledge.

Hall, S. (1988) *The Hard Road to Renewal*, London: Verso.

Hewitt, P. (1988) 'Impositions, Surrenders, and Sacrifices: a Therapist's View of the Unacceptable Side of Success'. Unpublished paper.

Hoover, K. and Plant, R. (1989) *Conservative Capitalism in Britain and the United States – A Critical Appraisal*, London: Routledge.

Hutton, W. (1995) *The State We're In*, London: Cape.

Ingleby, D. (1972) 'Ideology and the Human Sciences: Some Comments on the Role of Reification in Psychology and Psychiatry' in Pateman, T. *Counter Course*, London: Penguin.

Jones, B. (ed.) (1989) *Political Issues in Britain Today*, Manchester: Manchester University Press.

Lasch, C. (1980) *The Culture of Narcissism*, London: Abacus.

Levitas, R. (ed.) (1986) *The Ideology of the New Right*, London: Polity.

Lippmann, W. (1955) *The Public Philosophy*, New York: Mentor.

Meltzer, D. (1973) 'Pedagogic Implications of Structural Psychosexual Theory' in Meltzer, D. *Sexual States of Mind*, London: Clunie.

Meltzer, D. (1975) 'Adhesive Identification', *Contemporary Psychoanalysis* no. 11.

Meltzer, D. (1973) 'Permanent Revolution of the Generations' in Meltzer, D. *Sexual States of Mind*, London: Clunie.

Milner, M. (1955) 'The Role of Illusion in Symbol Formation' in *New Directions in Psychoanalysis*, Klein, M., Heimann, P. and Money-Kyrle, R.E. (eds), London: Maresfield.

Mitchell Waldrop, M. (1992) *Complexity – the Emerging Science at the Edge of Order and Chaos*, London: Penguin.

Ogden, T. (1985) 'On Potential Space', *International Journal of Psychoanalysis*, 66.

O'Hear, A. (1989) 'The University as a Civilising Force' in Ball, C. and Eggins, H. (eds), *Higher Education into the 1990s*, London: Open University.

Pilger, J. (1990) *Distant Voices*, London: Vintage.

Riviere, J. (1955) 'The Unconscious Phantasy of an Inner World Reflected in Examples from Literature', in *New Directions in Psychoanalysis*, Klein, M., Heimann, P. and Money-Kyrle, R.E. (eds), London: Maresfield.

Said, E. (1993) 'Representations of the Intellectual', in *The 1993 Reith Lectures*, London: Penguin.

Segal, H. (1955) 'A Psychoanalytic Approach to Aesthetics' in *New Directions in Psychoanalysis*, Klein, M., Heimann, P. and Money-Kyrle, R.E. (eds), London: Maresfield.

Segal, H. (1986) *Delusion and Artistic Creativity and Other Psychoanalytic Essays*, London: Free Association Books.

Tutu, N. (1989) *The Words of Desmond Tutu*, New York: Newmarket.

Wainwright, H. (1994) *Arguments for a New Left*, Oxford: Blackwell.

Wasik, M. and Taylor, R. (1995) *Blackstone's Guide to the Criminal Justice and Public Order Act 1994*, London: Blackstone.

White, J. (1992) 'Adolescence and Education in the 1990s', in *Idealism, Mastery and Futures*, Conference held by City University 1991, London: City University.

Wilding, P. (1994) 'The Debate about the Welfare State' in Jones, B. (ed.) *Political Issues in Britain Today*, Manchester: Manchester University Press.

Williams, G. (1989) 'Prospects for Higher Education' in Ball, C. and Eggins, H. (eds) *Higher Education into the 1990s – New Dimensions*, London: Open University.

Wilson, P. (1992) Higher Education and the Vanities' in Idealism, Mastery and Futures, Conference held by City University 1991, London: City University.

Winnicott, D. (1971) *Playing and Reality*, London: Penguin.

12

EXCITEMENT AND TENSION AT THE EDGE OF CHAOS

Ralph Stacey

The central theme that runs through the chapters of this book is encapsulated in the following question: What kinds of interventions should we be making in the organisations we belong to, or consult to in one way or another, so that those organisations will provide more creative ways of living for all of us?

As far as any organisation is concerned today, the issue of creativity is not some desirable addition to mere survival, nor is it confined to organisations in the education, health and social services sectors: all organisations face increasingly tough competition for resources and markets and in the end it is only the creative organisations that survive, for it is only the creative that develop new ways of playing the survival game. Creativity, then, is a central issue for all organisations. But is organisational creativity essentially linked to providing more creative lives for all of us? Or is the latter purely incidental to the primary need for creative and efficient organisations? The answer to this question depends, of course, upon the perspective one takes. I am going to suggest that this perspective depends heavily on how one conceptualises the systemic nature of individuals, organisations and societies. Today's dominant ways of understanding the nature of human systems do not seem to connect organisational creativity with the need to provide more creative ways of living for all of us, but there is an alternative systemic perspective that is growing in importance, which, I believe, does.

In this chapter, therefore, I propose to take a step back from the theme of kinds of intervention and focus instead on our understanding of the kind of system we are proposing to intervene in. I believe that this is a matter of major importance because beneficial interventions designed for one kind of system can turn out to be quite ineffective, even disastrous, for another kind. In other words, I want to focus on the underlying beliefs about the systemic nature of societies, organisations and individuals that inform the debate about appropriate intervention. I want to explore whether these underlying beliefs are helpful or obstructive in making sense of how we are intervening. And I propose to use some important insights into the nature of living systems that are coming out of the newly developing science of complexity as the vantage point from which to critique today's dominant frames of reference. I will suggest that these insights require some serious rethinking by those who adopt the unfettered free-market position, on the one hand, and those who believe that it is the responsibility of some central authority to design appropriate systems for us to live in, on the other. I will also argue that this rethinking is required at all scales, from that of society to that of an organisation and its parts.

Consider first the dominant frames of reference that condition the thinking and policy advice of those who have been most influential at the levels of both society and individual organisations over the past two decades and, in fact, much longer than that.

DOMINANT FRAMES OF REFERENCE

A striking feature of the dominant frame of reference today is its split nature:

- Two diametrically opposed explanations are both used to justify reliance on the market system, namely, neo-classical economic theories and Austrian economics;
- One kind of explanation of optimal functioning applies at the level of an industry, economy or society, namely, the invisible hand of the market, while another applies at the level of the individual organisation as well as at the level of the individual, namely, management and planning.

The national level

Those who dominate policy-making these days make the, by now little questioned, assumption that the force of competitive selection produces the nearest to optimal arrangements that we are likely to get to. This dominant view is derived from two sources.

Firstly, there is neo-classical economic theory which assumes that industries, economies and societies are linear systems in which a cause, taking the form of a change in their environments, produces an effect (or at least a limited number of effects), taking the form of some action that adapts the industry, economy or society to the change, so that stable equilibrium is restored. So, the systemic view is one in which the system is always moving toward stable equilibrium and is disturbed from that journey by perturbations and causes, out there in the environment. Intervention then takes the form of acting upon these environmental causes to prevent disturbances from stable equilibrium or to move the whole system to a new, more desirable stable equilibrium. This view about the nature of the

177

system that is an economy or society underlies classical, monetary, supply-side, Keynesian, and even communist economics and it supports the notion that central authorities can steer whole industries, economies and societies in a direction of their choosing. Neo-classical, Keynesian and communist economists differ, of course, in their judgement as to the extent of beneficial intervention in the operation of the market system, but none of them hold that it is pointless to intervene because all assume that the system they are dealing with is a linear one, drawn to stable equilibrium adaptation to the environment where long-term outcomes are knowable.

If we adopt this frame of reference, then, our interventions might take the form of national plans, or of national and regional industrial policies if we do not much like free markets. But even if we do, we will still use monetary policies, medium-term financial strategies, trade policies, trade finance subsidies, regulatory bodies, and so on to steer those markets. This whole perspective reflects its Newtonian origins, via Adam Smith. The Newtonian perspective is, of course, one that sees systems as machines moving in predictable ways. The machine that an economy is assumed to be works through the operation of the invisible hand of the market, which ensures that all acting in their own best self-interest will produce an optimal overall outcome. And where this invisible hand is being interfered with, central authorities can intervene successfully to redirect a market's development simply because the cause and effect links can be identified.

In many ways this is a comforting theory because it allows us to believe that a government is in control of national development, to some extent at least. Such a view also gives us someone to blame if we do not like what is happening. If we believe that the world works like this, we will be led quite naturally to a societal, economic and industrial science of quantities – we will think it important to measure, predict and monitor inputs and outputs in quantitative terms. We will believe that value and quality can be approximated by some quantity and measured because systems will display their value in their performance.

Secondly, there is Austrian economic theory whose most well-known proponents are Hayek (1948; 1982) and Schumpeter (1934). This school stresses the importance of entrepreneurs: Schumpeter talks about economic development as a gale of creative destruction in which entrepreneurs develop, through trial and error, products that people did not even know they wanted. Hayek talks about the economy as a system that is so complex that no member of it can fully understand it and yet, despite this, through their interaction in markets, essentially self-organising phenomena, they produce the emergent order of economic development. From the Austrian perspective, an economy would never reach equilibrium this side of death – the invisible hand of the market does not produce stable equilibrium at all but rather the disequilibrium of creative life. The Austrians see an economy as a non-linear system in which the links

178

between cause and effect are distant and difficult to detect: a system which evolves through competitive selection to produce a higher standard of living.

So the Austrians also originate in Adam Smith but they go down a disequilibrium rather than an equilibrium route. Darwin too utilised Adam Smith's notion of the invisible hand of competitive selection and later the neo-Darwinians applied this notion to random mutations at the level of the genes to explain evolution in nature. The Austrians adopted similar thinking, seeing economic development as the consequence of trial and error and, in that sense, random, entrepreneurial actions selected out by a ruthlessly competitive market. Just as neo-Darwinians do, Austrian economists accepted that such a process can account for the increasing complexity produced by evolution in both cases.

If one adopts the Austrian view of the systemic nature of an economy or a society then interventions should be restricted to the bare minimum, because if you cannot easily identify the cause of an effect, and if you cannot really understand the system, you had best let it take its own course. So, from this perspective, central authorities cannot steer industries, economies or societies and no one is in control of long-term developments – the invisible hand, the brute force of the market, is in control. On the whole, interventions at the industrial, economic and societal levels will simply make things worse. You will get the best possible result by leaving the system to the forces of competition simply because markets and economies are systems over which no one can be 'in control'. Where the market has been destroyed it should be restored and where it does not exist it should be created. There will be no call for measurement here – no science of quantities or, for that matter, of qualities either. Indeed, there will be the opposite call to remove red tape and free up individual entrepreneurial activity, where quality and value are matters for individual judgement.

This is an anxiety-producing view of the world and not surprisingly, therefore, it has never been all that popular.

Both of these perspectives have, at one time or another, been espoused by prominent UK government members. Which of the perspectives helps us to make the most sense of government policy over the past two decades?

The Austrian perspective would explain the huge denationalisation programmes and the attempts to turn public services into market places. It would also help us to understand the closure of large parts of the Central Statistical Office, because if you are not going to steer industries, for example, you do not need to measure their performance.

However, it seems that despite frequently quoting Hayek the government could not persuade itself to go quite as far as Hayek called for. According to Hayek, no one can be in control of a nation's development

179

and the government should, therefore, largely attend to the functioning of an impartial legal system and privatise and decentralise the rest. In many respects, however, the government moved in the other direction – it reduced the power of local authorities and through the enormous multiplication of unaccountable regulatory bodies that it appoints it has greatly increased its power. It intervenes in international trade. It intervenes in financial markets. It intervenes in many areas of national life. None of this intervention is justifiable from an Austrian perspective but it is from a neo-classical supply-side perspective. So to make sense of what the government is doing, using their own espoused explanations, we have to switch between two fundamentally contradictory theories. Both can be used to conclude that free markets are optimal, but rely on very different kinds, mutually exclusive kinds, of intervention. And nowhere in these theories is there much concern for value, for the intrinsic rather than the extrinsic performance-based value of beings. Any notions of value in these theories are based on measured performance or market success – there is no notion that, for example, each of us might have intrinsic value simply because we are beings. In the end, it is only the winners who matter.

The contradiction between neo-classical and Austrian economics reflects the origins of the two theories, for there is a contradiction between Newtonian and Darwinian views of the world. According to Newton, the inanimate systems of the universe are machines in which the same effects eternally flow from the same causes and what we see is endless repetition. However, according to neo-Darwinian theory, the animate systems on earth are cobbled together by chance – random mutations at the level of genes are selected out by the brutal forces of competition and all we see is collections of cells who are the winners.

The level of the individual organisation

The confusion is compounded when one moves to the level of an individual organisation. The dominant frame of reference at this level is quite clearly that of strategic choice. There is the ecology school of strategy, which argues that choice determines a particular constellation of competencies a firm initially acquires but then inertia, resistance and ignorance all lock it into that initial constellation and when the environment changes only those that by chance have the appropriate constellations survive. This very Darwinian theory has never attracted much support and most in government and in management at the organisational level subscribe to the strategic-choice view of things, whereby it is believed that the most powerful coalition in any individual organisation chooses a future state for their organisation and then oversees the actions required to realise their intention. The intention might take the form of a business plan, although nowadays it takes the rather more mystic form of a vision.

Now this process can only actually work if the most powerful are able to link their next actions to the long-term outcomes of their actions. If they are members of a system in which it is impossible to predict what the long-term outcome of their actions will be, then they cannot realise a prior plan or vision: instead, they will have to act and then deal with whatever emerges from that action.

So, the strategic-choice frame of reference makes the same unquestioned assumptions about the system the choice is applied to as does neo-classical economics, namely, that individual organisations are stable equilibrium systems just as economies are, for only then is it possible to make the predictions which make it possible for managers to connect their visions with their actions. It is not surprising that the strategic-choice school makes the same assumptions as neo-classical economics because the former is derived from the latter. From the strategic-choice perspective, one interprets business success as the realisation of some powerful, possibly charismatic person's plan or vision. One believes that the success is secured by implementing the plan which requires tightly controlled behaviour, measured and monitored within management information and control systems that employ damping feedback to sustain stability. These systems require comprehensive measurement and reporting against targets – they represent an organisational science of quantities.

Clearly, the UK government over the past 16 years has subscribed to this view and it has therefore pressed the approach across the whole spectrum of education, health, social service and other public sector organisations.

However, while this managerial strategic-choice process is reasonably consistent with the neo-classical perspective, it does not sit at all well with the Austrian economists. From the latter perspective, the economy is a non-equilibrium system whose future cannot be planned at all – it emerges out of random trial-and-error entrepreneurial action. Although the government has subscribed to an Austrian view of the economic system as a whole, it simultaneously adopts a view of the agents in that system – individual organisations – as entities capable of foreseeing outcomes and therefore capable of planning their futures. If all the agents can plan, and if a rather small number of them dominate the economy, as is the case, why can they not all get together and plan the whole? If no one is in control of the whole, how can we be in control of the parts? If there is no need to measure everything in sight for the national level, why must we measure everything in sight at the level of the organisation?

There is something really unsatisfactory about the dominant ways of understanding what kind of system we are intervening in that makes it impossible to make sense of what is going on in a way that resonates with our experience and how we feel about that experience.

The level of the individual

It makes little more sense at the level of the individual. The dominant frame of reference, the one that drives government policy, is based on the assumption that individuals must be completely responsible for their own and their immediate family's lives. If they are unable to cope it is largely because they have not exercised this responsibility properly – to a significant extent it is their own fault and they should not look to government to bail them out. Such a view of individual responsibility implies one of two things. Either individuals are like genes, the material upon which competitive selection operates, and interfering with this simply messes up the whole process of evolution producing weaker, less adapted strains of human being – a neo-Darwinian type of view of the place of the individual in the system. This is certainly consistent with the view that economies and societies cannot be controlled but have to be left to the invisible hand. But it is a totally repugnant view that few would espouse, presumably.

So, the assumption behind the dominant view of individual responsibility must be that it is in principle possible for individuals to take control of their own lives if they simply apply enough mental, emotional and physical effort to the matter. If it is possible in principle and they fail, then it is their own fault – a kind of Newtonian view of the place of the individual in the whole system. From this perspective an individual is also a controllable system moving toward equilibrium.

However, if you believe in an economy and a society that cannot be controlled but must be left to the invisible hand, how can you possibly believe that individuals can be in control of their own situation in such an economy or society?

Once again we must conclude that there is something completely unsatisfactory about today's dominant ways of understanding how societies, organisations and even individuals evolve.

The consequence of interventions based on the dominant perspective

We can see the kind of thinking I have described above at work in most of the UK's utilities. As examples, I will take the electricity and the water industries, simply because I have consulted to companies in both of these industries. Government policies have been much the same for both. In accordance with the belief in free markets, both industries were broken into separate regional companies and required to compete in artificially created markets and admonished to eschew bureaucracy and become entrepreneurial as the Austrians recommend. However, in both cases the result is regional monopolies rather than free markets so both are subject to bureaucratic regulation – justifiable from a neo-classical economics perspective. From this perspective, and an appeal to a mythology of how private sector firms are run, these utility companies are pressed to prepare both short- and long-term plans and to measure all aspects of their activities so that their performance can be measured and their managers and employees, as well as their shareholders can be rewarded accordingly – the strategic-choice view of management derived from neo-classical economics. While the government proclaims that the national economy is to be left to the market – which cannot be planned or measured all that much, as the Austrians suggest – they establish a framework for major utilities that is completely at odds with this view in that it requires companies within major sectors of the economy to plan their futures and meticulously measure their performance. What is the result?

Well, it is by no means clear that the supplies of water and electricity have got any better – some would say that the opposite is true. But the government's interventions have certainly had an impact on the lives of those who work in the utilities and use their products and services. Take the example of one of these utility companies I recently worked with.

The issue we focused on in our work together was this. Although opinion surveys showed that managers and workers were satisfied with their pay, and although absenteeism and staff turnover was low, there was a widespread feeling of unhappiness and depression at work. During a lengthy discussion it began to be clear why this might be. One after another of the participants in the discussion said that they felt that they could never perform well enough – no matter what they did, someone higher up told them to do better next time. This was a widespread view: 'In this place you can never satisfy; every success is turned into a complaint'.

They then began to talk about how it used to be. Before the changes, the elite, the most powerful group in the organisation, was the engineers – those who designed, built and maintained the facilities that produced what customers wanted. Now, however, they felt denigrated, emasculated and undervalued – the communities of practice that had existed to supply the wider community with life-giving water and energy had been broken. Power had shifted and the elite now were the customer services staff. They sat all day long in rows in front of computer screens, taking calls from complaining customers and responding to the repetitive complaints with repetitive replies that largely fobbed people off but occasionally compensated them for their inconvenience. That suddenly brought to my mind a conversation I frequently encounter – it is about how someone complained and was given a free dinner, a free weekend, a free flight, or some other free thing. The game is to find something to complain about and then see how expert one can become in extracting something free from the complaints staff. One then invites the amused admiration of family and friends for one's manipulative abilities.

The dynamics suddenly became clear. When we focus so singlemind-edly on competition, on satisfying the customer, on making the customer king, we encourage the customer to complain. The central focus of an organisation then becomes dealing with the complaints rather than supplying the product or service. This arouses insatiable greed on the part of the customer, who now competes to find fault and so get something for nothing. The consequence for an organisation caught in this is that its members can never do enough; they can never satisfy because greed is insatiable. Our focus on satisfying, on delighting the customer, starts off having favourable consequences but soon sets off the dynamic of complaint and greed which destroys the satisfaction of those working in the organisation that is supposed to be delighting the customers.

The irony is, of course, that all of us are both customers and members of organisations supplying customers. This point was powerfully made in a BBC documentary ('In Search of Power', BBC2, 21 January). It kept returning to the Meadowlands shopping centre near Sheffield, a structure whose domes made it look like some huge modern cathedral – a cathe-dral to Greed rather than God, perhaps. People in the centre were interviewed and one man said: 'When I come in here I have the power – I can refuse to buy people's goods and they must do as I want. But when I go to work I am simply a puppet who must do as he is told.' The presenter of the programme made a powerful point: if we exercise our power as customers to demand more, more rapidly and more cheaply, we unthinkingly impose on the supplier an imperative to be more flexible and move more rapidly. To achieve this, supplying organisations remove job security and diminish the level of empowerment for their employees while talking about increasing it. When we grab more power as customers, we set in motion a dynamic that disempowers us as workers in organisa-tions. The passive power of choice and refusing to buy generates the loss of true power, the value we get from our work.

Caught in this vicious circle of complaint and greed, this split between being all-powerful in one sphere and powerless in another, we turn to chance in the form of the national lottery. The glorification of the customer and the emphasis it leads to on measuring and rewarding performance so as to produce consistent certainty turns us to the very opposite, where mindless randomness is our most intense collective experience. The domi-nant recipe for creative organisations, defined as the successful, the winners, does not provide more creative lives for their members at all. Indeed, the reverse is largely true!

In the utility company I referred to above, this dynamic was recognised – the metaphor of the 'Wizard of Oz' was used by one participant in our conversation: the utility used to be like the scarecrow, having a heart but perhaps not that much brain, but now it was like the tin man, without a heart. This resonated with other members of the group, some of whom referred to the lion who was seeking courage and even more to the girl who was looking for home. This home was a place where the community of practice could be restored and where people would once again find value in their work, a value that comes from providing something vital and life-giving for the whole community rather than trying to cope with insatiably greedy complaints.

How are we going to go 'home again' to a psychological world of values and qualities rather than quantities? I believe that such a journey might start with a search for a more adequate understanding of the nature of the system we constitute when we interact with each other. It is the science of complexity, I believe, that can provide us with a deeper understanding of the systemic nature of individuals, organisation and societies and it is to this that we now turn.

THE SCIENCE OF COMPLEXITY

The first section of this chapter linked explanations of how economies and organisations function, with the theories in the natural sciences from which they were derived – those of Newton and Darwin in particular. It should not surprise us in the least, therefore, to discover that new theoretical developments in the natural sciences, which cast Newton and Darwin in a new light, should have revolutionary implications for our frames of reference when it comes to making sense of life in organisations.

The science of complexity is concerned with the behaviour of non-linear network systems consisting of large numbers of agents in which each agent employs some sets of rules, which we will call schemas, to interact with other agents in the system to produce joint action. For example, a colony of ants is a complex adaptive system and so is a flock of birds (Reynolds 1987) or a troop of baboons. And this is exactly what a human brain is (the agents being neurons), as well as the human mind (the agents being imaginal symbols), as well as a group, an organisation and a society (the agents being us). Note how an embodied brain nests in a mind, which nests in a group of minds, which nests in an organisation, which nests in a society, which nests in an international community, which nests in a natural ecology. This is a feature of all complex adaptive systems – one complex adaptive system, say, the species called frogs, interacts with another complex adaptive system, say, the species called flies, so forging a larger suprasystem, an ecology, which is itself also a complex adaptive system. What is a system at one level is an agent in a system at a higher level of aggregation. Within any system the agents co-evolve, and in doing so they affect the evolution of the system they are a part of. At all levels agents are determining their own survival strategies, and in doing so are affecting the evolution of the whole. This interconnectedness is crucial when thinking about the nature of an intervention – it compels us to remember not to ask for whom the bell tolls because it tolls for us. Immediately, this way of seeing things opens up what Brian Goodwin calls a science of qualities (Goodwin 1994). While a science of quantities is a way of understanding through measuring quantitative performance – a way of understanding a system by what it does – a science of qualities is a way of understanding a system by empathising with what it is. In the former, value is extrinsic and performance-based while, in the latter, it is intrinsic and arises simply because the system is, and is perhaps becoming something. The former describes a veal calf and measures its performance in some way while the latter tries to identify what it feels like to be a veal calf.

You can already see the potential of this way of seeing things in this non-linear, open-ended way in which agents each having their own structure co-evolve with other agents and systems, always partly creating what happens to them, as opposed to the linear perspective in which agents simply adapt to external changes, their internal structure being of little importance. From the non-linear, co-evolving perspective we see that the system features are the same, no matter whether you look at the level of the society or the level of the organisation or the level of an individual. It would be surprising, then, from this perspective, if one were to come up with an explanation which denied control at the level of the society but said you could control individual or organisational life. You would either be able to control the system at all levels or at none, simply because you are dealing with what is fundamentally the same kind of system. Explanations that do not see this are basically flawed and interventions based on them may well be misguided. We also see that because agents have internal structure they also have intrinsic value: they are not simply passive cogs in a mechanical system but active beings that constitute the system.

Consider now the profoundly important insights that are coming from the science of complexity.

The insights of complexity science

I am going to mention briefly a few of the most important insights that come from the science of complexity – to find out more, the reader is recommended to refer to Levy 1992; Gell-Mann 1994; Goodwin 1994; Kauffman 1995; Stacey 1991; 1992; 1996a; 1996b.

Creativity is possible only at the edge of chaos

Complex adaptive systems have, in very broad terms, three possible forms of behaviour open to them.

Firstly, when information or energy flows rather slowly through the system, when the connections between the agents are sparse and when the differences in the schemas driving agent behaviour are rather small, then all complex adaptive systems appear to operate in a state of stable equilibrium. Here their behaviour is predictable and it is possible to be in control of such a system simply because it endlessly repeats the same pattern of behaviour. This is a Newtonian world, a stable, ordered zone in which the system ossifies.

Secondly, when those control parameters – information/energy, connectivity, diversity – are set at very high levels, the system behaves in an unstable, explosive or random manner until it falls apart. This is the unstable, disordered zone in which the system disintegrates.

Thirdly, as the control parameters are increased so that the system moves from the ordered toward the disordered zone, it passes through a phase transition, and it does so just when the control parameters reach critical points in which there is rapid information flow, but not too rapid; rich connectivity, but not too rich; great diversity, but not too much. In this phase transition, at the edge of chaos, at the edge of system disintegration, the system produces endless variety and novelty. Here it is creative and alive and, in fact, it is only here that it is creative or alive – in both the ordered and the disordered zones the system eventually dies.

This state at the edge of chaos is a paradoxical one in which behaviour is both stable enough for the system not to fall apart and unstable enough not to get stuck in one pattern, and it is both of these at the same time. In this phase transition, the system can escalate tiny changes into major alterations in behaviour and this makes its long-term future radically unpredictable and therefore uncontrollable. It is the place where there is beauty, excitement and also tension.

Consider for a moment the profundity of this insight – complex adaptive systems are creative not when they are in stable equilibrium as the dominant economic theories would have it, but rather when they are far away from equilibrium at the edge of system disintegration. This is close to the Austrian view, except for one thing. At the edge of disintegration the long-term outcomes of an agent's next action are unknowable – there is therefore no guarantee whatsoever that the agent's action will have a beneficial outcome, and this applies whether the agent is an individual, an organisation, a government or a whole society. There are, therefore, no grounds at all for generally concluding that leaving things to individuals and organisations to slog it out in the marketplace will necessarily be an improvement upon actions of groups of people called the government. Only with hindsight will we be able to decide whether we like the outcome, and then we will not know what the alternative would have been.

The application to human systems

The sceptics will be saying by now that this might apply to ants, and perhaps even baboons, but certainly not to us, because we have free will.

We are conscious and self-aware and we can think systemically. Surely, the notion that we must operate at the edge of disintegration if we are to be creative is as plausible as the old wives' tale that genius lies at the edge of madness. Well, it is as plausible, of course, because genius does indeed lie at the edge of madness. There is support for this contention from psychoanalytic theory.

Melanie Klein (1975) distinguished between the schizoid-paranoid and the depressive positions. The schizoid-paranoid position is quite clearly a state of mental disintegration and we defend against occupying it through the employment of neurotic defences taking the form of repetitive and rigid behaviours. That surely is the ordered zone of the mind. The depressive position, however, lies between them and it is a position in which we can hold the ambiguities of existence – we can love and hate the same object. The depressive position is as paradoxical as the edge of chaos in any other complex adaptive system and it is very easy for us to tip from this depressive position into the schizoid-paranoid one of disintegration. Klein associated creative behaviour quite clearly with occupation of this depressive space – from the depressive position we can experience the guilt that drives us to make reparation, and that is the source of all creative behaviour.

Winnicott (1971) even used the term 'transitional' to describe the same space from his perspective. So transitional objects are manipulated, played with, in a zone intermediate between inner fantasy and outer reality, between the disintegrative and the ordered zones of the mind. He associated all learning and creativity with the ability to play with the very first symbol, the comfort blanket.

The same kind of distinction between ordered, disordered and intermediate zones has been identified in group behaviour. Bion's (1961) basic-assumption behaviour and the psychotic fantasies it gives rise to are clearly the disintegrative zone of behaviour for a group, while the kind of defences against learning identified by Argyris (Argyris and Schon 1978; Argyris 1990) and others constitute the ordered zone of operation for a group of people. A group can be creative only when it can occupy the space between the two. Since organisations and societies are aggregates of groups of people, there is every reason to expect to find such a space at the edge of disintegration at these levels too (Stacey 1996b).

Now consider what complexity science has to say about what happens in this space for novelty.

Self-organisation and the emergence of order out of the edge of chaos

At the edge of chaos the agents of the system self-organise to produce emergent outcomes. That is, each agent interacts with others following its own schema – it acts in its own best self-interest. As they all do this, they produce overall joint patterns of behaviour that cannot be explained in terms of the individual agents' schema rules. There is no one agent in control and yet through their spontaneous self-organisation they produce coherent patterns of behaviour – the system's behaviour is controlled, it does not sink into anarchy because at the edge of chaos each agent is taking into account the responses its actions are arousing from others. The agents and the system as a whole are learning as they act and it is this that produces coherent pattern and keeps anarchy at bay. However, while the system as a whole shows coherent pattern, this does not guarantee survival for individual agents or groups of them and it does not guarantee anything optimal for the system as a whole either. Agents and whole groups of agents can easily develop malfunctioning learning practices which trap them in repetitive patterns of behaviour which then open them up to destruction by competitors. Or, they may get caught up in other malfunctioning learning practices that tip them over the edge into chaos. Many simulations of complex adaptive systems (for example, Ray 1992) demonstrate waves of creative destruction as some groupings of agents are replaced by others.

This sounds exactly like neo-Darwinian views of evolution of life and the Austrian economic perspectives or, at least, the way in which those views and perspectives are widely understood. There is, however, a very profound difference. Neo-Darwinian and Austrian perspectives focus entirely on the role of competitive selection applied to random mutation while complexity science introduces the discovery of what seems to be a universal principle of cooperation. In the simulations of complex adaptive systems it has been found that while random mutation trial and error might be necessary to start the evolution of a system, it is rapidly overtaken in importance by cross-over replication. At lower developmental levels, species evolve by cloning and variety develops through random mutations in the genes. But at higher levels of development cross-over replication is used, that is, one agent has one half of the genetic code required in reproduction while another has the other half and they reproduce by mating, by a creative coupling or penetration of one agent by another. This method of cross-fertilisation – this creative act – has been shown to emerge spontaneously in complex adaptive systems. It has the effect of mixing up genes and so disrupting the reproduction process more thoroughly than random mutation in the cloning method. In other words, it makes more of a mess, it introduces more disorder and this performs the function of creating more variety and diversity and so avoiding being trapped into repetitive behaviour and the malfunctioning learning it represents. Now this cross-over replication is a cooperative process, although mate selection does also have its competitive aspects. What it does is use cooperation to develop agents that are then subjected to competitive selection.

189

Evolution is not driven simply by the brute force of competition, it is also driven by the gentle force of cooperation, or love – both are required if high levels of complexity, high levels of creativity are to be achieved. Evolution, then, is not driven purely by random mutation applied to independently functioning selfish genes, but much more significantly by the penetration and passionate embrace of one collection of genes by another – a collaborative and spontaneously self-organising act of creation.

So, spontaneous self-organisation of a system, a deeply cooperative principle of cross-fertilisation, develops the forms that are then subjected to competitive selection. This is very different from the purely competitive perspectives of neo-Darwinian evolution or of Austrian economics.

Playing at the edge of chaos

The simulations of complex adaptive systems reveal an intriguing feature of the process whereby they evolve. It was mentioned above that agents in a system behave according to schemas, or sets of rules. Those rules are coded into symbols, such as genes in the case of an organism, digital code in the case of a computer simulation, imaginal symbols in the case of a mind. When they reproduce, one agent in effect splices part of its symbol set onto a part of another agent's. That is certainly how it is done in computer simulations and in genetic reproduction and if you think about it, this is what mental cross-fertilisation means too – it is how we create a new generation of ideas in our minds.

Part of the symbol set making up schemas is used to construct the rules that drive the current survival strategy of the agent – we can call this the dominant schema, that which is currently being deployed for the serious purpose of actually surviving. However, this survival task may well not utilise all of the symbol set. There may be a left-over set that we can call the recessive schema. When the agents replicate, there will be a tendency to pass on rather unchanged the dominant schema because that is what is currently securing survival and agents not doing this will be selected out. Similarly, we hang on to ideas and beliefs while they appear to be working. But what happens to the recessive symbol set?

In simulations of complex adaptive systems (Ackley and Littman 1992) it is possible to watch what happens to the recessive schemas – while the dominant schemas stay much the same, as they should, the recessive schemas evolve in a trial and error way. While one part of the schema is working another is in a sense playing, and it is not being tested by competitive selection – it is being protected from such selection by the dominant schema. This might go on for some time until a viable alternative to the dominant schema emerges from this play in the recessive schema. It then suddenly takes over. Subversive play, no doubt exciting and full of tension, has resulted in a revolutionary substitution of the formerly dominant schema. A new schema has emerged, unpredictably, from playful, cooperative, protected interaction and now it will be tested by competition. If it were to be tested right at the beginning it would never get anywhere.

It is not at all fanciful to claim that this is what happens in individuals' minds, organisations and societies too. I have already referred to Winnicott's link between play and creativity in the individual mind. So we can quite plausibly think in terms of dominant schemas as rules about conducting the everyday life through which we survive, or not, as the case may be. The recessive schemas drive the fantasising and the play that are not necessary to perform day-to-day survival tasks. If we can hold the transitional space, the depressive position, then we can hold the anxiety of creative play. We can engage in true dialogue, we can use images, analogies and metaphors, we can engage in fantasies that do not at first make much sense. Here we are utilising the recessive schemas of our minds. And it is ultimately from such fantasising and playing that we might excitingly produce insights that change our dominant schemas and the way we behave. But this is destructive too, and so it provokes anxiety which we must find some way of holding if we are to play in the creative space. A similar description of creative life in a group can easily be constructed.

At the level of an organisation, it may be harder to see the parallel but not all that hard. All organisations are legitimate systems driven by dominant schemas. But all organisations also have informal, shadow systems that people spontaneously self-organise amongst themselves. There, driven by recessive schemas, they play in both creative and destructive ways. Such a shadow system is a place of tension and excitement, a learning community of practice, a covert political system, a psychodynamic system which is the source of, or the obstacle to, the creativity of an organisation (Stacey 1996a; 1996b).

So, if an organisation is to be creative, then it must occupy the phase transition at the edge of its own disintegration and this, it is clear, is a position of great anxiety. One way that members of an organisation can occupy this space is by proxy. This occurs when we project our own creativity into a charismatic, or even not such a charismatic leader, in return for that leader holding the anxiety of being creative, or even trying to be creative. Through this collusive specialisation in the occupation of the space for creativity, most of us can avoid the anxiety of creativity but pay the price of relatively uncreative lives. Or, we can take back our projected creativity and bear our own anxiety together as we collectively and individually occupy the space for creativity, at the edge of our own mental disintegration. Perhaps this participative occupation of the space for creativity has not happened, and still does not happen all that much, but it must surely be what we mean when we talk about organisations that are places where all of us can lead more creative lives. When we are considering the nature of interventions we should make to bring about such organisations, we must hold in our minds that such interventions are not simply the responsibility of those at the top – the interventions are our responsibility and they take the form of our taking hold of our own creativity and bearing the consequent anxiety ourselves. When trouble comes, we will have to bear the responsibility ourselves and not use our leaders as scapegoats. Organisations that provide us all with more creative lives are not painless utopias: when we find ourselves in a creative organisation it is a cause of both joy and pain.

THE IMPLICATIONS OF TAKING THE COMPLEXITY PERSPECTIVE

I have argued that the kinds of interventions we make in organisations flow from the perspective we take on the nature of human systems. If we take the kind of confused mixture of neo-classical and Austrian economics that has been in vogue for the last 16 years, then our interventions in organisations focus on creating a mixture of artificial markets and control devices that heavily emphasise measuring and monitoring – our focus is on quantities, for which we have developed an organisational science of quantities. The consequence appears to be the ignition of a vicious circle of complaining and insatiable greed in which we are passively empowered as customers and actively disempowered as members of the organisations through which we serve ourselves as customers – the one goes inevitably with the other. In our obsession with quantities and our neglect of values, we drive out the qualities of life that all the performance measuring is supposed to secure. We have gone so far down this route and created so much insecurity for ourselves as members of organisations, as opposed to individual customers, that there now seems to be a growing longing to somehow go back home, back to where the values were. But home is now very different and so are we: going home must mean returning to something left behind but in a different way – just as each time I return to my first home in South Africa I realise that I must find it afresh because each time both it and I have changed so much. I think this is where a new perspective, a new frame of reference comes in. We need to see home – the systems we are and the systems and values we create when we interact with each other – in a different way.

Complexity science yields a new and deep insight into the nature of complex adaptive systems and the processes through which they evolve. If living systems – and these include individual humans and their groupings into organisations and societies – are to evolve creatively, and they must if they are to survive, then they must operate at the edge of disintegration. They are all brought to this state at critical levels of information flow, agent connectivity and schema diversity. In addition to this, however, human systems are also highly sensitive to the differences in power between agents and the way those differences are used and this has a bearing on the level of anxiety that a system can contain. At critical points of anxiety containment and power differentials, human systems occupy the space at the edge of disintegration. If the anxiety is avoided they fall back into the stable zone, and if the anxiety is not contained they tip into the unstable zone. (These notions are developed more fully in Stacey 1996a; 1996b.)

When organisational and societal systems are at the edge of disintegration it is possible for playful activity to proceed in the recessive schemas of members' minds, behind the protective facade of the dominant schemas. In other words, members of organisations and societies then play in potentially creative ways in an informal shadow system while carrying out, in their legitimate system, the day-to-day tasks necessary for immediate survival. The role of creative play in the shadow system is a subversive one – ultimately it will replace parts at least of the dominant system.

This is an explanation that holds at individual, organisational and societal levels. At none of these levels is it possible for anyone to be 'in control' over the long term. At all of these levels, creative new directions emerge from a cooperative process of spontaneous self-organisation to which competitive selection is then applied. Both competition and cooperation must drive the system if it is to survive.

This is a very different perspective to the one based on competitive selection, upon the forces of the market, alone. Unbridled competition would destroy creativity because, in its early stages, creativity is play that must hide behind some dominant schema and must be protected from competitive selection. The question of whether we are to hold the anxiety of occupying the space for creativity participatively or by proxy, as we have usually done, is quite clearly posed.

The complexity perspective is one that focuses our attention on:

● The importance of cooperation as passionate, connective, exciting acts of spontaneous self-organisation that take place in tension with competition but do not imply the absence of competition;

● The importance of protecting exciting, playful, fantasising activity from the severity of competitive selection in our organisations because such playfulness is the birth of creativity;

● The critical nature of connectivity, diversity, patterns of power use and modes of anxiety-containment in establishing the conditions for creativity;

● The science of qualities rather than simply the science of quantities: that is, a mode of knowing that considers what it is like to be another entity rather than simply to measure its behaviour, a mode of knowing that honours the intrinsic value of simply being, rather than the extrinsic value of performing;

- New ways of conceptualising organisations as being controlled through the learning responsiveness of members rather than through the powerful being 'in control';
- The close connection between creativity and the need to hold rather than avoid the anxiety that this gives rise to.

What does all of this suggest about the kinds of intervention we should be making in our organisations to make life more creative for all of us – the question with which we started this chapter? Well, the free-market camp point to the similarity with Austrian economics and proclaim that they are already doing it, while their opponents focus almost exclusively on the insight about cooperation and connectivity and call for harmony and limitation of competition and conflict. And those who simply cannot abandon the central interventionist notion seek to use the new science to identify new ways of staying 'in control' – to use minor chaos to control major chaos, for example. These are all rather familiar ways of 'going home', homes that I think are no longer there.

I believe that if we really start thinking about organisations and society from a complexity perspective, rather than seeking to use it to sustain existing preconceptions, we will reach very different conclusions about the kinds of interventions that make sense. They would have to do with creating conditions in which people can play and reflect together on what they are doing. Leadership intervention will have more to do with containing anxiety than telling people what to do or trying to hoodwink them with plans and visions. Members of organisations might be less inclined to collude with their leaders in the fantasy that the latter are in control and are to be blamed when things go wrong. We will consider more carefully how we can protect playful, creative activity and be much more cautious about naively exposing everything to market competition. We will start to focus on how we can collectively occupy the space for creativity at the anxiety-provoking edge of disintegration. Once we abandon the fantasy that we can be in control of the long-term future of our organisations we might abandon the fantasy that we produce quality by measuring something. Then, perhaps, we might focus on what quality really is. By starting to think and talk and interact with each other in different ways, we will change the emergent patterns of our experience because we are, and when we interact with each other we form, complex adaptive systems in which spontaneous self-organisation can amplify small interventions to produce major new emergent patterns of behaviour.

REFERENCES

Ackley, D. H. & Littman, M. (1992) 'Interactions between Learning and Evolution', in Langton, G. C. (1992) *Artificial Life II*, Santa Fe Institute Studies in the Sciences of Complexity, vol X, Reading, Mass.: Addison-Wesley, pp. 501–2.

Argyris, C. (1990) *Overcoming Organizational Defenses: Facilitating Organiza-tional Learning*, Boston: Allyn and Bacon, Prentice-Hall.

Argyris, C. and Schon, D. (1978) *Organizational Learning: A Theory of Action Perspective*, Reading, Mass.: Addison-Wesley.

Bion, W. R. (1961) *Experiences in Groups and Other Papers*, London: Tavistock Publications.

Gell-Mann, M. (1994) *The Quark and the Jaguar*, New York: Freeman & Co.

Goodwin, B. (1994) *How the Leopard Changed its Spots*, London: Weidenfeld & Nicolson.

Hayek, F. A. (1948) *Individualism and Economic Order*, Chicago: University of Chicago Press.

Hayek, F. A. (1982), *Law, Legislation and Liberty*, London: Routledge & Kegan Paul.

Kauffman, S. A. (1995) *At Home in the Universe*, New York: Oxford University Press.

Klein, M. (1975) *The Writings of Melanie Klein*, London: Hogarth Press.

Levy, S. (1992) *Artificial Life*, New York: First Vintage Books.

Ray, T. S. (1992) 'An Approach to the Synthesis of Life', in Langton, C. G. (1993) *Artificial Life III*, Santa Fe, New Mexico: Addison-Wesley, 371–408.

Reynolds, C. (1987) 'Flocks, Herds and Schools: A Distributed Behavioural Model', *Computer Graphics* 21, July: 25.

Schumpeter, J. A. (1934) *The Theory of Economic Development*, Cambridge, Mass.: Harvard University Press.

Stacey, R. (1991) *The Chaos Frontier: Creative Strategic Control for Business*, Oxford: Butterworth-Heinemann.

Stacey, R. (1992) *Managing the Unknowable: The Strategic Boundaries Between Order and Chaos*, San Francisco: Jossey Bass. Also published in the UK as *Managing Chaos*, London: Kogan Page.

Stacey, R. (1995) 'The Science of Complexity: An Alternative Perspective for Strategic Change Processes', *Strategic Management Journal*, August.

Stacey, R. (1996a) *Strategic Management and Organisational Dynamics* (second edition), London: Pitman.

Stacey, R. (1996b) *Complexity and Creativity in Organisations*, San Francisco: Berrett-Koehler.

Winnicott, D. W. (1971) *Playing and Reality*, London: Tavistock Publications. Reprinted 1993, London: Routledge.

INDEX